Affective Tourism

This book brings together, explores and expands socio-spatial affect, emotion and psychoanalytic drives in tourism for the first time. Affect is to be found in visceral intensities and resonances that circulate around and shape encounters between and amongst tourists, local tourism representatives and places. When affect manifests, it can shape-shift into emotions such as fun, joy, fear, anger and the like. When it remains a visceral force of latent bodily responses, affect overlaps with drives, as expounded in psychoanalysis. The aim of the title, therefore, is to explore how and in what ways affects, emotions and drives are felt, sensed and performed in tourism encounters in places of socio-political turmoil such as Jordan and Palestine/Israel, with a detour to Iraq.

Affective Tourism is highly innovative as it offers a new way of theorising tourism encounters, bringing together, critically examining and expanding three areas of scholarship: affective and emotional geographies, psychoanalytic geographies and dark tourism. It has relevance for tourism industries in places in the proximity of ongoing conflicts as it provides in-depth analyses of the interconnections between tourism, danger and conflict. Such understandings can lead to more socio-culturally and politically sustainable approaches to planning, development and management of tourism.

This groundbreaking book will be valuable reading for students and researchers from a number of fields such as tourism studies, geography, anthropology, sociology and Middle Eastern studies.

Dorina Maria Buda is a Rosalind Franklin Fellow and Assistant Professor in the Department for Cultural Geography at the University of Groningen in the Netherlands. Her scholarship in geographies of tourism revolves around interconnections between affect, emotion and psychoanalysis. Adopting a critical approach, she particularly focuses on tourism in areas of socio-political turmoil.

Contemporary Geographies of Leisure, Tourism and Mobility

Series Editor: C. Michael Hall, Professor at the Department of Management, College of Business and Economics, University of Canterbury, Christchurch, New Zealand

The aim of this series is to explore and communicate the intersections and relationships between leisure, tourism and human mobility within the social sciences.

It will incorporate both traditional and new perspectives on leisure and tourism from contemporary geography, e.g., notions of identity, representation and culture, while also providing for perspectives from cognate areas such as anthropology, cultural studies, gastronomy and food studies, marketing, policy studies and political economy, regional and urban planning, and sociology, within the development of an integrated field of leisure and tourism studies.

Also, increasingly, tourism and leisure are regarded as steps in a continuum of human mobility. Inclusion of mobility in the series offers the prospect to examine the relationship between tourism and migration, the sojourner, educational travel, and second home and retirement travel phenomena.

The series comprises two strands:

Contemporary Geographies of Leisure, Tourism and Mobility aims to address the needs of students and academics, and the titles are published in hardback and paperback. Titles include:

Routledge Studies in Contemporary Geographies of Leisure, Tourism and Mobility is a forum for innovative new research intended for research students and academics, and the titles are available in hardback only. Titles include:

Affective Tourism
Dark routes in conflict

Dorina Maria Buda

Routledge
Taylor & Francis Group

LONDON AND NEW YORK

First published 2015
by Routledge

2 Park Square, Milton Park, Abingdon, Oxon OX14 4RN
711 Third Avenue, New York, NY 10017, USA

Routledge is an imprint of the Taylor & Francis Group, an informa business

First issued in paperback 2017

British Library Cataloguing in Publication Data
A catalogue record for this book is available from the British Library

Library of Congress Cataloging in Publication Data
Buda, Dorina Maria.
Affective tourism : dark routes in conflict / Dorina Maria Buda.
pages cm
Includes bibliographical references and index.
1. Dark tourism. 2. Tourism—Psychological aspects. 3. Tourism—Middle
East. I. Title.
G156.5.D37B84 2015
306.4'819—dc23
2014046186

ISBN: 978-1-138-82246-7 (hbk)
ISBN: 978-1-138-08390-5 (pbk)

Typeset in Times New Roman
by Swales & Willis Ltd, Exeter, Devon, UK

Pentru Ileana și Ioan Buda

Contents

PART IV
Re-tour   **153**

Figures

Acknowledgements

I have been waiting a long time to *properly* thank Anne-Marie d'Hauteserre, who took me seriously as a researcher, lecturer and intellectual, long before I even deserved it. Her encouragement and support put me on the path that eventually led to writing this book. Sometimes, life has a *funny* way of surprising us with all sorts of situations. I am lucky enough to have had the support of great people when addressing such situations: Inge Hutter, Lynda Johnston, Mirjam Koster-Wentink, Joseph Daniel Lema, Alison McIntosh, Frank Vanclay and Kees Vermeij. Thank you for having helped me when I most needed it. Without their support, I would have not been in the position to finish this book.

A project like this is a collective endeavour and I am indebted to many people. First and foremost, I am most grateful to the many participants in this research project. Their time and stories have made this research possible. Their willingness to share their emotions, thoughts, reflections and photographs allowed me to explore what it is so special, so dark and so colourful about emotions and tourism that *moves* us. Promises of anonymity prevent me from naming my participants, but I extend my greatest debt to all of them.

I have been very fortunate to be a doctoral researcher in the Geography and Tourism Programmes at the University of Waikato in Aotearoa New Zealand from 2008 to 2012. I am grateful for the programmes' research grant. The doctoral research fund at the Faculty of Arts and Social Sciences in the same university contributed substantially to my field trip in Jordan, Israel and Palestine in 2010. I must also thank the Waikato International Doctoral Scholarship Committee for their financial support. I wish to particularly acknowledge Gwenda Pennington for her support with searching and applying for funds.

I am grateful to Dr Barbara Porter and all the staff at the American Centre for Oriental Research where I was hosted during my fieldwork in Amman. The staff at the W. F. Albright Institute of Archaeological Research in Al Quds/Jerusalem also deserve special thanks for their hospitality during my stay in 2010.

My thanks to individuals are too numerous to list in full, but here are some people to whom I am particularly thankful. I especially thank Anne-Marie d'Hauteserre (again) who, unwaveringly, accepted to read my manuscript and provided excellent feedback. Peter Groote, Bettina van Hoven and Otto Sestak offered valuable comments on various chapters. I wish to acknowledge Frank Vanclay for his support polishing the book proposal.

Colleagues, friends and family all have an important role in the production of this book. I am thankful to those who have, in their respective ways, contributed to this book. My colleagues in the Tourism and Geography Programmes at the University of Waikato were very supportive during my doctoral research. I would like to especially thank Heather Morrell for helping me navigate the wonderful world of references. I am also thankful to Max Oulton for his cartography work. Special thanks go to Lynda Johnston for her support, guidance and invaluable insights. As one of the doctoral supervisors, she was generous with her time and provided excellent advice regarding academic matters. Both my doctoral supervisors, Anne-Marie d'Hauteserre and Lynda Johnston, have been a real inspiration for me. It has been a rewarding experience to have them on my supervisory panel.

Colleagues in the Department of Cultural Geography at the University of Groningen were particularly welcoming when I joined the faculty in 2013. I would like to thank for their warm collegiality: Agnes van den Berg, Jeannette Brondsema, Peter Groote, Bettina van Hoven, Jelmer Jeuring, Debbie Lager, Philippe Hanna, Tialda Haartsen, Paulus Huigen, Erik Meijles, Lidewij van der Ploeg, Koen Salemink, Frank Vanclay, Dirk Strijker, Gwenda van der Vaart and Gerd Weitkamp. The team at Library Zernike at the University of Groningen, especially Marianne van Os, have also been really helpful.

Many thanks to some of my friends for their keen interest in my projects and for their friendships: Carmen Bârsan, Paul Colcer, Flaviu Dragomir, Amro Gazawi, Mariana and Dorel Moga, Alexandra Pop and Paula Simuţ. Otto Sestak, Ligia Tomoiaga, and Rodica Ţurcanu from North University of Baia Mare, Romania – my alma mater hold a special place in my heart for having taught me love of knowledge.

I would like to thank Emma Travis, Philippa Mullins, Jeanne Brady, Elizabeth Kent, Thomas Newman and the entire team for their editorial support.

My deep and lasting appreciation go to my wonderful parents Ileana Buda and Ioan Buda, who have always supported me, believed in me and encouraged me to study. This book is dedicated to them, without their continuous and unwavering support the book would not have been possible. Mami şi tati vă mulţumesc din suflet pentru tot sprijinul şi dragostea neconditionată pe care mi le-aţi oferit mereu.

To all who have assisted me, I offer my heartfelt thanks.

Part I
Packing and setting forth

1   Packing light, feeling down

This book introduces and critically examines *affective tourism* – the ways in which affects, emotions, and feelings are accessed, felt, experienced and performed in encounters between touring bodies and places. Theories of affect, emotion, psychoanalysis and tourism are brought together to explore dark tourism routes in places of socio-political turmoil such as Jordan, and Palestine/Israel. The intention is to interject two novel concepts in tourism studies: socio-spatial affect and psychoanalytic drives. Affect is to be found in visceral intensities that circulate around and shape encounters between tourists, local tourism representatives and places. Affect can manifest in resonances of emotions such as fun, joy, fear, anger and the like. When it remains a visceral force of latent bodily responses, affect overlaps with drives as they are expounded in psychoanalysis.

Engaging in affective tourism provides opportunities for psychoanalytic drives, especially the death drive, to be accessed in places of ongoing socio-political turmoil. The psychoanalytical concept of the death drive refers to a constant force, a nuance of affect, at the junction between life and death, which is not understood in a biological sense of physical demise of the body, nor in opposition to life. Affective encounters in conflict and danger-zones, the scope of this book, can be more critically explored and understood through the lens of the death drive. As an in-depth ethnographic account, this book traces experiences of tourists and local tourism industry representatives in Jordan and Palestine/Israel. Drawing on in-depth interviews, ethnographic observations, and written and photographic diaries, this book offers a multi- and interdisciplinary investigation of affect, emotion and the death drive in the spatial and socio-cultural context of tourism.

With this region of Jordan and Palestine/Israel in focus, and to illustrate the potential of affective tourism, I address the following questions: how are places in (the proximity of) conflict affectively experienced and performed in tourism? What emotions and senses circulate amongst and between tourists and local tourism industry representatives in such places? How do politics of affect and emotion shape tourism encounters in places of conflict?

To address these questions, I have three objectives. First, I critically examine affective and emotional geographies – that which is sensed, felt and performed in places of ongoing socio-political conflict. Feeling fear, shock, anger and engaging haptically with these places provide a disruption of some dominant dichotomies in tourism studies such as peace/war, safety/danger, fun/fear and life/death. Second, I argue that by travelling to such dangerous places, some tourists reflect on, negotiate and purge their own family memories and embedded traumas, a process explained using the psychoanalytic concept of the death drive. Third, I unravel connections between tourism, danger and ongoing socio-political turmoil so as to exemplify tourists' affective performances in conflict places. Theorisations of tourism in such places of ongoing socio-political turmoil and conflict – danger-zone tourism – are situated within the sub-field of dark tourism.

This book advances the call for an affective and emotional turn in tourism studies as it explores dark-tourism performances in dangerous places. I define this type of tourism as danger-zone tourism and employ Adams's explanation of the term being 'tourism to tumultuous locations, places that are not necessarily the sites of declared wars but are nevertheless sites of *on-going* political instability, sites where there is at least an imagined potential of violent eruptions' (Adams, 2001, p. 268, emphasis in original). Tourism in areas of danger and conflict has received scant attention. This book goes some way towards filling this gap. My intention is not only to show that danger-zone tourism exists as practice, but also to discuss some danger-zone tourists' embodied, emotional, affective and sensuous experiences in areas of ongoing conflict.

I draw on works in geography,[1] cultural studies,[2] and sociology[3] to explore affects, emotions, feelings and senses generated by and in a 'danger-zone'. Such an examination offers new ways of understanding affective and emotional performances in danger-zone tourism. I employ Sigmund Freud's (trans. 1938, trans. 1984) and Jacques Lacan's (trans. 1977a, trans. 1977b) psychoanalytic theories of the death drive to show how danger-zone subjectivities disrupt some prevailing binaries in tourism studies such as safety/danger, peace/war, fun/fear and even life/death.

Throughout this book, the phrase 'areas (in the proximity) of an ongoing conflict' will be used so as to express the difference between Jordan, which is in the proximity of the conflict, and Palestine/Israel, which is at the heart of the conflict. Using this strategy, I do not intend to set up a binary – in/near the conflict – but to point out that what is considered to be 'in' and what is considered to be 'near' the conflict is never clearly separate. On the one hand, Jordan signed a peace treaty with Israel in 1994, which I wish to acknowledge by treating Jordan in the proximity of the Israeli–Palestinian conflict and not directly involved in the conflict. On the other hand, Jordan has a considerable population of Palestinian descent; thus the conflict does not merely happen in the neighbouring area, but has emotional and political implications for most Jordanians. This book is a story of some tourists, local tourism industry representatives, and myself in danger-zones of conflict. Having lived for approximately six months in Jordan and Palestine/Israel in 2009 and 2010, I was exposed to some tourists' experiences of these places, but also to daily life in the proximity of conflict, to some locals' daily habits, joys, and struggles.

A Romanian woman abroad

I have moved around a lot in my life, and my body hates it. It loves the rituals of everyday life, and hates the thought of disruption. . . . This is not a tale of woe, nor even very unusual, but the experience does provide me with ample evidence of a strange little strain of shame: the body's feeling of being out-of-place in the everyday. It is a shame born of the body's desire to fit in, just as it knows that it cannot. 'You're not from here': the slip of tongue, the flash of ignorance faced with an entirely different arrangement of the everyday. It is no big deal, compared to the experiences of others violently uprooted. It is just a little shaming from within fed by the desire to be unnoticed, to be at home in the everyday of someone else's culture.

(Probyn, 2004a, p. 328)

I empathise with Elspeth Probyn's emotions. I have also moved around a lot in my life. Over the past twelve years, I have lived in eight countries. I have a bittersweet feeling being a foreigner in somebody else's country. I love it and I hate it. I love the 'new-ness' that each country brings into my everyday life, but I hate most of the emotions and feelings that come with every new environment. Like Probyn I feel shame, but also fear, and at times frustration. Probyn's shame refers to her body originating from the colonial centre, hence she feels shame as she represents the colonial power even when she is against it. For Probyn, shame is a way of navigating everyday life in a complex postcolonial country.

My shame has nothing much in connection to the post/colonial. Romania, my country of origin, has never been a colonising country, and it was also not colonised in the way Aotearoa New Zealand, Australia, or parts in the Middle East were and some still are colonised. Romania is a country that bears the signs of invasions from the Roman, Ottoman and Austro-Hungarian Empires and two world wars. The country was a satellite of the Soviet Union, but never part of it.

Here I want to introduce and locate myself and answer the question I ask myself and I am frequently asked by others: what was I, a Romanian woman, doing in the 'Middle East' while studying in Aotearoa New Zealand? Unravelling some of my emotions and thoughts does not always prove to be easy. 'How did you end up in New Zealand? Why did you choose New Zealand?' In a way New Zealand chose me. I echo here similar feelings shared by Frohlick (2013), that, however trite it may seem, sometimes field sites *do* choose us.

I knew I did not want to research anything related to my home country Romania and this particular point generates my feeling of shame. I am ashamed because of my decision not to research a topic related to Romania, thus I feel I am not 'a good Romanian'. Perhaps, I should have turned my attention to topics connected to social justice that could have societal relevance for Romania. But I did not want to, and this unwillingness brings me shame. I feel intense emotions in relation to anything that has happened in Romania after the 1989 revolution when the Communist Party was overthrown. I feel too passionately and strongly about my country and feared I would not be able to manage this passion and these emotions. This is partly why I opted not to research a Romanian social and cultural aspect.

Why do I feel shame in connection to this? I understand shame, as Probyn describes it in the introductory quote, to be 'the body's feeling of being out-of-place in the everyday'. I felt out-of-place in and because of the four locations connected to this book – New Zealand, Jordan and Palestine/Israel, and Romania. The shame that I felt in New Zealand was akin to the shame that reconceptualises the everyday. Having lived, worked and studied in Hamilton, Aotearoa New Zealand from 2008 to 2012 when this book project started, I felt shame because of my own disinterest and ignorance at some of the aspects that represent a 'typical' New Zealand 'everyday'.

In the Netherlands, where I currently reside, I am still ashamed because of my accent. In Probyn's case, it is 'the slip of the tongue' that betrays her being from somewhere else. In the United States, where I lived for 18 months prior to relocating to New Zealand, native English-speaking friends and colleagues would tell me that I have a 'strong' and 'harsh'-sounding Romanian accent. I speak English fluently but with the occasional grammar and vocabulary mistakes. This I feel as a stigma, both in my 'casual everyday' but also in my 'academic everyday', in which my every 'slip of the tongue' is sanctioned.

Being a young, female researcher in Jordan and Palestine made me confront shame differently than in the United States and New Zealand. I remember that in July 2010, the second time when I travelled from New Zealand for my fieldwork in Jordan and Palestine/Israel, I experienced somatic spasms. The way Probyn writes about her body hating disruptions of the everyday, loving the rituals of the daily routine and having entered somatic spasms when she immigrated to Australia resonate with the ways I feel my body reacts as it is moving around a lot, and especially when I reached my 'field site'.

In the Middle East, I was a single, eastern European woman trying to collect information while unaccompanied in public. My 'eastern-ness' represented an aspect from which I could negotiate similarities. During the 1970s and 1980s, Romanian universities hosted many Arab students; this was a point of commonality upon which I tried to capitalise, so as to diminish my out-of-place-ness. In some instances, being a single woman from eastern Europe meant to some locals that I was available for more than collecting data for my project, thus sexual innuendos were made with which I was not comfortable at all and which exacerbated my shame. I wanted to run away, to hide, but I could not. There was nowhere to hide. These innuendos made me feel ashamed.

These feelings of shame, followed by desires to be invisible and disappear contradict my desire to tell stories of the everyday I lived in other places and stories of my travels. But who wants to listen to my stories of shame, joy and embarrassment?

In a way, this book is also 'a telling of my stories' lived in Aotearoa New Zealand, Jordan, Palestine, Israel, Romania and other places. The storyline of this book moves back and forth between my own experiences in the region as a tourist/researcher; my observations of what tourists and local tourism workers do and feel; what they say themselves (their words recorded during interviews, conversations and electronic messages) about their activities and feelings, and my interpretations of their activities and feelings. This is very briefly the beginning of my 'shameful' story, a story which I will detail in the following chapters, a story entangled with other stories shared by tourists I met, by Jordanians, Palestinians and Israelis I interacted with in this region whereby conflict, danger, tourism and the everyday mingle in intricate ways.

Fieldwork 'in conflict'

'In conflict' refers to the 'in-the-trenches type of geography' (Dowler, 2001, p. 154) that I conducted during my fieldwork. The particular place of my fieldwork – Jordan and Palestine/Israel – is considered an area (in the proximity) of an ongoing conflict (please see Figure 1.1 as an example of a site where fieldwork was conducted). There are accounts of 'dangerous' fieldwork in areas of conflict in geography (Dowler, 2001), anthropology (Begley, 2009; see also Nordstrom & Robben, 1995 for a series of case studies) and sociology (Lee, 1993; see also Lee-Treweek & Lingokle, 2000 for further case studies). Throughout the fieldwork I gathered data not only from tourists but also from local tour guides, tourism company owners, managers and government officials. I wanted to unravel the *tourism–danger–conflict* nexus, explore emotions, felt and performed, in an area (in the proximity) of ongoing conflict and understand the ways affect circulates in such places.

Figure 1.1 Fieldwork at the Baptismal Site in Jordan.
Source: Dorina Buda, 2010.

I travelled to Jordan for the first time in April 2009. For the second stage of the fieldtrip, I travelled to Israel, Palestine and Jordan from July to November 2010. On both occasions, the region was deemed stable and safe. My 2010 travels, especially to and in Israel and Palestine, however, were considered dangerous and 'in a war zone' by a New Zealand insurance company. For a month spent in Israel and Palestine, I was insured (and charged accordingly) with an extra 'war coverage'.

In tourism, studies about areas of danger and conflict deal mostly with the quantitative aspect of numbers and percentages of tourists and expenditure being dramatically reduced during war and conflict, such approaches discuss marketing techniques to attract tourists once the conflict has ended (Bar-On, 1996; Mihalič, 1996; Fallon, 2003; Thapa, 2003). Such studies have not engaged with methodologies used beyond the analyses of statistics and numbers prior and after violent troubles occurred. One exception is Pitts's (1996) research on the 1994 Chiapas uprising in Mexico. He travelled to the region a few days after a ceasefire was declared, but skirmishes between armies were still common. The author used interviewing as one of his methods of data collection. I also used interviewing to collect data in Jordan, Israel and Palestine. More specifically, I employed individual and small group interviews, photographs, written diaries and participant observation. Online methods, such as instant messaging and interviews by electronic mail, were also used to recruit and interview participants.

A researcher's diary was kept throughout the whole fieldtrip in which I would write daily my participant observation notes related to tourists', tourism industry representatives', and my own emotions and senses in the field. I also took more than one thousand photographs, some of which will be analysed here. To gain more insights into emotions, feelings and affects some people experience in tourist places in a region of ongoing socio-political conflict, I also examined photographs tourists electronically mailed me upon return to their home countries. Use of this visual method is also meant to counterbalance the 'very wordy worlds' (Crang, 2003, p. 501) produced by verbal and written methods.

A brief numerical inventory of people involved in this project lists 79 participants, of which 25 were international tourists and 29 tour guides in Jordan and Palestine. The remaining 25 were governmental officials, tourism company owners or representatives, taxi drivers and even Franciscan monks working in the tourist attraction of Mount Nebo in Jordan. With the 25 international tourists, I conducted ten individual face-to-face interviews, three small group interviews and six online interviews. Eleven tourists, upon return to their home countries, provided non-commercial photographs, and four tourists provided short written diaries. Tour guides in Jordan and Palestine/Israel were also key respondents in this research. Thus, 24 tour guides from Jordan and five from Palestine took part in this project. With them I organised 24 individual interviews and one small group interview (Figure 1.2 depicts a room inside Petra Visitors Centre where some individual interviews were carried out, and Figure 1.4 shows the Wadi Rum desert where some group interviews took place). Three tour guides in Jordan also kept short photograph diaries. Information provided by other respondents, such as government officials and tourism company owners and managers will also be discussed in Part III 'Destinations: affective routes in "Middle Eastern" tourism'.

Figure 1.2 Conference room in Petra Visitors Centre in Jordan.
Source: Dorina Buda, 2010.

Figure 1.3 Petra Visitors Centre in Jordan.
Source: Dorina Buda, 2010.

Figure 1.4 Wadi Rum desert in Jordan.
Source: Dorina Buda, 2010.

The interviewing language was English, as tourists and local Jordanian and Palestinian respondents were able and willing to converse in English. For me and for most of my participants, whether local Jordanians, Palestinians or some international tourists, English is not our first language. Yet, they seemed to have felt at ease speaking with me and were not embarrassed at the occasional 'grammar mistakes'. Likewise, I do not speak Arabic, I am not from the region, and so immersion in Jordanian and Palestinian societies or blurring the insider/outsider status was never a question for me. Observing ethical guidelines, I would always hand in a project information sheet and a form agreeing to participate detailing, amongst others, confidentiality, anonymity and participant rights. In this book, most participants were given a pseudonym.

When I arrived in Jordan and Palestine/Israel, I could not exactly specify in advance just what form my fieldwork would take. I could not be sure of how I would be able to engage international tourists, tourism industry representatives and government officials in Jordan and Palestine/Israel, given also the contentious aspect of the ongoing Israeli–Palestinian conflict. In this respect it is argued:

> The whole reason for doing research is to find out something about the setting, and it is quite possible that some of the things that we do not know about the setting impact upon the design and conduct of the research we carry out. To a certain extent, then, social research methods have always had to be adaptive.
>
> (Hine, 2005, p. 2)

These assertions ring very true in the case of my research, in the sense that I had to adapt, change, or cancel altogether some aspects of the planned methods as imposed by the unique settings of Jordan and Palestine/Israel. I planned to interact both with individual and 'package' tourists. Pre-packaged tours around Jordan and Palestine/Israel are not longer than four to a maximum of seven days. Thus, I expected that recruiting tourists on pre-packaged tours would be challenging. Before the fieldtrip, my intention was to recruit tour guides and owners of tourism companies who could facilitate my travelling along with tourists on package tours. A limitation of this project, that I have had to acknowledge, is the fact that interacting with tourists on package tours in Jordan and Palestine was out of my reach. Negotiations with tourism companies or tour guides to have access to such tourists were unsuccessful. All tourist participants in this project were individual travellers who organised their trips by themselves.

Tourism geographies of affect and emotion

What emotions are provoked by being in a place of an ongoing conflict manifested on all levels: cultural, social, political and economic? How do danger-zone subjectivities perform emotionally in places of ongoing conflict? What bodily senses are engaged by tourists in the middle of conflict? The term 'subjectivities' is used to refer to spatio-temporal positions we take 'in regard to ourselves as subjects' (Probyn, 2003, p. 290). The argument is that subjects are interpellated by practices of different ideological systems, according to Probyn. This interpellation of individuals as subjects means that people inhabit different spaces at different times embodying different subjectivities. 'Conflict subjectivities' in times and places of ongoing socio-political turmoil are performed in affective, embodied, emotional and sensuous ways by tourists and tourism industry workers. I offer a different way of understanding subjectivities in tourism studies, which is founded on geographies of affect and emotion.

'Our first and foremost, most immediate and intimately *felt* geography is the body, the site of emotional experience and expression *par excellence*', it is maintained in social and cultural geography (Davidson & Milligan, 2004, p. 523, emphasis in original). Emotions and affect *take place* within, around, and between bodily spaces. Affects, emotions, and senses cannot be divorced from the body. Tourism studies have increasingly engaged with the body and embodiment theories.[4] There is also a 'growing intellectual interest' in the sensuous tourist subject, maintain Crouch and Desforges (2003, p. 6). It is surprising, therefore, that there is scarce engagement with affects, emotions and feelings in tourism. I would say that in tourism studies we *'pack light luggage'* when it comes to affect and emotion. This particular aspect makes me *'feel down and blue'* and makes me wonder why have affect and emotion been ignored for so long?

Marginalisation of emotion in geography, for example, more than a decade ago, was in part due to the fact that 'thinking emotionally is implicitly cast as a source of subjectivity which clouds vision and impairs judgement, while good scholarship depends on keeping one's own emotions under control and others' under wraps' (Anderson & Smith, 2001, p. 7). Currently, the same can be argued for tourism studies whereby knowledge production has been grounded on objective, rational, detached and masculinist approaches. There are limited understandings concerning tourist subjectivities; tourists, 'their' activities, motivations, and practices have been mostly essentialised and universalised.

Emotions and emotional relations tend to be relegated to the private and/or personal realm. Tourism knowledge production so far has been concerned by and large with 'the economic', which is seen as something apart from emotions. Tourist encounters, however, are lived through fun, fear, excitement, joy, pain, and so on. The power of affective and emotional engagements should no longer be ignored in tourism studies. Since 2001, when Anderson and Smith published the above quoted editorial, geography has increasingly engaged with emotions. Geographers now confidently assert that there is 'a surge of interest' in emotions (Davidson & Milligan, 2004, p. 523) and attest to strong evidence of 'a recent and rapid rise in engagement with emotion' (Davidson et al., 2008, p. 1).

Tourism studies are a long way away from experiencing such 'a welling up of emotion', to use Davidson and Milligan's (2004, p. 523) expression. The affective and emotional turn in geography stands proof that there is considerable 'positive recognition that emotions *already have* an important place in our own and others' work' (Bondi et al., 2005, p. 1, emphasis in original). More than being a 'shiny new "object" of study' or a 'passing academic fad' (Bondi et al., 2005, p. 1), emotional geographies and geographies of emotions prove that emotions *matter*.

This book addresses the 'affective and emotional gap' in tourism studies. It adds to the scarce literature that considers emotions in tourism studies and responds to these researchers' calls for more engagement with emotions (Johnston, 2005b, 2007; Tucker, 2007a, 2007b; 2009; Waitt et al., 2007). I particularly address Tucker's (2009) assertion that 'It is . . . necessary to examine closely the emotional and affective or bodily dimensions' (p. 447), if researchers aim to understand better tourism encounters. This project also contributes to 'the spatiality of emotions' (Waitt et al., 2007, p. 249) and demonstrates how danger-zone subjectivities experience places (in the proximity) of ongoing conflict through embodied emotions. I advocate for an affective and emotional turn in tourism studies akin to the one in socio-cultural and feminist geography. There is considerable engagement with the critical aspect in tourism studies; thus continuing this critical turn could be further inspired by the affective and emotional turn in geography. Affective tourism – tourism of affects, emotions and drives – recognises and deals with affectual connections, divisions and engagements. These become more poignant in tourism places of socio-political conflict and possible danger.

In Jordan, I analyse sanitisation practices that take place in tourism spaces. I unpack the idea that despite Jordan being portrayed as a 'peaceful' country, it is much more volatile than dominant discourses suggest. The assertion of Jordan as 'an oasis of peace and stability' is brought about by the existence of conflicts at Jordan's border. This sanitisation process is also resisted from within Jordan by some tour guides working near the borders with Palestine/Israel. The politics of the ongoing Israeli–Palestinian conflict is intimately linked with an emotional politics through the anger, fear and frustration felt by some Jordanian tour guides.

In Palestine/Israel, and as a result of the ongoing Israeli–Palestinian conflict, I examine emotional and sensed encounters between bodies and places as a defining characteristic of danger-zone tourism. I focus on tourists and guides at the separation wall, refugee camps and checkpoints. Fear is analysed in connection to the sense of touch. I illustrate how haptic geographies – bodies touching places and places touching bodies – in some Palestinian tourist places prompt fear and anger. Emotions matter; so do bodily senses through which tourists make sense of and feel places and spaces. I pay special attention to the haptic sense, and examine how danger-zone tourists touch places, how places touch tourists, and how soldiers touch tourists in an area (in the proximity) of ongoing conflict.

As I move beyond a binary approach and acknowledge the tight connections between affect, emotion, feeling, sensing and psychoanalytic drives, special attention is paid to fear as embodied, socially constructed and performed in danger-zones. On the interrelation between tourist discourse and fear, Albert Camus writes:

> What gives value to travel is fear. It breaks down a kind of internal structure . . . stripped of all our crutches, deprived of our masks . . . we are completely on the surface of ourselves. . . . This is the most obvious benefit of travel.
>
> (Camus, cited in Phipps, 1999, p. 81)

Apart from adventure tourism which thrives on fear, danger and adrenalin, fear has been, so far, treated mainly as an unwanted emotion. I open for discussion fear as (an intentionally) sought emotion that can make one feel alive. I discuss the fear that, as Camus wrote, breaks down internal structures, strips people of crutches, deprives them of masks, and thus leaves danger-zone subjectivities on the surface of themselves.

Geographies of psychoanalysis in tourism

Tensions and connections between affect, emotion and drives are tackled through theories of affect and theories of psychoanalysis. The link between affect and drives has been considered by geographers interested in psychoanalysis, affects and emotions (Kingsbury, 2010, 2014; Thien, 2005; Thrift, 2004, 2008; Pile, 1996, 2010). The focus is on the psychoanalytic concept of the death drive, as I aim to theorise the intangibility and ineffability of affects. The death drive explains the junction between life and death. Affect, in connection with the death drive, is that raw possibility before emotions are felt and expressed.

Examining psychoanalytic, affective and emotional geographies in danger-zone tourism leads to understanding how binary oppositions such as fun/fear, peace/war, safety/danger and life/death are disrupted. Danger-zone tourism, as a facet of dark tourism, refers to tourism in areas of political turmoil intimately connected to outbursts of frequently violent conflicts. While dark tourism mirrors growing social interest for tourist experiences in sites related to death, disaster and atrocity (Lennon & Foley, 2000; Ryan, 2005; Sharpley & Stone, 2009a), danger-zone tourism speaks of active engagements with politics of conflict, disasters and atrocities. Such engagements are tackled as I bring together, examine and expand psychoanalytic theories with geographies of affect and emotion in tourism studies. Psychoanalytic theories of the death drive offer a good route to understanding danger-zone performances in areas of dangerous, ongoing political conflict. The death drive blurs the boundaries of the life/death dualism, and also contributes to disrupting other binaries, such as fun/fear, safety/danger and peace/war.

Binaries, as forms of categorisations, represent not only means of dealing with complexity, but also a way to create individual and collective identities (Cloke & Johnston, 2005). The main philosophical, socio-spatial and political shortcomings of a binary approach is the expression of power favouring one term over the other 'when the supposed opposites are in fact mutually constitutive' (Cloke & Johnston, 2005, p. 14). The sides of the dualisms are indeed interrelated and the logic of binary oppositions leaves no interstitial space 'for any middle ground or shared identities' (Johnston, 2005a, p. 122). One way of breaking free from binary understandings is to adopt a multifaceted approach through which to overcome binary assumptions of either/or (Cloke & Johnston, 2005). Dualisms such as fun/fear, safety/danger and peace/war are, like almost all categories, socially constructed – 'they are created, not given' (Cloke & Johnston, 2005, p. 2). Dualisms are formed, with one having positive status and the other side being negatively defined. In relation to the epistemological relation between the two sides of a dualism, Johnston writes:

> If one side is represented by 'A', then its opposite will not be something from a different set of category relations, say 'B', but rather will be a conceptualization of what 'A' is not, say 'A-' . . . this is a mode of knowing in which A has a positive status and only exists in relation to its other.
>
> (Johnston, 2005a, p. 122)

Fun, safety and peace are the 'positive' constructs, while fear, danger and war are their 'negative' counterparts, defined only within the limits of the positive terms. I wish to consider that in danger-zone tourism the subordinate pole of the binary is not valorised – that is, danger-zone tourists do not simply reverse the hierarchy of the dualisms, as this would leave the binary in place. Some danger-zone tourists subvert and resist these binaries when travelling to places of ongoing conflict by engaging affectively and sensuously *in* and *with* these places. Along with these socially constructed binary oppositions, the life/death dichotomy is also unsettled by tourists in danger-zones. Compared to the rest of the above mentioned binaries, life/death together with 'distinctions between human and non-human, or between animate and inanimate, or between land and water may be considered natural in the sense of being pre-given or existing outside any imposed categorisation involving human thought' (Cloke & Johnston, 2005, p. 2). Although, Cloke and Johnston continue, even these distinctions have been debated. The death drive exists at the border between life and death and when accessed, the life/death dichotomy is troubled.

The *tourism–conflict–danger* nexus

Tourism and conflict are widely considered to be mutually exclusive. The separation of tourism and conflict is held in place by an overarching discourse, which claims that tourism can only thrive in tranquil and peaceful conditions (Hall, 1994; Hall et al., 2003; Pizam & Mansfeld, 1996). I analyse the emergence of academic interest in danger-zone tourism within the theoretical framework of dark tourism. Two decades ago, dark tourism – that is, tourism to sites associated with death, disaster and atrocity – was largely ignored (Dann, 1998; Lennon & Foley, 2000; Seaton, 2009). Dark tourism has now caught the attention of both the academic world and that of the wider public.[5] In April 2010, a conference on 'Death/Dark/ Thanatourism' was organised in New York, sponsored by Transitions: A Center for International Research in the Humanities and Social Sciences. There is also an Institute for Dark Tourism Research affiliated with the University of Central Lancashire in England.

In 1996, the *International Journal of Heritage Studies* published the first special edition on dark tourism, in which the authors drew attention to this significant yet ignored type of tourism (Seaton, 1996). Since then, one new special issue has been published (see Biran & Hyde, 2013). Lennon and Foley undertook initial research on heritage and atrocity without having 'a semantic label' to allow them to 'conduct fieldwork without the fear of misunderstanding' (1996, p. 195). They considered the term 'dark tourism' only as a working title for their project. The intention was to later adopt another term for a more inclusive approach to this concept. The authors have, instead, continued to use the phrase 'dark tourism' ever since, and the term has entered tourism studies vocabulary.

Since these first theoretical inceptions, a considerable body of work on dark tourism has been published. Lennon and Foley's book (2000) *Dark Tourism: The Attraction of Death and Disaster* seems to be the forerunner of this increased interest in dark tourism. Seaton analyses battlefield visits to Waterloo as a form of thanatourism according to 'a sight sacralisation model' (1999, p. 130). The author maintains that the site is invested with a semi-religious mystique and sacralisation, which have turned Waterloo into a pilgrimage site for dark tourists. In a different study, together with Dann, Seaton contextualises 'slavery tourism' 'within a framework of thanatourism, dark tourism and dissonant heritage, a field which in turn poses several questions for further research into this new and exciting phenomenon' (Dann & Seaton, 2001, p. 1). They have also published an edited book on *Slavery, Contested Heritage and Thanatourism*. On the same topic of tourism and 'presentation of urban slavery', Litvin and Brewer (2008, p. 73) consider the concept of thanatourism to argue that 'plantation slavery' in Charleston, South

Carolina, has been rather inadequately re/presented. Other case studies have been discussed in dark tourism/thanatourism literature such, as Alcatraz in the US and Robben Island in South Africa (Strange & Kempa, 2003), the Buried Village in New Zealand (Ryan & Kohli, 2006), and Fort Siloso in Singapore (Muzaini et al., 2007), amongst many others.

Holocaust tourism – that is, visits to 'sites associated with Nazism and the Jewish Holocaust' (Lennon & Foley, 2000, p. 23; Pollock, 2003) – is also part of the wider field of dark tourism. Some authors consider tourism to Holocaust sites such as Kraków-Kazimierz or Auschwitz-Birkenau in Poland as part of a 'dissonant heritage condition . . . in which there is a lack of congruence in time or space between people and their heritage' (Ashworth, 2002, p. 363). Definitions of dark tourism and/ or thanatourism have been extended and adapted to fit each of these case studies.

By and large, research on dark tourism remains descriptive, driven by managerial, marketing and business considerations, and portrays dark tourists as passive consumers of death, disaster and atrocity devoid of emotions, feelings and senses. This is a summation of the critique that I level not only at dark tourism, but also at the field of tourism studies. I do this throughout the book and more specifically in Part II, 'Introducing Affect in Tourism'.

In the *International Journal of Heritage Studies*' first special edition on dark tourism mentioned above, Seaton, at the end of the concluding section, brings the following critique:

> The central paradox of Dark Tourism is that, like much popular journalism, it addresses desires and interests which are not supposed to have a legitimate existence within the secular, moral discourse of the 20th century which is why it is frequently presented as heritage, education or history.
>
> (Seaton, 1996, p. 224)

In a study on the 'dark side of tourism', Dann writes:

> There are apparently many tourists who are not simply motivated by the personal danger and risk of adventure and sport (climbing the Himalayas for instance), but who wish the excitement of visiting a current trouble spot, such as Beirut or Algiers . . . Since death is inevitable, and the death wish is so universal (at least according to Freud), why not anticipate the Grim Reaper as a ludic form of presocialization?
>
> (Dann, 1998, p. 7)

It is timely, therefore, to consider that 'desires and interests which are not supposed to have a legitimate existence within the secular, moral discourse of the 20th century' were acknowledged and addressed beyond the 'heritage, education and history' perspectives. Danger-zone tourism in places and times of turmoil, has scarcely made it within the realm of academic research, and tourists travelling to places of political conflicts are looked upon as morbid ghouls. Tourism in areas of ongoing political turmoil is briefly mentioned in the literature of dark tourism as an extreme and bizarre form of travel; its protagonists, danger-zoners, are considered to be 'in the vanguard of dark-tourism' (Lennon & Foley, 2000, p. 9). The danger generated by an ongoing socio-political conflict is considered to be a deterring factor for tourists. This dominant discourse has been seldom questioned. When it has been questioned, practices of travelling to places of ongoing conflict are described as 'morbid or ghoulish' (Sharpley, 2005, p. 216). In this book, it is argued that, despite widely held beliefs, there are tourists who, consciously attracted or not, travel to places of socio-political unrest. Their practices and experiences can be understood within the wider subfield of dark tourism. I offer such examinations beyond the possible sarcasm displayed by Dann's question above: 'why not anticipate the Grim Reaper as a ludic form of presocialization?' I consider it appropriate that danger-zone tourism should be brought from the margins of the dark tourism debate to closer to the core, by in-depth engagements with theories of affect, emotion and psychoanalysis.

Book outline

The book enacts the touring circuit and consists of four parts. Part I is titled 'Packing and setting forth', Part II 'Arrival: encounters with affect in tourism', Part III 'Destinations: affective routes in "Middle Eastern" tourism', and Part IV 'Re-tour'. Each part contains chapters, which I outline below.

Part I, 'Packing and setting forth', includes this first and introductory chapter, 'Packing light and feeling down'. Here I have laid out the background and main claims of this book, most importantly, that affective tourism is performed by subjectivities who engage in emotional, affective and sensuous encounters in danger-zones of conflict. I argue that affects, emotions and drives need to be considered in the production of tourism knowledges. I propose that the death drive be discussed in connection with geographies of emotions and affects to further explore and understand tourism experiences in areas of ongoing conflict. In considering emotions, affects and the death drive, some dualisms that underpin tourism studies such as safety/danger, fun/fear, peace/war and life/death are disrupted.

The theories that underpin this book are discussed in Part II, 'Arrival: encounters with affect, emotion and darkness in tourism', which comprises Chapters 2, 3 and 4. Within the critical turn in tourism studies, scholars engage reflexively with research. It is within the space of this critical turn that most studies, that seek to disrupt hegemonic and masculinist approaches to/in tourism, are produced. Being reflexive about 'our' emotions as tourism researchers, as well as integrating studies of affects, emotions, bodily senses and drives felt and performed in tourism contexts, can bring new and exciting possibilities to the critical turn in tourism studies.

In Chapter 2, 'Touring affect', I draw on socio-spatial theories of affect and emotion to conceptualise critical geographies of tourism in places and times of ongoing turmoil. In Chapter 3, '"Psychoanalysing" tourism', psychoanalytic explorations (more specifically of the death drive) are introduced to offer in-depth understandings of subjectivities in danger-zones. Dark-tourism literature is discussed in Chapter 4, 'Routes in dark tourism', to frame theorisations of danger-zone tourism in Jordan and Palestine/Israel. I argue that considerations of affect, emotion and psychoanalytic death drives add in-depth understandings of danger-zone tourism in particular, and tourism studies in general. This chapter's main focus is to show that one can theorise a tourism practice irrespective of the danger and conflict 'tormenting' a region, which are so far considered to be deterring factors.

Part III, 'Destinations: affective routes in "Middle Eastern" tourism' includes Chapters 5–8. In Chapter 5, I locate 'the Middle East', offering a brief historical, geopolitical background for the region. In Chapter 6, 'Around Jordan – Switzerland of the Middle East?', I discuss the ways the Israeli–Palestinian conflict is sanitised in Jordan. I challenge the image of the 'oasis of peace' or 'Switzerland of the Middle East' that governmental officials and tourism industry representatives have constructed of Jordan. Emotions and the politics of the relations between Jordanians, Israelis and Palestinians are intimately linked. In this chapter, I unpack such dis/connections by examining the emotions felt and performed by Jordanian tour guides.

Chapter 7, 'Crossing into the West Bank: it's all political and emotional in Israel/Palestine', focuses on tourism and emotions in Palestinian tourism spaces. I examine the political aspect that pervades tourism in Palestine. 'Icons' of the ongoing Israeli–Palestinian conflict, such as the separation wall still being built, refugee camps, and crossing points have become tourist sites of fascination and frustration. I discuss haptic encounters at these sites by analysing the narratives of Palestinian tour guides and international tourists.

Chapter 8, 'Between a rock and a hard place: a brief detour to Iraq', brings together geographies of psychoanalysis, emotions and affects to argue that fear makes one feel alive. I draw on Freudian and Lacanian conceptualisations of the death drive to argue that danger-zone subjectivities assert and disrupt the life/death dichotomy along with other binaries such as safety/danger, fun/fear and peace/war.

Part IV, 'Re-tour', contains Chapter 9, the concluding section of the book. Here I return to the initial argument that affects, feelings and emotions should be considered more prominently in the production of tourism knowledges. There is much ado about the critical turn in tourism studies, and considerations of the affective, emotional and psychoanalytic aspects can add further critical and reflective understandings of tourism practices and theories.

Notes

1 Anderson & Smith, 2001; Davidson et al., 2005; Davidson & Milligan, 2004; Johnston 2005b, 2007; Waitt et al., 2007.
2 Ahmed, 2004a, 2004b, 2010; Gregg & Seigworth, 2010; Massumi, 1993, 2002a, 2002b; Probyn 2003, 2004a, 2004b; Ngai, 2005.
3 Clough, 2003; Clough & Halley, 2007.
4 Andrews, 2005; Edensor 2000, 2001, 2007; Johnston, 2001, 2005b, 2007; Macnaghten & Urry, 2000; Pritchard et al., 2007; Veijola & Jokinen, 1994.
5 Biran & Hyde, 2013; Dunkley, 2007; Dunkley et al., 2011; Knudsen, 2011; Lennon & Foley, 2000; Lisle, 2007; Muzaini et al., 2007; Sharpley, 2005, 2009; Sharpley & Sundaram, 2005; Stone, 2006; Stone & Sharpley, 2008; Rittichainuwat, 2008; White & Frew, 2013.

Part II

Arrival

Encounters with affect, emotion and darkness in tourism

2 Touring affect

> The increasing significance of affect as a focus of analysis across a number of disciplinary and interdisciplinary discourses is occurring at a time when critical theory is facing the analytic challenges of ongoing war, trauma, torture, massacre, and counter/terrorism. If these world events can be said to be symptomatic of ongoing political, economic, and cultural transformations, the turn to affect may be registering a change in the cofunctioning of the political, economic and cultural.
>
> (Clough, 2007, p. 1)

In this chapter I wish to argue the case for an affective and emotional turn in tourism studies as I show that affects, emotions, feelings and senses matter, yet they have been conspicuously ignored in tourism studies. Given the fact that tourism experiences, encounters and performances are lived through feelings and emotions, one would think that tourism studies abound with research on what feelings are, how they work, what they do with tourists and in tourism, and what they mean – but this is hardly the case. In the humanities and social sciences (philosophers from Aristotle to Baruch Spinoza; cultural studies scholars such as Sara Ahmed, Brian Massumi, Sianne Ngai and Elspeth Probyn; contemporary geographers such as Liz Bondi, Joyce Davidson, Christine Milligan, Steve Pile and Mick Smith amongst many others), and in the medical sciences (psychologists and neurobiologists from William James to Antonio Damasio) have tackled affect, emotion and feeling in their respective fields. As pervasive as they are in the lived life and abundantly debated in other disciplines and fields of study (Gouk & Hills, 2005), these remain under-researched in tourism.

Some of these forays, mostly in medical, ethical and psychological fields, consider emotions as natural entities suitable for scientific quantification. The affective and emotional turn that I advocate in tourism studies calls for a more fluid, cultural and spatial reading of affect and emotion as gut-wrenching intensities. Critical debates that consider social and cultural constructions of affects, emotions, feelings and senses should figure more prominently in tourism studies. Arguably, such debates have been marginalised through the gender politics of research, wherein the academy is conditioned to principles of distance, objectivity and rationality (Pritchard et al., 2011). Affect, embodied emotions and feelings are judged as unscientific, pretentious, or evasive. These are highly gendered and political issues. In tourism studies, the gendered politics of knowledge production has been the main reason why these have been ignored. Cognitive and universalising considerations of emotions as quantified and quantifiable variables are critiqued here in favour of a genuine expressing of, and dealing with, affective and emotional attachments in tourism studies. The human world is constructed, lived, experienced and performed through emotions; so too are travel and tourism. Affective and emotional encounters define touring people and places as affect and emotion travel with and through bodies, in places and between objects.

Detached, objective, rational and business-oriented research has been valued and implicitly masculinised. While this landscape timidly begins to change in tourism, engagements with affective and emotional subjectivities remain largely devalued and feminised. The affective and emotional turn in tourism studies seeks to *feel and fill* this gap.

Moving in affect

We exist, move and tour in worlds infused with affect, emotion and feeling. In the social sciences, affect and emotion are hotly debated, with critical theorists, cultural critics and human geographers inviting a turn to affect starting early 1990s (Clough, 2010). The call to turn affective was launched as re/action to perceived limitations in post-structuralism, postmodernism (which declared the 'waning of affect' according to Frederic Jameson) and deconstruction (often considered 'truly glacial', and therefore the emotion-less part of post-structuralism, as Rei Terada points out). More recently, the focus in critical cultural, social and spatial theories has been on dis/connections and circuits between affect and emotion and a 'return to the subject as the subject of emotion' (Clough, 2010, p. 207). I want to argue for those approaches to be advanced in tourism which regard affect as pre-individual, *other than* conscious, vital and bodily forces shaping the tourist body's capacity and willingness to move, to be im/mobile, to connect to others and with places (Seigworth & Gregg, 2010). Affect as intensity, sometimes forceful as in psychoanalytic studies of trauma, neurosis and death drive, sometimes subtle, transpiring in everyday geographies, is both of the ordinary and of the *extra*-ordinary. Emotions as subjectively felt states, expressed *in* and *through* the body, both individually and collectively, are connected to social, cultural and political currents. Focusing on such considerations in tourism should also be a 'harbinger of and a discursive accompaniment to the forging of a new body' (Clough, 2010, p. 207), a 'new' emotional and affective tourist body.

As concepts, affect and emotion pair 'dangerously close', with affect being a felt familiarity 'seemingly knowable despite not having objective tangibility' (Dewsbury, 2009, p. 20). As a phenomenon, affect is akin to an invisible felt presence, like 'a force field . . . something known to be there, but equally intangible in being not quite there' (p. 21). When affect can be manifest, as it is only partly expressible and able to be 'captured' in communicable terms, it can shape-shift into emotions. Emotion and affect belong to different registers, logics and orders, with emotion being 'subjective content' and 'qualified intensity', and affect being intensity itself (Massumi, 1995). Ngai (2005) summarises the difference:

affects are *less* formed and structured than emotions, but not lacking form or structure altogether; *less* 'sociolinguistically fixed', but by no means code-free or meaningless; *less* 'organized in response to our interpretations of situations', but by no means entirely devoid of organization or diagnostic powers.

(Ngai, 2005, p. 27, emphasis in original)

The vitality, ubiquity and pervasiveness of affects offer considerable routes and resources to access and tackle emotional geographies (Bondi, 2005). Affect is treated as non-reflective and challenging cognition, especially with non- or more-than-representational geographers having sought to shift attention away from representations of affect and emotion feeling to 'feelingness itself' (Bondi, 2005, p. 443). The authority of individual and located emotions has, however, not been properly challenged. Non-representational approaches run the risk of turning affect into something extra-ordinary, too detached from everyday articulations of emotion. The distinction between affect and emotion is considered by some to be more 'a modal difference of intensity or degree, rather than a formal difference of quality or kind' (Ngai, 2005, p. 27). Others contend that while emotions and affects have been used somewhat interchangeably in the social sciences, there are significant differences, disagreements, or even a split, a 'relationship/non-relationship' between affect and emotion (Pile, 2010).

Emotions cross boundaries, making them unstable; emotions are expressed, while affects are 'inexpressible' and therefore 'unable to be brought into representation' (Pile, 2010, p. 8). Pile maintains that this split between emotion and affect poses important questions about the ways these are to be understood. He draws on geographies of psychoanalysis to offer an explanation of the relationship between affects, emotions and feelings by proposing a three-layer cake model. In this model, Pile (2010) considers affect a quality of life and the deepest level before and beyond (pre-) cognition, always interpersonal; feelings are the middle layer since they can be expressed at a conscious level, but are mostly tacit and intuitive remaining at a pre-cognitive level. The third level – the most visible and expressed one – is the one of socially constructed emotions, which, at the cognitive level, are 'expressed feelings, being both conscious and experienced' (p. 9).

On the contrary, to avoid the awkward split between emotion and affect, Bondi (2005) draws on the theory and practice of psychotherapy to discuss the gap between emotions and affects, and between feelings and their representations. She warns of 'the twin pitfalls of equating emotions with individualised subjectivity and conceptualising affect in ways that distance it from ordinary human experience' (Bondi, 2005, p. 441). In the same vein of considering affect as having psychological nuances, Thien (2005) writes about an 'affective turn in social and critical thought' (p. 450). Affect's psychoanalytic connotations are also recognised by Thrift (2004; 2008) as one of the four facets of affect, along with affect as embodied practice and knowledge; naturalistic affect and having an interactive capacity; and affect as neo-Darwinian based on physiological change and evolution.

These psychoanalytic connections to affect and emotion are useful to frame theoretical links between death drives, anger, fun, fear and the like in tourism.

The inexpressibility of affects represents the overlapping point with psychoanalytic death drives and *jouissance*, which I discuss in more detail in the next chapter. When affect remains that ineffable, invisible presence and unassimilable intensity, it overlaps with the drives as understood in psychoanalysis. Affect, and its distinction from emotion, is arguably meant to address a basic psychoanalytic problem of differentiating between 'first-person from third-person feeling, and by extension, feeling that is contained by an identity from feeling that is not' (Ngai, 2005, p. 27).

Tourism, a field of the in-between after all, ought to tackle transactions and transitions from one pivot to the other, from affect to emotion via feeling, sensing and back. Affective tourism is about interstitial spaces, of passages in which affect intensifies, acquires density in and outside expression. Affects morph into emotions, feelings become intentions 'for forceful or unambiguous action . . . and amplify their power to diagnose situations' (Ngai, 2005, p. 27). More specifically, affective and emotional geographies of tourism – that which is sensed, felt and performed especially, at tourist sites in the middle of or in the proximity of some danger-zones – trouble binary oppositions in tourism studies such as safety/danger, fun/fear, peace/war, and life/death.

Emotions in tourism

The subjective experience of emotions becomes most obvious in tourism since tourism moves people (Picard, 2012), not only in a physical sense, but also emotionally and affectively. The word itself – emotion – comes from Latin *emovere* 'to move out or move away'. Initially the term meant physical movement or migration and until the nineteenth century it continued to refer to 'moving, stirring agitation in a physical sense' (Gouk & Hills, 2005, p. 17). Historical and etymological developments of emotion show that before the eighteenth century in English there were no 'emotions' as such, but 'passions' and 'affections', with a focus on passive sufferings and endurances linked to the Crucifixion (Richards, 2005). Later, the term 'passion' was substituted with 'emotion' as the focus shifted from passivity to activity, to '*being moved* to some action' (Richards, 2005, p. 53, emphasis in original). Emotions, however, are not only about movements, but also about attachments, connections and divisions (Ahmed, 2004b). Movement and attachment are significantly interrelated, in that movement 'connects bodies to other bodies . . . attachments take place through movement' (p. 11). These attachments and dis/connections between touring bodies and places are at the core of my argument of turning to affect and emotion in tourism.

Tourism studies employ a wonderfully eclectic approach to exploring life, cultures, societies, places and spaces. Affective tourism is, therefore, not couched in any big discourse or theory. Like other authors, such as Crouch (2012), my attempt is to go beyond category-driven thinking and research, especially beyond the binary thinking so entrenched in tourism with its pervasive dichotomies of home/away and host/guest. I do feel inspired by critical tourism researchers Irena Ateljevich, Anne-Marie d'Hauteserre, Alison McIntosh, Nigel Morgan,

Annette Pritchard; by feminist and cultural geographers such as Liz Bondi, Lynda Johnston, Bettina van Hoven, Robyn Longhurst, Deborah Thien, Gordon Waitt; and by cultural anthropologists like Susan Frohlick. I also find inspiration in the works of Sigmund Freud, Jacques Lacan, and psychoanalytic geographers such as Paul Kingsbury, Steve Pile and Heidi Nast. I particularly like Crouch's approach whereby 'I am sensitive to theory but not coerced by it' (2012, p. 2).

Perhaps, instead of arguing for a turn to affects, emotions and drives in tourism studies, one should ask for a *re-turn* to a previous call for more recognition of emotions in tourism studies launched a decade ago – a call that seems to have remained, by and large, unanswered. Jamal and Hollinshead maintain that 'The omission of studies and narratives which locate . . . "emotion" in tourism, whether that of the tourist or the host, is a problem which has been noted and addressed by very few scholars' (2001, p. 67). Omitting or relegating emotions to the margins might after all not be too surprising and *ipso facto* shows that they are at the centre of thought itself, as deconstruction stances would explain (Ahmed, 2004b).

Disparate accounts of emotions in tourism have been recently published.[1] Performances in lesbian tourism geographies are examined through the spatial and political productivity of pride and shame in gendered and sexualised bodies (Johnston, 2007). Shame and pride are further explored and proven to open and close moral gateways in joint management strategies of national parks in Australia, since travelling, walking, climbing, touching and being touched by Uluru, for example, are lived through emotions (Waitt et al., 2007). Travelling to Uluru, some feel a type of everyday shame (Probyn, 2004a). Shame and discomfort in a tourist encounter in the Turkish village of Göreme are also recognised and discussed by a tourism researcher (Tucker, 2009). I am in agreement here with Tucker, who argues: 'if we are to understand tourism encounters more fully, it is necessary to examine closely their emotional and bodily dimensions' (p. 444). It is this call for a closer engagement with emotional and bodily dimensions to which affective tourism – and the affective and emotional turn in tourism studies that I advocate – responds.

Some studies in tourism view emotions as variables in quantitative approaches. Research on satisfaction and loyalty in regards to emotions has received attention from tourism scholars employing business and managerial methodologies (Bigné & Andreu, 2004; Faullant et al., 2011; Yüksel & Yüksel, 2007). In tourism management scholarship, emotions tend to be considered as biologically hardwired, subject to cognitive processes and treated as items that can be measured using mathematical formulas and numerical analysis models. Emotions are furthermore examined as separate from affects, feelings and senses.

Critical approaches in tourism recognise the importance of emotions and their potentially cathartic impacts. Accounts of dark tourism present the ways anxiety, death and danger are commoditised as products and experiences at dark sites focusing mainly on 'merchandising and revenue generation' (Lennon & Foley, 2000, p. 12). Narratives in thanatourism are discussed to capture in more depth the emotional experiences of 25 tourists who toured First World War battlefields in Somme and Ypres (Dunkley et al., 2011). There is even a brief mention of the psychoanalytic concept of voyeurism connected to emotions in thanatourism, but the authors seem to be slightly reticent to fully engage with it: 'Whilst there may well be elements of voyeurism in their encounters, battlefield tours emerge as complex, deeply meaningful and in some cases life-changing experiences for the individuals involved in this study' (Dunkley et al., 2011, p. 866). In spite of this conclusion, surprisingly, engagements with affects, emotions, feelings, senses and drives are missing in dark tourism. Yet I remain hopeful for a possible affective and emotional turn in tourism studies in general, and dark tourism in particular. Delving into dark tourism's commodifications of anxiety, death and danger requires in-depth explorations of affect, emotion and embodied senses, which have been to a great extent ignored. Experiences of those in the vanguard of dark tourism – danger-zone tourists – are tackled in the following through the lens of fear encountered head-on in a place of ongoing conflict.

Fear: between affect and emotion

Fear has received unrivalled attention in the social sciences.[2] My aim is to delve into fear which some tourists feel in areas (in the proximity) of an ongoing conflict such as Jordan and Palestine/Israel. I examine fear as affective forceful intensity circulating in places of conflict. Fear is not to be objectified or classified into negative/positive, basic, primary, or derivative since 'Fear is not only objective circumstance but also subjective response' (Tuan 1979, p. 210). Fear is relational (Pain, 2010, 2014); it permeates bodies, and crosses boundaries, rendering them unstable and uncertain.

My attention also turns to fear as an intentionally sought emotion having different layers and nuances which might not all be 'negative', since the study of fear 'is not limited to the study of withdrawal and retrenchment . . . it also seeks to understand growth, daring and adventure' (Tuan, 1979, p. 10). Seeking, consciously or not, to feel fear in a locale of ongoing conflict is not meant to be another form of hegemonic imposition, or enhancing the post/colonial gaze in the region. Thus, I acknowledge and unpack the contradictory and paradoxical position of such tourists who (may) contribute to the ongoing existence of danger and conflict. I argue that some tourists seeking fear to make them feel alive can sometimes generate pro-social action. Fear seems to be spatio-temporally pervasive as we live again in 'a time of fears', of fears that are:

> socially and culturally recycled [and] may be seen as a sediment of a past experience of facing a menace point blank – a sediment that outlives the encounter and becomes an important factor in shaping human conduct even if there is no longer a direct threat to life or integrity.
>
> (Bauman, 2006, p. 3)

The ubiquity of fear is most fearsome especially when fear has no clear address or cause, when fear is diffuse and scattered. Dangers one is afraid of could be 'real' or 'imagined', and when there is mismatch between the real and the imagined, the value of fear comes into question. Three kinds of 'fearful' dangers can be described (Bauman, 2006). First, there are dangers that threaten the body and the possessions; second, dangers that jeopardise the stability of the social order connected to security of livelihood or survival, and third, dangers that put at risk one's place in the world connected to social hierarchies, class, gender, ethnic and religious identities. Fear itself has been re-interrogated as having interior and exterior aspects (Pile, 2010), or working according to 'inside-out' and 'outside-in' models (Ahmed, 2004b). Fear is felt inside in the body, it moves then outside, in the direction of other people and objects, and later might even return to its initial subject. This is the 'inside-out' model of fear (Ahmed, 2004b). The 'outside-in' model is of a fear that permeates interior as well as exterior subjectivities. It originates from an outside moving in and is formed of socio-cultural accumulations of previous menacing experiences, which connects bodies to places and holds the social body together.

Menacing experiences of danger and fear seem to be intimately interlinked, both described in gloomy shades as giving rise to *ugly feelings* which compared to 'aesthetic emotions' are 'the rats and possums rather than lions' in the 'bestiary of affects' (Ngai, 2005, p. 7). These 'negative' and 'nasty' connotations notwithstanding, fear is the key emotion debated in philosophy from Aristotle to the present. In this book, fear, instead of being unwanted, seeks to recycle some of this 'nastiness' for its productive confrontation with dangers in times and places of conflict and turmoil. This can lead to different understandings of tourist subjectivities. To be sure, I am not using 'nasty' and 'negative' as absolute attributes of emotions; I acknowledge that polarities 'positive and negative', 'good and bad' bear judgemental weight. The notions of 'emotional polarity' or 'emotional opposites' and even of 'emotional valence' have been scrutinised. This is not to say that there are no valences or contrasts, but there exist a variety of such polarities and nuances (Solomon & Stone, 2002).

I argue in favour of an existential fear or a fear that makes one feel alive which permeates and disrupts binary oppositions such as danger/safety, fear/fun, death/life and peace/war in Palestinian and Jordanian danger-zones. Fear possesses productive potentials in cases whereby it encourages us to confront dangers or when 'it propels us to remove ourselves from danger' (Solomon & Stone, 2002, p. 420). In the context of visiting an area of ongoing conflict such as Palestine/Israel and Jordan, fear could propel some people to remove themselves from danger by confronting it point blank. Fear in such a context can generate anger, which in turn can challenge 'the status quo and motivate pro-social action, defined as either direct helping or righteous behaviour in the interest of less fortunate others' (Henderson, 2008, p. 30). Anger's 'political salience' challenges the idea that 'negative and ugly emotions' 'necessarily lead to negative socio-political outcomes and should, therefore, be avoided' (Henderson, 2008, p. 29). I join scholars (such as Ngai, 2005; Henderson, 2008; Probyn, 2004a, 2004b; Saville, 2008) who challenge the 'negativity' of emotions such as anger, fear, or shame.

Fear felt by some tourists in an area of political turmoil can awaken anger and/or shame, for example. Experiencing anger at one or all parties involved in a conflict, meant to address perceived injustice (Henderson, 2008), brings about a feeling of being alive. In some cases, anger is not directed towards anyone, but is internalised and then it can become shame. Anger, fear and shame bear disparaging connotations. Challenging shame and its treatment as a 'bad' emotion, Probyn (2004a, p. 329) argues that 'shame is immensely productive politically and conceptually in advancing a project of everyday ethics'. Shame as affect explains what 'the feeling body does in shame' (p. 330), whereas shame as emotion, privileges cognition. Conversely, a focus on anger as emotion rather than affect, favours descriptions of anger with a 'cognitive bias' rather than a 'biological bias' (Henderson, 2008, p. 28).

A debate of fear as affect or as emotion will always get off-track. Fear is specific to particular ways of engineering which is not wholly resistant to reconfiguration, to moving from the individual to the social and back, and shape-shifting to and from intangible intensity. The equivocal, in-between status of fear, anger and shame ought to be capitalised on so as 'to recuperate some of these negative affects for their *critical* productivity' (Ngai, 2005, p. 3, emphasis in original). While avoiding romanticising such dysphoric affects, these do seem to fuel spatio-temporalities in turmoil, crisis and conflict.

My defence of fear felt, experienced and performed in times and place of turmoil and conflict is, however, guarded. I argue that existential fear experienced both by tourists and local tourism industry representatives can be extremely productive socially, spatially, politically and conceptually in advancing affective tourism in places of turmoil. For tourists, existential fears awaken the senses and the consciousness of life lived in (the proximity of) an area of ongoing conflict. For local tourism industry representatives, existential fears are transferred to tourists. Existential fear – a nuance of fear that makes one feel alive – is a mixture of emotion and affect wherein affect is interwoven into the emotion of fear and also reconfigured by emotional engagements some tourists have with place. Fear as affect is ubiquitous, is 'raw possibility, between all those things that comprise life as we know it' (Saville, 2008). It is the ways human bodies sense, touch and are touched by fear, that engagements with places in socio-political conflict are formed.

Touch! Sense! Feel!

Is tourism out of touch with touch? Have tourism researchers/geographers forgotten 'touch'? In human geography, it has been argued that vision's hegemony has been challenged, that the 'empire of the senses' is on the rise and 'touch has come to have considerable intellectual currency' (Dixon et al., 2012, p. 131). In tourism studies, the focus on vision, visuality and visual metaphors has not really shifted to considering interconnections within the whole sensorium, between senses, sensations, emotions and feelings (van Hoven, 2011). Tourism researchers have ignored touch: we are very simply and literally out of touch. To forget touch, it is bemoaned by others (Paterson, 2005), means to ignore the body with its sensuous senses, to favour the eye (abstracted visualism) to the detriment of the hands and feet (haptic experience).

Since Veijola and Jokinen (1994) and Johnston (2001) enquired whether the body can be written into tourism studies, there has been increasing, but still insufficient, academic interest in the bodily character of tourist experiences. Embodiment and subjectivity connected to the sensuous, sensual and sensorial in tourism studies pose new issues about ways to conceptualise social, cultural and spatial formations of tourism (Crouch & Desforges, 2003). Instead of exploring individual sensory geographies of taste, touch, smell, or sound, for example, some authors argue for the overall consideration of the sensual, and sensuous nature of travel and tourism as a whole to understand the construction and performance of tourist subjectivities (see Crouch & Desforges, 2003). While such endeavours are highly needed and welcome in tourism, I argue for 'adding in' geographies of different senses that could lead to a more critical, affective, emotional and sensuous interpretation of tourist subjectivities. These sensuous geographies of tourism have been to a great extent ignored and forgotten.

Touch is the most intimate sense and also the most reciprocal of the senses, since 'to touch' always implies 'to be touched' (Rodaway, 1994). Scratching the surface of the immediacy of tactility, there is a whole haptic system, which feels beyond the cutaneous experience of the skin (Paterson, 2006). The haptic system, a concept borrowed from perceptual psychology, comprises three aspects (Paterson, 2009a): first, the kinaesthetic ability of the body to feel its own motion; second, proprioception or the sense of internally felt sensation and exterior perceptions, and third, the sense of balance, bodily re/orientation and inertia connected to the vestibular system.

'Haptic' is a word that is derivative of the Greek term '*haptikos* = able to come in contact with' which in turn comes from the Greek '*haptein* = fasten' (Oxford English Dictionary, 2011). Haptic refers to the sense of touch, but it avoids the superficial assumptions that 'touch geographies are only the sensuous experiences of the fingers' (Rodaway, 1994, p. 41). Haptic refers to the largest and most decentred human bodily system of feeling and perception that deals with touch (Obrador-Pons, 2007). Thus, it plays a major role in the intersubjective formation and circulation of affect and emotion. Touch is 'ambiguous' in its ability to simultaneously be receptive and responsive, active and expressive, thus to touch always implies being touched which 'assumes an open orientation to the experience of touching, actively converting raw sensation into synthetic affects of fear, calm, tenderness' (Paterson, 2004, p. 170).

This complex hapticality cuts across several systems of perception and brings together touch with the visual, the aural and the olfactory in synaesthesia through which the body feels, experiences and performs place and time (Dixon et al., 2012). The mingling between vision and touch – a visuo-haptic collocation – (Paterson, 2006) is intensified when physically manipulating virtual as well as material objects. Physical touch is complemented by the proximity and intimacy of material objects, places and bodies. Touch, beyond its physicality and tactility of the skin, becomes an awareness of temperature, pressure and locomotion (Obrador-Pons, 2007; Straughan, 2012). These play an important role when engaging in and with tourist places and activities.

Some tourists in Spain, for example, engage haptically with a nudist beach as wind and sand are felt by the skin (Obrador-Pons, 2007). These feelings of temperature, texture and movement are part of a sensuous haptic system, whereby the skin and whole body is touched and touches. Likewise, when hiking and bear-viewing in the Canadian Great Bear Rain Forest, tourist experiences are 'framed by the haptic for, at all times, wind and weather touched our skin thus warming, cooling, moistening or stroking us' (van Hoven, 2011, p. 43). Leisure aquatic activities such as scuba diving are also performed through the touch of the water, whereby 'the texture, temperature and spatiality' (Straughan, 2012, p. 22) of water is felt and embodied suspending and enfolding the diving body. In this context 'touch operates as part of a hapticality' which is 'a kinaesthesia that allows the body to feel its positionality in space' (Straughan, 2012, p. 20).

These same aspects of tactility, pressure, temperature and movement are considered in the argument that the hot desert air in Jordan produces a haptic shock through which place, the lowest geographical point on earth near the Dead Sea, is felt. In Jordan, Israel and Palestine, a region plagued by continuous socio-political turmoil, this haptic shock is embodied and reverberates in the aural and visual as tourists in the area engage their sensorium – that system of sensory values which is rarely articulated in words, but nevertheless felt and performed. In Palestine/Israel, fear is felt as 'touching intensity' of anticipated unpleasantness. Touch in connection to this nuance of fear in the West Bank is analysed in more detail in Chapter 7.

In dark and danger tourism, touching and being touched by danger and conflict bring about performances of fears, which reside at the border between an interior and exterior self. These tend to be felt inside, but generated by outside events in a danger-zone. Feeling and performing affective tourism show how tourist/host, safety/danger, fun/fear and peace/war binaries are asserted and disrupted in some danger-zones in Palestine/Israel and Jordan, such as checkpoints and the separation wall. Haptic tourism geographies – bodies that touch places, places that touch bodies, and bodies that touch each other – could generate fear, anger and even disdain. Touching and being touched by danger, fear, conflict and even death have the potential not only to disrupt and destabilise these above-mentioned dichotomies, but also to generate pro-social action. Danger-zone tourism is contingent upon an array of fears, which are not totally 'negative', but could be regarded as a productive haptic engagement with place and people in regions of political turmoil.

Touching between bodies and places in danger-zones brings about 'a new awareness of Life', as danger and death are sometimes felt to be lying in wait: 'It is the thrill felt by the individual when immersed in an ordeal and in control of the danger being faced – a mixture of fear and intoxication, of emotion and sensation' (Le Breton, 2000, p. 2) that is sought and that brings the body, metaphorically, to life. Fear and death are important ingredients in danger-zone tourism, in particular, and dark tourism in general. Flirting with danger or even death leads to an increase in emotion 'as a "voluptuous panic" that totally thrills' (Le Breton, 2000, p. 4). It is this voluptuous panic that is brought about by the death drive and understood as desire to satisfy fantasies. At the interface formed between touching and touched, an entire system of haptic sensations is set in motion in danger-zone tourism. Haptic sensations help translate drives and instincts stemming from un/ conscious desires and fantasies. Fears and the system of haptic sensations are generated in the workings of death drives and desires for *jouissance*, aspects that I detail in the following chapter.

Notes

1 See Buda et al., 2014; Dunkley, 2007; Dunkley et al., 2011; Johnston, 2005a, 2005b, 2007, 2012; Mitas et al., 2012; Mura, 2010; Picard & Robinson, 2012; Shakeela & Weaver, 2012; Tucker, 2007b, 2009; Waitt et al., 2007.
2 Fear has been explored from various perspectives: political fear (Robin, 2004), liquid fear (Bauman, 2006), women's fear (Bankey, 2002; Listerborn, 2002), agoraphobia (Davidson, 2002), phobias of nature or bio-phobias (Davidson & Smith, 2003), fear of crime, fear of violence (Pain, 2014), fear of death (Tuan, 1979) and the list can continue.

3 'Psychoanalysing' tourism

> Psychoanalysis is a controversial account of mental life and a troublesome form of knowledge. Unsurprisingly, therefore, there are no accepted psychoanalytic concepts which can be easily transposed into, superimposed onto, or mapped alongside, geography – regardless of the kind of geography.
>
> (Pile, 1996, p. 81)

Affect and emotion in tourism can be further explored via psychoanalytic routes. By and large, tourism studies have left aside psychoanalysis as a form of knowledge to interpret and understand various tourist experiences, especially those involving fantasy, desires, drives and the unconscious, amongst others (Buda, 2015). Examples of previous engagements with psychoanalysis in tourism research are scarce. The politics of enjoyment in Jamaican tourism, for example, is analysed employing Lacan's psychoanalytic concepts of *jouissance*, the pleasure principle, the Other and fantasy (Kingsbury, 2005). In another project, Freudian and Lacanian psychoanalytic concepts of symptom, ego, defence and fantasy are used to examine discourses of risk, security and anxiety in US travel magazines in the months following the September 11, 2001 events (Kingsbury & Brunn, 2003, 2004).

In an earlier study of tourists flocking to Princess Diana's grave in Althorp, England, the psychoanalytic concept of catharsis is used to question whether 'morbid tourism [is] an expression of an inner purification' (Blom, 2000, p. 34). More recently, drawing on psychoanalytic sociology, Freudian and Jungian concepts of the Id instincts of sex, aggression and the Superego are proposed in tourism research to explore deviant tourist behaviour (Uriely et al., 2011). Such research adds, as the authors argue, to the literatures of 'sex tourism, drug tourism, dark tourism, heritage tourism, ecotourism, volunteer tourism, risk and terror in tourism, adventure tourism, sport tourism, as well as backpacking, pilgrimage and sea–sand–sun vacationing' (p. 1053). The study briefly mentions emotions objectified and categorised as positive/negative in relation to the concept of sublimation:

> The use of adaptive defense mechanisms, such as sublimation (the transformation of negative emotions or instincts into positive actions, behaviors, or emotions) and altruism (offering service to others that brings personal satisfaction) can help explain participation in normative tourist activities.
>
> (Uriely et al., 2011, p. 1053)

In another recent study, the psychoanalytic concept of voyeurism proved useful to examine a dark tourism account of a tourist jailed in Iran for three weeks (Buda & McIntosh, 2013). Psychoanalysis with some of its key concepts such as (counter)transference, castration, libido, narcissism, desire, phantasy, and the drives, amongst many others, offers ways to tackle experiences in dark tourism, to penetrate and make (even if partial) sense of unconscious irrationalities. 'The science of the unconscious mind' as Freud defined psychoanalysis, investigates processes that are almost inaccessible in any other way and has become a distinct scientific discipline, a discipline that is yet to be given a chance in tourism studies (Kingsbury, 2005). Affective tourism proposes psychoanalysis as a potential route to explore tourism experiences in areas of ongoing socio-political turmoil. My claim is that the uncanny juxtaposition of tourism with ongoing conflict can be more critically understood via psychoanalytic death drives. Through the intersection between psychoanalytic theories, and geographies of affect and emotion, I intend to deconstruct connotations such as 'morbid' and 'ghoulish' attached to those who (are enticed to) travel to places of danger and conflicts.

'Driven by death': Sigmund Freud and Jacques Lacan in danger-zones

Driven symbolically by death – the death drive, or the metaphorical 'pleasures of death' arguably 'enjoyed'/experienced by tourists in a region of continuous turmoil – presents tourism studies with a puzzle. One way to tackle this puzzle is through the death drive. This psychoanalytic 'enjoyment' in the death drive refers to a surplus pleasure that is 'elusive, ineluctable, painful, overwhelming and fascinating' (Kingsbury, 2005, p. 119). My goal like Kingsbury is not to merely superimpose the death drive on tourism studies, but to call for a genuine engagement with this concept so as to examine and understand, more critically, tourist experiences. Psychoanalytic theories on the death drive, I claim, offer exciting avenues to examine affective tourism performances in areas of dangerous, ongoing political conflict. Like Pile (1996) cited above, I agree that psychoanalysis in general, and the death drive in particular, provide a productive yet contentious lens to tackle mental, affective, or emotional life. The death drive and other psychoanalytic concepts are not easily interjected in tourism studies, irrespective of the type of tourism. Critical tourism, however, is hoped to welcome such endeavours more heartily.

I propose the death drive so as to theorise the inexpressibility of affect that circulates in such places. In this way, I also contribute to the scarce and so far cursory debates between tourism studies and psychoanalysis. The death drive connects life and death; when accessed, the life/death dichotomy is troubled, and along with it further dualisms – fun/fear, safety/danger and peace/war – are also disrupted. The death drive refers 'quite concretely to the detritus of memories embedded in our flesh through family myths and archaic traumas' (Ragland-Sullivan, 1995, p. 94). I use the death drive to allude to this purge of memories ingrained in bodies through family hi/stories which some re/experience when in a place of danger and ongoing conflict. As I introduce the death drive in tourism studies, I mainly turn to Ragland-Sullivan's (1987, 1992, 1995) and Boothby's

(1991) interpretations of Freud's and Lacan's theories. Readings of both Freud's and Lacan's work are vast; likewise psychoanalysis offers extensive understandings of affective, emotional and mental life. Apart from Ragland's and Boothby's works, I also draw on geographers' use of psychoanalytic theories in human geography (see Bondi, 1999a, 1999b, 2002, 2003, 2005; Kingsbury, 2003, 2004, 2005, 2007, 2009a, 2009b; Pile, 1991, 1996, 2010). I limit my account to these authors so as to confine and better manage the insertion of this potentially controversial concept into tourism research. Explorations of the death drive within the context of critical tourism research should not be regarded as clinical but conceptual. The death drive is not an essentialist and organicist concept. There is no innate, inborn death drive; rather we, humans as cultural and social beings are afflicted with the death drive.

Freud's death instinct versus death drive

Apart from being 'a troublesome form of knowledge', psychoanalysis formulated by Freud and Lacan was written mainly in German and French respectively. This poses the problem of translating their works into other languages. We are reminded of 'the proverbial Italian tag *traduttore traditore*' (Ragland-Sullivan, 1995, p. 1, emphasis in original), which literally means 'translator traitor'. This conveys the idea that the translator could improperly transmit the meaning and spirit of a text from one language into another.

Freud's term '*Todestrieb*' is translated as death instinct, and the word 'instinct' is unfortunate, if not inappropriate, because *Todestrieb* has little to do 'with the patterned, spontaneous behaviour of animals that we think of as "instinctual"'(Boothby, 1991, p. 229). The word '*Instinkt*' is used to render innate animal responses, the word '*Trieb*' is employed to convey 'an elemental impulse or striving that is radically unspecified with respect to its aims and objects' (Boothby, 1991, p. 229). Thus, the problem of translating Freud's *Todestrieb* as death instinct or death drive poses, to authors, the challenge of interpreting the term conceptually. It is argued that *Todestrieb* = death drive remains a highly ambiguous and controversial concept in Freudian work, as it exists at the threshold between the psychical and the somatic, the 'inarticulate strivings of the body' (Boothby, 1991, p. 102), between life and death. Freud (trans. 1984) maintains that the hypothesis of death instincts should be further re-interrogated in close association with life instincts. Freud's theory on the death drive remains sketchy, as he did not develop his thoughts on *Thanatos* (death) and death drive, beyond understanding it in equal opposition to *Eros*, that is, sexual and life drives (Ragland-Sullivan, 1995).

Freud (trans. 1984) arrived at the conclusion of the existence of a death drive through the concept of 'repetition compulsion' (*Wiederholungszwang*) in the article entitled 'Beyond the pleasure principle'. Repetition compulsion represents the tendency to repeat in dreams, memories, or through transference, repressed and therefore unpleasant experiences (Boothby, 1991). Freud contends that most of what is experienced again as a result of 'the compulsion to repeat must cause the ego unpleasure, since it brings to light activities of repressed instinctual impulses' (trans. 1984, p. 308). He goes on to argue that what brings 'unpleasure' – explained as increase in psychic tension – to one system can bring pleasure, satisfaction – decrease in tension – to another. Thus, his theory on the compulsion to repeat repressed, unconscious and unpleasant experiences does not contradict the pleasure principle, which Freud considered to be at the core of the psychic processes. The homeostatic principle of pleasure explains the tendency for equilibrium, harmony and diminution of tension and was thought to be the basic principle of life instincts. In addition to life instincts and *beyond this pleasure principle* another force was discovered, a force towards death, conflict and disintegration – the death instinct.

Unlike repressed wishes, which store pleasurable memories in the unconscious, this repetition compulsion that Freud discovered 'recalls from past, experiences which include no possibility of pleasure, and which can never, even long ago, have brought satisfaction even to instinctual impulses which have since been repressed' (trans. 1984, p. 291). This explanation of the compulsion to repeat is useful in analysing death drives and desires in connection to affect, which move in and between people and places in turmoil.

The compulsion to repeat experiences that were unpleasant at any time or at any level of the psyche happens mainly in dreams and in the transference process between analyst and analysand (the patient in psychoanalysis). This led Freud to assert that there is a '"*daemonic*" force at work' (trans. 1984, p. 307, emphasis in original) that overrides the fundamental concept of the pleasure principle. This 'daemonic power', an intensity of affect, explains that 'everything living dies for internal reasons – becomes inorganic once again – . . . that 'the *aim* of all life is death' and, looking backwards, that 'inanimate things existed before living ones' (Freud, trans. 1984, p. 311, emphasis in original).

From Freud to Lacan

Lacan reworked Freud's theory on the death instinct. Freud had resorted to biological explanations to present life instincts in opposition to death instincts. Lacan offers a different interpretation of the death drive as one not rooted in biology and threatening the biological organism, but being 'the inertia of *jouissance* which makes a person's love of his or her symptoms greater than any desire to change them' (Ragland-Sullivan, 1995, p. 85). It is maintained that the death instinct was not thoroughly developed by Freud, remaining in an embryonic and sketchy state (Boothby, 1991; Braunstein, 2003; Dean, 2003; Ragland-Sullivan, 1995; Sarup, 1992).

It has been suggested that there might have been two reasons why Freud dropped his theory on the death drive. First, it might have been to appease his colleagues offended by the existence of a drive towards death. Second, even though Freud discovered the death instinct/drive, he could not fully explain the concept (Ragland-Sullivan, 1995). This driving force towards death 'operates from the beginning of life and appears as a "life instinct" in opposition to the "death instinct" which was brought into being by the coming to life of inorganic substance' (Freud, trans. 1984, p. 334). Freud himself might have been shocked by his own conclusion that human beings are driven by death and not by the pleasure principle, a principle which I explain below (Boothby, 1991).

Lacan's conceptualisations of the death drive, however, cannot be understood separately from those of Freud. Freud's ideas on the death drive might have been embryonic, but 'cannot unproblematically be traced back to biological sources' (Boothby, 1991, p. 229). Lacan himself criticises such interpretation, explaining that 'What Freud calls Trieb is quite different from an instinct' (Lacan, cited in Boothby, 1991, p. 29). The Freudian concept of the drive refers to a force, a striving that remains equivocal 'bearing within itself a reference to the effects of psychological structures that function independently from any basis in biology' (Boothby, 1991, p. 229).

Lacan's *jouissance* in the death drive

Returning to Ragland's (1995) tag of *traduttore traditore*, she introduces the idea that Lacan is not a translator for the Francophone world increasingly interested in Freud's theories, but an emendator, that is, a scholar who corrects or removes faults and blemishes, and even suggests a different reading. Lacan himself proclaimed his 'return to Freud' and reworked Freud's texts according to his own critical and radical rereading. Freud's most radical and pivotal concept, the death drive, retains an important position in Lacan's work as the French author declares it to be 'the key point for grasping the essential import of psychoanalytic discovery' (Boothby, 1991, p. 14). Lacan himself argues:

> This notion [of the death drive] must be approached through its resonances in what I shall call the poetics of the Freudian corpus, the first way of access to the penetration of its meaning, and the essential dimension, from the origins of the work to the apogee marked in it by this notion, for an understanding of its dialectical repercussions.
>
> (Lacan, trans. 1977a, p. 102)

In spite of the importance Lacan attributes to the death drive, his thoughts on this notion are spread throughout 50 years of teaching without having written a sustained discussion in which his ideas could be clearly grasped. Such seems to have been Lacan's intention as he directly discouraged readers from expecting a traditionally structured theory, he warns that 'My Écrits are unsuitable for a thesis, particularly for an academic thesis: they are antithetical by nature: one either takes what they formulate or one leaves them' (Lacan, cited in Boothby, 1991, p. 15). The evocative power of his thoughts and writings impact psychoanalysis and his evolving ideas on the death drive can be followed throughout his entire work.

From the very beginning, Lacan rendered clearly that the notion of the death drive is not grounded in biology: 'we all know very well that it [death drive] is not a question of biology, and this is what makes this problem a stumbling block for so many of us' (Lacan, trans. 1977a, p. 102). It is argued that Lacan rids Freud's work of the traces of biologism that dominated classical psychoanalysis by conceptualising human subjectivity connected to speech and afterwards with language (Dean, 2003). Lacan reworked Freud's death drive as a primordial drive aimed towards the unity of the ego, not towards decay of the biological organism. Regarding misreadings of Freud's *Todestrieb* as death instinct and implicitly connected to biologism, Lacan writes:

> The notion of the death instinct involves a basic irony, since its meaning has to be sought in the conjunction of two contrary terms: instinct in its most comprehensive acceptation being the law that governs in its succession a cycle of behaviour whose goal is accomplishment of a vital function; and death appearing first of all as the destruction of life.
>
> (Lacan, trans. 1977a, p. 101)

As part of this project, Lacan redefines 'psychic negativity' (Dean, 2003, p. 248), particularly the concept of the death drive in relation to *jouissance*. *Jouissance* has no adequate translation in English; 'enjoyment' expresses one meaning contained in *jouissance*, that is, 'enjoyment of rights and property' (Sarup, 1992, p. 98), but it does not convey the sexual pleasures of the French term. Pleasure is used to translate the concept of '*plaisir*' which is different from *jouissance*. Pleasure (*plaisir*) functions according to homeostatic principles 'whereby through discharge, the psyche seeks the lowest possible level of tension' (Sheridan, 1977, p. x). *Jouissance* transgresses such principles of homeostasis. This in-between space of transgressions represents the connection between *jouissance*, affect and emotion. Operating beyond pleasure, *jouissance* overlaps with instances when affect is felt but is unrepresented intensity beyond emotion, when it is 'temporarily *prior* to the representational translation of an affect into a knowable emotion' (Pile, 2010, p. 8, emphasis in original). *Jouissance* translated on a conscious level is pleasure; likewise, when affects penetrate from their location in the 'non-cognitive' and 'non-psychological' layers into the 'pre-cognitive' and 'cognitive' levels, they become feelings and emotions respectively (Pile, 2010, p. 9).

While *jouissance* is a multifaceted notion that eludes precise definition and a strong grasp, three perspectives from which to explore this unruly concept are provided (Ragland-Sullivan, 1995, p. 9). First, *jouissance* in connection to pleasure. From this perspective, *jouissance* is understood as excessive, if not paradoxical, pleasure, which can generate divergent feelings of being 'overwhelmed or disgusted', while at the same time being 'a source of fascination' (Fink, 1995, p. xii). When *jouissance* goes beyond pleasure (*plaisir*), it reveals an 'exquisite pain' (Sarup, 1992, p. 99), or a 'paradoxical form of pleasure that may be found in suffering' (Dean, 2003, p. 248). This is not to say that *jouissance* is masochism understood as pleasure in pain; *jouissance* represents unconscious pleasures that become pain. When *jouissance* becomes conscious, it turns into pleasure (Sarup, 1992). It is contended that *jouissance* takes place 'when physical pain becomes unphysical pleasure . . . *Jouissance* like death, represents something whose limits cannot be overcome' (Sarup, 1992, p. 100). To explain *jouissance*, it is worth considering the following example: 'while listening to music the other day I burst out crying without knowing why. *Jouissance* begins where pleasure ends' (Sarup, 1992, p. 99).

Second, *jouissance* as a set of beliefs and knowledge suppositions effected in the generation of *jouis-sens* signifiers, which refer to a surplus enjoy-me(a)nt. '*Jouir de* something' refers to profiting from a thing, an object, or property, whether owned or not, its usufruct or surplus value (MacCannell, 1992). Enjoyment, as a context-specific translation and usage of *jouissance*, provides a useful lens to question the critical turn in tourism studies through theorisations of the politics of enjoyment (Kingsbury, 2005).

Third, *jouissance* linked to repetition of drives. Lacan argues that which generates pleasure during the first moment turns into displeasure during the second moment of repetition. Thus, repetition turns pleasure into displeasure, which is the loss of pleasure. Pleasure, however, 'remains as a fixation, as a trace in memory and gives body to fantasy . . . pleasure is retrieved via repetitions that constitute fantasies of eradicating loss' (Ragland-Sullivan, 1995, p. 89). The aim of the repetition is to compensate for that loss, but at the very moment of repetition *jouissance* is lost and in trying to recuperate it we only retrieve parts of *jouissance*. Lacanian repetition represents the desire to repeat patterns by which one hopes to achieve *jouissance*.

This drive of repeating known patterns through which one aims to reach *jouissance* is useful to explain the desires of people who live in close proximity to a socio-political danger-zone to visit another such spot in a different part of the world. Repeating the known, however, cannot satisfy desire for the new, for change, because this gives individuals 'the consistency of the expected', which is valued above everything else (Ragland-Sullivan, 1995, p. 90). Some people desire new emotions and experiences. Craving for change through the familiar cannot be satisfied, thus some people seek excitement in different locations, in dangerscapes across the world. The desire to travel to what is perceived as a dangerous place of death and disaster does not speak of a wish for death understood as the demise of the body; it indicates a quest for *jouissance* through the death drive and disruption of the opposition life/death.

Desire is a continuous force, fundamentally eccentric and insatiable (Buda & Shim, 2014). In Freudian psychoanalysis, *Wunsch* (translated either as 'wish', or 'desire') is an impulse towards fulfilment of an unconscious wish (Freud, 1979). In Lacanian work, *désir* is 'desire of the Other' (Lacan, 1977a), mostly linked to the object that causes it rather than the object that would seem to satisfy it (Sheridan, 1977a, p. viii). Desire is used by Lacan to explain the death drive through fantasies of one's own death. Fantasising one's own death is linked to fear of death, or of one's disappearance, which is 'the first object that the subject has to bring into play in this dialectic [of desire]' Lacan (trans. 1977b, p. 214). He further maintains that the fantasy of one's own death is first used and manipulated by the child in the love relations with the parents and offers an explanation based on desire and lack:

> One lack is superimposed upon the other. The dialectic of the objects of desire, in so far as it creates the link between the desire of the subject and the desire of the Other . . . this dialectic now passes through the fact that the desire is not replied to directly. It is a lack engendered from the previous time that serves to reply to the lack raised by the following time.
>
> (Lacan, trans. 1977b, p. 215)

Such explanations are brought into discussion here to examine some (danger-zone) tourists' desires to travel to places of turmoil in connection to fear that makes one feel alive and provides an affective sense of immortality. This may be accessed and performed through the death drive which, it is argued, provides an affective source of energy and vitality since 'it is death that sustains existence' (Boothby, 1991, p. 300).

Lacan's two deaths and three registers

The death drive disturbs the life/death dichotomy and connects the two deaths that Lacan conceptualised: first, a physical 'animal death of the body', and second, a metaphorical death whereby 'the subject is eclipsed by the signifier, thus being castrated or alienated within the language imposed on the biological organism' (Ragland-Sullivan, 1992, p. 57). Regarding these two deaths, Lacan claims that 'it is not enough to decide on the basis of its effect – Death. It still remains to be decided which death, that which is brought by life or that which brings life' (trans. 1977a, p. 308).

Lacanian death drive connects the 'two deaths' while being located at the junction of the three registers: the Imaginary, the Symbolic and the Real, tied in a Barromean knot. The three rings in the Barromean knot are so arranged that if any one ring is removed, it results in three disconnected rings, breaking the mutual link that holds them together. Using such an image to explain the three registers and their interrelation, Lacan emphasised the mutual co-dependence of the registers on one another. Generally speaking, these form the fundamental dimensions of psychic subjectivity.

Briefly presented, the Imaginary comes from the French adjective '*imaginaire*' turned into a noun, which Lacan used to explain ego-formation in the mirror stage whereby the child identifies with images of another, whether an image of itself in the mirror or another age-related child. This order tends to be associated with people's experiences in mundane (non-psychoanalytic) reality. That which one imagines and experiences such as felt emotions, envisions of the thoughts and feelings of others are closely linked, if not driven, by speech and language. Such socio-cultural and linguistic dynamics fall under the realm of the Symbolic. Language is entwined with traditions, rituals, customs, rules, laws and the like existent in cultural, social, political and economic systems, which form the collective symbolic register. To individual subjects, the Symbolic manifests in and through mediation of these socio-linguistic processes.

Whatever is not present in the Imaginary and Symbolic reality, whatever is hidden, beyond, behind and beneath awareness, appearance and representation is the domain of the Real. The Real drives us, yet the Real is the terrain of that which cannot be expressed. This is not to say that the Real is completely outside experience since it 'governs our activities more than any other' (Lacan, 1977b, p. 60). The Real cannot exist without the barrier of the Symbolic, which represents our desires and feelings through language. The Real designates what might be considered as total fullness and blissful purity of the being. It is the topology of where the drives, especially the death drive reside. It cannot, however, be contended that the death drive belongs solely to the agency of the intangible and inexpressible Real. The three Lacanian orders are not static concepts as 'at each moment each may be implicated in the redefinition of the others' (Sarup, 1992, p. 105).

Such aspects are further discussed and exemplified later in this volume in Part III, 'Destinations: affective routes in "Middle Eastern" tourism', where I analyse narratives of fear of death, family memories and archaic traumas. Possibly accessing death drives, some tourists (seek to) feel fear. Seeking, intentionally or not, to feel fear disrupts the fun/fear and life/death oppositions, as attested by some tourists.

4   Routes in dark tourism

More and more tourists, it seems, are winding up in places they shouldn't be. Some travel to war zones or countries their government has warned them not to visit. Robert Reid is an editor with the travel guide series, Lonely Planet. Marco Werman asked him why people are heading to dangerous places.

Marco Werman: Now, are you finding this to be true as well, that more people are heading to dangerous places, Robert Reid?

Robert Reid: I think so ... what's happening is, stories come back from places like these and there's more places where people are going and people become interested.

Marco Werman: ... I mean, are Caribbean cruises and bus tours of Italian medieval sites really that boring?

Robert Reid: [laughter] Well, you know, I think they are not boring. I think a lot of people like to search out authentic experiences with individuals and sometimes that will mean going to a place where you hear overwhelmingly negative things ... Like those [three US] hikers that were caught [on July 2009] very near the Iraq–Iran border and what happened there is a little unsure [Iran accused them of illegal entrance and links to US intelligence], but they went into the northern part of Iraq, which is very different from the south which we see in the news a lot.

(Werman, 2009)

This excerpt is part of an interview between Marco Werman, a presenter of Public Radio International's *The World* and Robert Reid, an editor with the *Lonely Planet* travel guides, which was aired in November 2009 on radio stations in the US, and is also available online. The two interlocutors discuss the increased interest in tourism to dangerous places. I start with this example to point out that tourists travel to dangerous places and it is timely that this form of tourism is given more academic attention. In defining tourism that thrives in tumultuous times and in places of (imagined) danger as danger-zone tourism, Adams (2001) also calls for more academic attention to this under-researched genre of tourism. She describes danger-zone tourists being enticed by political unrest.

In her research on danger-zone tourism in South East Asia, especially in Indonesia and East Timor, Adams interviewed some tourists amongst whom were several policy planners, social science teachers and activists who visited dangerous places. The author notes that 'their pilgrimages to strife-torn destinations are not for professional purposes but rather for leisure, although in some cases the professional identities of danger-zone tourists are related to their leisure pursuits' (2001, p. 266). In subsequent publications (2003, 2006), Adams draws further attention to this ignored form of tourism especially in relationship to postcolonial cities in South East Asia. Thus, I want to point out that no tourism scholar or any other social science researcher, to my knowledge so far, has responded to Adams's call for further exploration of this form of tourism. Reviewers of her work considered danger-zone tourism 'an intriguing study' (Wearing & McDonald, 2003, p. 753); such an 'intriguing' topic, however, remains underexplored.

Prior to Adams coining the term 'danger-zone tourism' (2001), tourism to perilous places 'which include towns of terror from the past as well as dangerous destinations of the present' (Dann, 1998, p. 3) was considered one of the five forms of dark tourism. In this fivefold model of dark sides of tourism, Dann also includes 'houses of horror', 'fields of fatality', 'tours of torment' and 'themed thanatos'. Houses of horror represent buildings associated with violent ends as well as tourism edifices of death display such as 'dungeons of death' or 'heinous hotels'. Fields of fatality refer to places where 'fear, fame or infamy' is commemorated, such as battlegrounds, holocaust sites and cemeteries of celebrities. The fourth category of dark tourism sites – 'tours of torment' – pertains to group visitation of dark attractions such as 'sites of mayhem and murder'. Themed thanatos relates to 'morbid museums and monuments to morality' (p. 3).

Exploring connections between tourist discourse and tourist death, it is maintained that some tourists, especially backpackers, actively seek death and danger in their travels. In this respect 'Death itself becomes a macabre and fascinating tourist site' (Phipps, 1999, p. 83), which, however paradoxical it may appear to some, is not a new phenomenon. Mitchell, for example, describes 'how, in 1830, entrepreneurs from Marseilles took tourists to Algiers to watch the colourful spectacle of the ongoing French bombardment of that city from the comfort of a large barge at sea' (Mitchell, 1991, cited in Phipps, 1999, p. 83). Travel to witness political executions and public hangings would attract large crowds of British people in the nineteenth century and prices for seats would vary according to the proximity to the action. This form of travel represents 'the strongest and, in modern Western societies, the most morally proscribed' (Seaton, 1996, p. 240). Death, danger and ongoing political turmoil have been an impetus for travel for a long time. This practice of travelling to potentially dangerous places of ongoing socio-political conflicts, however, has not been adequately theorised in tourism studies.

Danger-zone tourism: in the vanguard of affect

Danger-zone tourism refers to travel to areas of socio-political, sometimes violent, turmoil. This can encompass two motivational nuances, one being travel precisely *because of* the conflict; and the second, travel *in spite of* the conflict. Irrespective of motivational reasons, at the core of danger-zone tourism are the affects, emotions and senses felt, performed and circulating in places of ongoing conflict and/or turmoil. The dominant academic discourse – that few people want to experience political conflicts or any dangerous, ongoing conflict for that matter – is prevalent in tourism literature. The practice of travelling to areas of socio-political conflict is, however, on the rise:

> It is not difficult to explain the increase in Dark Tourism to conflict zones over the past 15 years. Firstly, the intensification of globalization has made every part of the world instantly recognizable, accessible and understandable. This is especially the case with sites of conflict – the repetitive framing and circulation of war zone imagery within the news media.
>
> (Lisle, 2007, p. 334)

Tourism scholarship is still partly based on rational modernist thought, therefore one could understand the manner in which endeavours of travelling to a tumultuous place in politically dangerous times are relegated to the margins of academic research. Dark tourism is a concept made famous by Lennon and Foley's (2000) book, *Dark Tourism: The Attraction of Death and Disaster*. As the title suggests, dark tourism refers to travel to sites of death, disaster and atrocity, which 'posit questions, or introduce anxiety and doubt about modernity and its consequences' (Lennon & Foley, 2000, p. 12). The authors maintain that for a site to be considered a dark site, the events of death, disaster and atrocity should have taken place in the 'living memory' 'of those still alive to validate them' (p. 12) starting with the First World War and the sinking of the *Titanic*.

For the authors, dark tourism represents an 'intimation of postmodernity' as they discuss different instances of dark tourism such as holocaust tourism, tourism to graves or sites of murder of famous people, and tourism to war memorial museums. While not entering any discussions over the implications of postmodernism/postmodernity or postmodern tourism, as the authors assert, they do recognise the significance of the global–local juxtaposition and the space-time collapse brought about by global communication technologies in defining dark tourism.

Regarding Lennon and Foley's book on dark tourism, Lisle argues that the 'numerous and potentially interesting case studies are rendered superficial by their resistance to theorizing, and they frame the figure of the tourist as entirely passive' (2007, p. 334). I would add that dark tourists are portrayed as being devoid of feelings, emotions and senses. Those who visit dark and dangerous places 'during moments of death, disaster and depravity – those in the vanguard of "dark tourism"' (Lennon & Foley, 2000, p. 9) are ignored in Lennon and Foley's analysis. This is because those in the vanguard of dark tourism are not mass tourists and cannot generate enough economic profit (Lennon & Foley, 2000). Another critique is that the authors 'do not engage with important literature in voyeurism and the consumption of danger' (Lisle, 2007, p. 334). Lisle's own timid engagement with the psychoanalytic concept of voyeurism to analyse 'Dark Tourism to conflict zones' (2007, p. 334) gives hope that psychoanalysis could be utilised in tourism studies.

Affective danger-zone tourism shows the socio-cultural, spatial and political productivity of affects, emotions and drives experienced and performed in areas of conflict. Geographies of affect and psychoanalysis are useful to examine tourists' embodied feelings, emotions and engagements with places and spaces of ongoing conflict. They show how and what subjectivities feel, think and perform when confronted with 'darker sides of life on tours'. I argue that danger-zone tourism speaks of death drives in the Lacanian sense, understood as desire for *jouissance*, that is, satisfaction of drives and fantasies. The death drive blurs the boundaries of the life–death dualism when touring 'dangerous destinations of the present' (Dann, 1998, p. 3), even though Freud saw them as a sensible dichotomy that can explain 'the rich multiplicity of the phenomena of life' (Freud, cited in Boothby, 1991, p. 4). Being driven towards metaphorical deaths, tourists confront danger and fear in areas of turmoil. Danger-zone tourist subjectivities engage death drives and affectively experience ongoing socio-political conflicts.

More recent edited collections on dark tourism (Sharpley & Stone, 2009a; White & Frew, 2013) continue to avoid psychoanalysis and affect. This might be because it is 'undoubtedly morbid curiosity, voyeurism or *schadenfreude* [which] may be the principal driver of tourism to certain dark sites' (Sharpley, 2009, p. 17, emphasis in original). Once again, those in the vanguard of dark tourism, those with 'an "interest" . . . to dice with death in dangerous places' (p. 14) are abandoned. Such 'morbid' and 'voyeuristic' interest might give rise to 'deviant feelings' unworthy of academic study.

Sharpley's descriptions of dark tourism rely on 'the presumed fascination in death and dying' (p. 7) or tourists' interests in 'the seemingly macabre' (p. 10). This hesitant mention of fascination not only with death as a commodified exhibit, but also with 'dying', alludes perhaps undesirably, to those in the vanguard of dark tourism, to danger-zoners, those visiting places during moments of death and ongoing danger. For this author, flirtation with death, dying and the macabre is mainly presumed, and in very few and 'extreme' instances is actually existing and occurring. These are considered 'the darkest or more intense form of dark tourism [whereby] tourists seek to integrate themselves with death, either through witnessing violent or untimely deaths, or in the extreme perhaps, travelling in the knowledge or expectation of death' (Sharpley, 2009, p. 18). There is little attempt made to delve beneath the surface of this extreme and more intense form of dark tourism, that is, danger-zone tourism. Its importance is perhaps only marked as an aspect of class differentiation (Sharpley, 2009), with no mention of the affective, emotional and sensuous aspects.

There is an eclectic and disparate range of terminology that shows the growing academic interest in death-related forms of tourism, but from which danger-zone tourism is missing. Apart from the more often employed term of 'dark tourism', there also exist other names to denominate the intersection between tourism, conflict, danger and death such as 'thanatourism', a macabre form of special interest tourism (Dunkley, 2007; Seaton, 1996), conflict tourism (Warner, 1999), morbid tourism (Blom, 2000), grief tourism (Sharpley, 2005), battlefield tourism (Dunkley et al., 2011; Ryan, 2007a, 2007b), and war tourism (Smith, 1996). The following subsections discuss these terms in connection to danger-zone tourism.

Dark tourism versus thanatourism in danger-zones

Tourists have long travelled to sites of conflicts, atrocities and death, but academic interest in tourism to such places increased only at the end of the 1990s. Travel in its inception was assimilated with risk-taking and fear for one's physical integrity, as robbers usually plundered the travelling caravans. To actively take part in wars, such as, for example, the crusaders fighting the War of the Cross, was another reason people used to travel to remote places in the eleventh and twelfth centuries.

During the Middle Ages, travel for European Christians mostly took the form of religious pilgrimages. Jerusalem, Rome and Santiago de Compostela were the three most important destinations visited by large numbers of Christian pilgrims. Rome, for example, in 1300 attracted around 300,000 religious pilgrims (Holden, 2005). For the Jubilee celebrations in 1500, another 300,000 moved through Rome in spite of the rule of a contested pope, Alexander VI. Travel to religious places such as Jerusalem in the eastern Mediterranean region to conquer, and then rule, occurred during the Crusades from the eleventh century through to the thirteenth. Travel in order to spread Christianity to and within 'pagan' places also occurred during the Middle Ages. In these instances, travelling was accompanied by violence and war that built up and added to instability in Jerusalem and the whole region. Thus, understood from this vantage point, travel in pre-modern times can be considered a precursor to danger-zone tourism.

The word 'travel' comes from the Latin verb '*tripaliare*' 'to torture with a tripalium [a three-staked torture instrument]' (Raccah, 1995, p. 11), which later entered the French language as '*travailler*' meaning work, everyday work. In English, 'travail' has the meaning of 'an unpleasant experience or situation that involves a lot of hard work, difficulties and/or suffering' (Hornby et al., 2005, p. 1634). With time, the word 'travail' was used to describe people's feelings while undertaking long journeys. It was considered 'a real travail' to walk or ride wagons for days in a row in fear for one's life and belongings as attacks by robbers were common (Holden, 2005). This connects travelling to distant places to issues of risk-taking, violence and danger.

There have been several attempts to define and label travel to places related to disasters, dangers and death. Thanatourism is defined as travel to locations whereby actual and/or symbolic encounters with death are possible (Seaton, 1996). Dark tourism limits the boundaries of the concept to events that happened in the twentieth century and that question the project of modernity (Lennon & Foley, 2000). A matrix is proposed, with shades of grey tourism ranking from pale to black depending on supply and demand (Sharpley, 2005). Other usages have stretched such definitions so as to fit the phenomena under analysis of their respective case studies (Preece & Price, 2005; Ryan & Kohli, 2006; Smith & Croy, 2005; Warner, 1999).

Throughout this book I use the term 'dark tourism' and not 'thanatourism'. In more recent research (Dunkley et al., 2011) the term 'thanatourism' is preferred. This is because dark tourism is argued to be an unhelpful term with negative connotations, which 'undoubtedly arouses curiosity, makes good newspaper headlines' and hints 'at ghoulish interest in the macabre or, perhaps, an element of *schadenfreude* on the part of the tourist' (Sharpley & Stone, 2009b, p. 249, emphasis in original). I resist such evaluations that assign negative connotations to dark tourism and hint at ghoulish and macabre interests. A preference for one term over the other, in this case of thanatourism over dark tourism, risks constructing thanatourism as 'good', 'acceptable' and academic, while dark tourism is the 'bad' and 'undesirable' counterpart. My aim is to prevent the construction of a dark tourism/thanatourism conceptual binary. By portraying dark tourists in general and danger-zone tourists in particular as embodied, emotional and sensuous, who have meaningful experiences in areas of danger, death and ongoing conflicts, I intend to disrupt disparaging considerations of dark tourism as negative, ghoulish and macabre.

The generic, mundane set phrase 'dark tourism' seems to have gained broader acceptance in the literature, compared to the more technical term 'thanatourism' (Smith & Croy, 2005). The relative simplicity of the set phrase is in contrast with the multiplicity of aspects that define this concept. The difference lies not on a linguistic level, as the debate is not over which word best relays the meaning of the same concept. Thanatourism and dark tourism are two related concepts, but differ in their employment of the temporal aspect (Seaton, 2009). Dark tourism is an intimation of postmodernity because of memorialisation, commodification and industrialisation aspects, which accompany fascination with death as an explicit motivation to travel. For thanatourism, pilgrimage is the earliest form of travel associated with death. Interest in death as part of the travelling experience is, therefore, not a phenomenon of the modern or postmodern world. People have long travelled to battlefields, cemeteries, mausoleums, and death/murder sites.

Thanatopsis, the contemplation of death, has always been present in human life. From the Middle Ages to the nineteenth century, this was well supported by symbolic representations and material objects meant to keep thoughts on death alive in people's awareness (Seaton, 1996). The concept of thanatopsis also refers to the factors that generate these thoughts and the response to these stimuli. Thanatopsis, therefore, refers to thoughts of one's own death as well as death of others, irrespective of the distance in time and space. 'Dark tourism is a travel dimension of thanatopsis' which Seaton (1996, p. 240) calls thanatourism. Thanatourism develops alongside a continuum of intensity, depending on motivation as well as knowledge and interest in death. The highest and purest form of this type of tourism is travel out of sheer fascination with death. At the other end of the continuum is the visitor motivated by knowledge of the dead who was in one way or another related to the tourist.

Drawing on De Quincey's article 'On murder considered as one of the fine arts' (cited in Seaton, 1996), Seaton contends that interest in death is a taste shared by all humans to a greater or lesser extent. The premise underlying both De Quincey's article and death-related tourism, Seaton argues, is the 'act or event which might be deplorable or repugnant from a moral point of view [but] could have considerable attraction as a spectator experience' (1996, p. 234). Explaining murder as a fine art within the system of values and beliefs that condemns anything shocking and repugnant, the article convinces that it is a matter of taste. Such abject and repugnant matters can actually be a source of private pleasure.

This type of tourism, more than providing private pleasures, has also 'become the subject of commercial practice . . . with an ability to create products for monetary profit . . . on a global scale' (Ryan, 2005, p. 188). Advances in technology have contributed to the compression of time and space, which have helped spread this phenomenon thus bringing death, disaster and atrocity live into people's homes and in their living memories. The media, films and accounts of breaking-news events all help stimulate dark tourism. The global–local juxtaposition represents a drive to this phenomenon. Dark tourists cannot, therefore, be totally divorced from the viewing public. The public incorporate these media commoditisations into their lives and later seek tourist experiences to feed the sense of 'familiarity' provided by the media.

Fascination with the abject, morbid, strange and bizarre seems to highlight the postmodern aspect of dark tourism:

> It thus appears that while 'dark tourism' initially is focused upon sites of horror and destruction, its extension towards the bizarre, the morbid and the strange begins to either dilute the original concept, or to change the nature of the original concern of death.
>
> (Ryan, 2005, p. 188)

Likewise, the postmodern perspective of danger-zone tourism emphasises flirtation with death, danger and conflicts. Danger-zone tourism, like dark tourism, disrupts the modernity–postmodernity debate. Danger-zone tourists cross safety/danger, peace/war, fun/fear and life/death boundaries as they engage in emotional, affective and sensuous experiences in places of ongoing conflicts. It can be argued, following different aspects of death-related tourism, that danger-zone tourism is an offspring of both post/modern dark tourism and pre/modern thanatourism. Danger-zone tourism can, therefore, be studied from different perspectives: premodern, modern, postmodern and post-structural.

Postmodern and post-structural approaches contribute to understanding performances of danger-zone tourist subjectivities as emotional, affective and sensuous in ongoing socio-political conflict zones. Postmodernity and post-structuralism, if properly understood, struggle to 'free knowledge' from the shackles of dialectic dualism (Oakes & Minca, 2004). Rationalising the world in dichotomic concepts is a modern habit, which lays the foundation of the modern mechanisms of power. The postmodern and post-structural approaches provide researchers with tools to problematise and subvert dichotomies (Oakes & Minca, 2004). To fully understand affective danger-zone tourism we must move beyond the 'truly glacial' (Terada, 2001) aspects of post/modernism and post/structuralism. This move beneath and beyond is rendered possible by affect, emotion and psychoanalysis.

Danger-zone tourism, understood as experiencing or flirting with conflict, death and danger, brings about an engagement with death drives which tear down dualisms such as safety/danger, fun/fear, war/peace and life/death. I maintain that danger-zone tourists move beyond understanding death, disaster and atrocity of the past to flirting with conflicts of the present. Danger-zone tourism reflects affective, emotional and sensuous mobilities, the shifts in the apprehension of travelling which does not mean anymore 'sight-seeing' but 'sight-involving' (Boniface, cited in Ryan, 2005, p. 188) and even *sight-feeling* and/or *site-feeling*. Danger-zone tourism, therefore, mirrors a turn to affect and emotion, a fascination with feeling in places of turmoil whereby dualisms are torn down and their boundaries are crossed.

The phenomenon of danger-zone tourism expands beyond contemplating death, disaster and tragedies in history, into affective involvement in the politics of conflicts. Paraphrasing Tarlow (2005), danger-zone tourism seems to be the dirty little secret of tourism. Dark tourism or thanatourism were not recognised forms of tourism more than a decade ago. Likewise, danger-zone tourism is currently tucked away in an inconspicuous place. There is a certain denial from tourism scholars to peel away its layers. The dominant discourse remains that 'few people would want to experience the fog of war first hand' (Tarlow, 2005, p. 52), or the fog of any conflict for that matter and for a site, even a dark site, to become a tourist attraction, it needs to be safe and secure. From this perspective, dark tourism seems to belong more to late modernity, as it carries a 'glacial' imprint of the rationality in the safety/danger dualism. Danger-zone tourism can be better understood from affective, emotional and psychoanalytic standpoints, as it tries to accept and embody feelings and desires to meet death, danger and socio-political conflicts head-on.

It has been argued (Mestrovic, 1991; Oakes & Minca, 2004; Rojeck, 1993; Uriely, 1997) that modernity is about searching for fun tourism, sun, sand and relaxation; postmodern tourism takes the quest for fun to other, 'alternative' places. Basing his theory on Boym's (2001) forms of nostalgia, Tarlow discusses 'tourism nostalgia' whereby 'the traveler seeks to heal from past hurts by travelling back in time . . . it is touching danger without actually being in it' (2005, p. 52). Dark tourism is a form of virtual nostalgia; it is finding the danger in the safe (Tarlow, 2005). The differentiation is between 'authentic history (continuing and therefore dangerous) and heritage (past, dead and safe)' (Urry, 1990, p. 110). Danger-zone tourists are the ones interested in experiencing and *feeling*, the ongoing, dangerous history, while challenging the 'banality of evil' (Tarlow, 2005). Dark tourists are rather '*homo videns*' who prefer to remain on the safe side of 'heritage, past, dead and safe history'. Danger-zone tourists partake in history, continuing and therefore possibly dangerous, especially when socio-political turmoil is involved.

Conflict tourists

Conflict tourism is considered 'a variant of dark tourism . . . visits to places made interesting for reasons of political dispute' (Warner, 1999, p. 137). Tourists who engage in such visits have been termed in a variety of ways: conflict tourists (Warner, 1999), danger-zoners (Adams, 2001), politically oriented tourists (Brin, 2006) and war tourists (Pitts, 1996; Smith, 1996, 1998). These are some of the types of tourists that I explore in this section.

War tourists are those for whom political conflicts represent the principal factor for visiting or travelling in a region and their main motivation is to 'experience the thrill of political violence' (Pitts, 1996, p. 224). In a project on tourism in Chiapas immediately after the Zapatista uprising in 1994, it was found that besides journalists who rushed to the scene, a considerable number of conflict or war tourists flocked to Chiapas: 'just like drivers on the interstate stretching their necks trying to get a glimpse of "what happened" at a wreck scene, these individuals wanted to be part of the action' (Pitts, 1996, p. 221). Chiapas was still attractive to war tourists as long as there continued to be some degree of unrest, but as political turmoil stabilised in the region war tourists were no longer lured there (Pitts, 1996).

This type of tourists is changed by the danger (or lack thereof) of a political situation. If, prior to any outbreak of violence, a destination appeals to tourists valuing safety and tranquillity, then, during time of unrest, war tourists will most probably be enticed to the region. Those war tourists described by Pitts share similarities with danger-zone tourists in considering an ongoing conflict an enticement rather than a deterrent. Pitts's choice of terminology could be confusing since 'war tourism' as coined by Smith (1996) was referring to tourism in sites of past wars. In her research, Smith (1998) uses the term 'war tourism' to analyse the 'touristic impacts of World War II' (p. 203), such as tourists' fascination with cemeteries, battlefields, military zones and the like. For Smith (1996), war tourists visit sites of past wars, cemeteries, monuments and so forth; her explanation does not convey the idea of travel to present tumultuous places.

War tourists pay reverence to the dead, satisfy their curiosities and learn more about an ended war or conflict, while danger-zoners experience ongoing conflicts first-hand. War tourism positions the events of danger in the past following the cessation of conflict; danger-zone tourism implies travel to areas of danger for and during the conflict. Danger-zone tourism develops in current spatio-temporalities of ongoing socio-political turmoil in a region (Adams, 2006). Attention here is not on tourism to places of past wars and battles such as cemeteries, mausoleums, battlefields and the like. Danger-zone tourism concentrates on engagements with/ in potentially dangerous places of the present that bring about a range of feelings and emotions. The focus is on affective, emotional and sensuous performances in tourism places of ongoing conflicts.

The ongoing Israeli–Palestinian conflict is argued to be an impetus, rather than an impediment, for some tourists to visit Jerusalem. Political instability, and therefore danger, are considered enticing factors for tourists. There are politically oriented tourists who 'come to the city not just despite its troubled reality, but sometimes even because of it' (Brin, 2006, p. 215). These politically oriented tourists in Jerusalem are of three types. First, solidarity tourists show their support for one side or the other involved in the Israeli–Palestinian conflict.

Second, activist tourists who join organisations that actively promote peace. The third type is the intrigued tourist, for whom the conflict is an attraction. These types of politically oriented tourists are examined from the perspective of 'perceived risk and consequent decision-making process when contemplating a travel destination' (Brin, 2006, p. 222).

Jerusalem 'lies in the focus of the Israeli–Arab Conflict and especially the Israeli–Palestinian Conflict' (p. 223), which undoubtedly prompts tourists and tourism industry workers to feel and perform a range of emotions connected to the ongoing conflict. Affective and emotional implications of such visits in Al Quds/ Jerusalem need to be given more attention. The city's status is still hotly debated by scholars and politicians across a range of disciplines. Jerusalem or more precisely east Jerusalem is hoped to be the capital of a future Palestinian state, an aspect that impacts tourism discourses in the region. Brin, also a tour guide by profession, mentions 'the large Palestinian population which resides in the eastern quarters of Jerusalem refuses to recognize Israeli rule and wishes to see its part of town become the capital city of a future independent Palestinian state' (p. 224). In a subsequent publication, Brin acknowledges his apparent 'inclination towards the Israeli and Zionist narrative' (Brin & Noy, 2010, p. 19), as the authors analyse the politics of tour guiding in a Palestinian neighbourhood in Jerusalem.

Engaging with grief, horror and morbidity in tourism

During travels to places of danger and death, some tourists pay homage and grieve for the victims memorialised in place. The term 'grief tourism' has entered the dictionaries and tourism literature. It has gained prominence in 2002 when two schoolgirls were murdered by their school caretaker in the village of Soham in Cambridgeshire, England (Maxwell, 2004). A grief tourist is 'a person who travels specifically to visit the scene of a tragedy or disaster' (Maxwell, 2004, para. 1). This form of tourism is distinguished from disaster and dark tourism. Disaster tourism is identified as travel to places affected by natural disasters, such as the South East Asian tsunami of 2004 or Hurricane Katrina of 2005. Grief tourism is considered to have 'very disparaging overtones, compared by some to the practice of rubbernecking' (para. 3).

The most frequent explanation for people's interest in death and danger-related forms of tourism is their 'inherent morbid or ghoulish interest in the suffering or death of others' (Sharpley, 2005, p. 216). Some dark tourism researchers (Preece & Price, 2005; Sharpley, 2005) explain that this morbid interest in death might be just a simple curiosity in the unusual, or a form of postmodern tourism. People's attraction to and demand for morbidity-related events and places have been on the rise in the last decades (Blom, 2000). Human beings have been increasingly fascinated, frightened and enticed by sudden and/or violent events. Tourists seek new experiences and places to satisfy the need for sensation (Blom, 2000). Within tourism literature, there are a number of tourist classifications based on motivations, supply-and-demand patterns, behaviour and activities amongst others. One typology, however, has been excluded: 'those who seek the unknown and the frightening, a category which can be related to the type of attraction that is not planned . . . those who are drawn in some way to the morbid and that which often causes us unease and anxiety' (p. 30).

Critical attention should be paid to tourism that 'on the one hand focuses on sudden violent death and which quickly attracts large numbers of people and, on the other, as an attraction-focused artificial morbidity-related tourism' (p. 33). This aspect of morbidity in tourism plays on terror, horror, death and danger. At the turn of the third millennium, Blom contended that from a western European perspective, life was relatively safe and secure, but dull and monotonous. This created a craving for 'the opposite' place where life was lived vividly and dangerously. Drawing on Breuer's and Freud's psychoanalytic theories on catharsis, Blom maintains that people from western European societies were confronted with a lack of identity. Such people would seek identification and purification through participation in other peoples' (eastern and/or Third World) lives and places. Tourists flocking to Princess Diana's grave in Althorp, England, are explained to be engaging in morbid tourism 'focusing on accidents and sudden violent death [which] are being produced and consumed in ever growing numbers' (p. 29).

The post- or neocolonial western European stance notwithstanding, Blom's innovation in tackling tourism to sites of accidents and violent deaths through the lens of psychoanalysis is acknowledged. Psychoanalysis has been a long time coming in tourism. Such studies are useful and lay the foundation for further genuine considerations of emotions, affects, feelings and senses. Affective tourism, advocated in this book, delves into the scholarship on affective, emotional and psychoanalytic geographies. This is meant to enhance critical spatial understandings of affect and emotion in tourism as socio-culturally constructed, rather than grounded in biological processes.

Part III

Destinations

Affective routes in 'Middle Eastern' tourism

5 Locating the 'Middle East'

The 'Middle East' is a politically charged, western European, colonial construct (Daher, 2007). The eastern Mediterranean region has been known along the centuries under various names: Bilad al Sham, Mashreq, the Levant, the Orient, the Near East, the Middle East, the Near East and North Africa (NENA), the Middle East and North Africa (MENA). All these terms represent geopolitical and cultural categories that can be contested and scrutinised in terms of their origins and meanings. They reflect privileged standpoints and discursive practices that facilitated their formation and circulation (Daher, 2007). Most of these names encompass the contemporary territories of Jordan and Palestine/Israel, case studies discussed in this book. In this context chapter, I briefly examine some of these terms. I then introduce Jordan and Palestine by presenting some geographical, historical and political considerations about the area. This brief and descriptive geopolitical framework sets the stage for examinations of affective danger-zone tourism in this region.

The two Arabic terms 'Bilad al Sham' and 'Mashreq' have emerged from within the region, while the rest of the terms listed above 'have been part of colonial or neo-imperial *imagineering* of the region' (Daher, 2007, p. 3, emphasis in original). The local geographic term 'Bilad al Sham' has been in usage for more than a thousand years and refers to the land of the eastern Mediterranean region (Daher, 2007). The Eurocentric concept of the Middle East brings forth and conjures dis/continuities and transformations within this region. I am not from within the region, but together with others (Daher, 2007; Hazbun, 2008; Jacobs, 2010), I also point to the Eurocentric and colonial connotations of the concept.

Bilad al Sham refers to Greater Syria, encompassing contemporary countries of Jordan, Palestine, Lebanon and Syria. The term is ideologically and politically connected to pan-Arabism, or more broadly to ethnographic, cultural, and regional aspects of the region. It is maintained that Bilad al Sham expands beyond national boundaries or discourses, being very much a living and functioning concept (Daher, 2007). Another concept produced within the region is Al Mashreq al Arabi, which literally means 'Arab East'. This term refers to the current countries of Jordan, Lebanon, Syria and Palestine. Its counterpart the 'Arab West' is called Al Maghreb al Arabi and encompasses the countries of Libya, Algeria, Tunisia and Morocco. Countries such as Saudi Arabia, Kuwait, Bahrain, Qatar, the United

Arab Emirates, Oman and Yemen are part of the Gulf and the Arabian Peninsula. Egypt and Sudan are part of Wadi al Neel (the Nile Valley) (Daher, 2007).

The 'Levant' is another colonial concept, of French origins, commonly used to describe Lebanon and Syria (Milton-Edwards, 2007), or more broadly an area of trading contact 'between the cosmopolitan citizens of the Mediterranean and the Arab populations inland' (Jacobs, 2010, p. 316). In tourism literature, it is used to conjure up exotic images of the eastern Mediterranean region, which continue to inform orientalist and colonialist imaginaries (Jacobs, 2010). In spite of the area's rich religious and cultural heritage, picturesque landscapes, and imposing archaeological ruins, tourism development has been thwarted by ongoing socio-political turmoil (Hazbun, 2008, p. 77).

The 'Orient' is another term used to refer to the Middle East. A debate on entanglements between tourism and orientalist discourses represents a whole topic in itself worthy of another book project. Briefly though, in the eighteenth and nineteenth centuries, the word 'orientalism' had two major meanings. On the one hand, it referred to the works of 'the orientalist' dealing with languages and literatures of the Orient, Turkey, Syria, Palestine, Mesopotamia and Arabia, and later on also India, China and Japan, and even the whole of Asia (Macfie, 2000). On the other hand, it was used to mean a specific feature and style associated with 'the East'. Socio-political uprisings in large parts of Asia and Africa started to challenge and undermine western European domination: the 1906 Iranian revolution, the 1908 Young Turk revolution, the First World War and the annihilation of the German, Austrian, Russian and Ottoman Empires, the 1919 nationalist movement in Egypt. These laid the foundation for the future attack on orientalism all through the twentieth century. By the end of the Second World War, orientalism became a heavily charged concept and referred to:

> a corporate institution, designed for dealing with the orient, a partial view of Islam, an instrument of Western imperialism, a style of thought, based on an ontological and epistemological distinction between orient and occident, and even an ideology, justifying and accounting for the subjugation of blacks, Palestinian Arabs, women and many other supposedly deprived groups and people.
>
> (Macfie, 2000, p. 2)

These intellectual transformations were challenged by military and political events such as: the independence of India in 1947, the Algerian uprising in 1952, the British withdrawal from Egypt in 1954, and the collapse in 1958 of the Hashemite regime in Iraq supported by the British. On the intellectual front, orientalism was assaulted from different perspectives: orientalism as part of imperialism, which aimed to colonise Third World peoples; orientalism as a lens of understanding and interpreting Islam and Arab nationalism; orientalism as a hegemonic system (Macfie, 2000; Said, 2003).

Challenges to and deconstructions of orientalism have undergone a major shift after the first publication of Said's book *Orientalism* in 1978. His book questioned the mysticism and exoticism previously attached, to the Orient, and unveiled the term's pejorative and political connotations. In his preface to the fifth edition of the book, Said writes:

> I should say again that I have no 'real' Orient to argue for. I do, however, have a very high regard for the powers and gifts of the peoples of that region to struggle on for their vision of what they are and want to be. That has been so massive and calculatedly aggressive an attack on the contemporary societies of the Arab and Muslim for their backwardness, lack of democracy, and abrogation of women's rights that we simply forget that such notions as modernity, enlightenment and democracy are by no means simple and agreed upon concepts that one either does or does not find, like Easter eggs in the living room.
>
> (Said, 2003, p. xiv)

Orient has come to encompass the Indian subcontinent and eastern Asia, in addition to the Arab and Muslim countries in the western part of the Asian continent. Orientalism and Middle East, as concepts, present overlapping views. Following Said's (2003) argument, I use Middle East to emphasise that neither (middle) East nor West have 'any ontological stability; each is made up of human effort, partly affirmation, partly identification of the Other' (p. xii). Said also uncovered and problematised stereotypes linked to 'the Arabs' who for 'the West', he claims, are:

> first of all, as one in their bent for bloody vengeance, second, psychologically incapable of peace, and third, congenially tied to a concept of justice that means the opposite of that, they are not to be trusted and must be fought interminably as one fights any other fatal disease.
>
> (Said, 2003, p. 308)

This sharp tone characterises most of Said's critique of orientalism and arabism. He also asserts that to date Arabs remain an entity forming 'the Arab world'. Indeed, writing about the Arab world as a homogenous area, is still present in tourism studies (Scott & Jafari, 2010; Steiner, 2010). 'This Arab and Muslim world' engages in Islamic tourism, a new tourism trend, which has emerged after 9/11 to compensate for geopolitical uncertainties (Neveu, 2010). In Jordan, for example, this new phenomenon has prompted the government to draft new strategies meant to help rebuild holy sites all over the country (Neveu, 2010).

This book on affective danger-zone tourism in Jordan and Palestine treats the Arab world as a polemic and politically charged term which obfuscates 'regional realities, social histories of various towns, villages, and cultural landscapes' (Daher, 2007, p. 2). I acknowledge that discourses on the Arab or Muslim world render invisible multiple identities within the region and construct it as a collective entity to the West. Some tourists are enticed by this 'conflation' of everything Arabic and Muslim.

It is argued that tourism is mostly a capitalist ideology, with the majority of tourists originating in developed and 'wealthy nations like the United States, Canada, Australia, New Zealand, Israel, Germany, the United Kingdom, France and Spain'

(McRae, 2003, p. 242). Such tourists broadly embrace a 'right to roam' (Franklin, 2001, p. 126), a mindset 'encased in a consciousness of colonization' (McRae, 2003, p. 242). While I acknowledge the validity of such claims, in my analysis of danger-zone tourism in Jordan and Palestine, I intend to challenge readings of tourists as performing a 'Western colonising gaze'. My intention is to show that experiences in places of ongoing conflict, whether of tourists, locals, or anyone else in between, should not 'simply re-perform the perversions of colonization' and do not always reinforce 'a gaze on "primitive indigenous people"' (p. 238).

Jordan and Palestine: geopolitical and historical considerations

The Hashemite Kingdom of Jordan and the West Bank (of the River Jordan) in Palestine represent a suitable setting for my research on affect and danger-zone tourism. Both areas are geographically and politically connected to the ongoing Israeli–Palestinian conflict (Robins, 2004). The West Bank is located in the heart of the conflict and is one of the points of contention between Palestinians and Israelis. Amman, Jordan's capital, is about 60 kilometres away from Al Quds/ Jerusalem and even closer to other Palestinian towns such as Jericho, for example. Politically speaking, Jordan can be considered to be in the proximity of the conflict and not in the middle of it, because of the peace treaty signed with Israel in 1994. The fairly large number of citizens of Palestinian descent living in Jordan, however, makes the conflict a very sensitive and emotional situation for the country.

Jordan, Palestine and the neighbouring countries – Israel, Lebanon, Syria and Iraq – make up a complex geopolitical tapestry of the Middle East (see Figure 5.1). The Israeli–Palestinian conflict has been ongoing for well over six decades. Iraq was one of the main targets of the 'war on terror' beginning in April 2003, and at the time of writing (2014), bombings are still common and frequent, kidnappings and attacks on military and non-military personnel are daily occurrences (BBC, 2011). Jordan, Lebanon and Syria are countries where there is a great possibility that the troubles in Iraq and Palestine/Israel spill over. For example, at the southern border of Lebanon on 3 August 2010, there was a skirmish between the Israeli and Lebanese armies in which two Lebanese soldiers and a journalist were killed. This was one of the most violent incidents since the 2006 war. With fears of the conflict being intensified, the United Nations peacekeeping force in south Lebanon intervened to negotiate the situation (*Jordan Times*, 2011). The end of 2010 and the beginning of 2011 brought great havoc to several countries in the Middle East such as Bahrain, Libya, Syria, Yemen and also Jordan. In Jordan during the protests in January 2011, there were no casualties, but thousands took to the streets to protest over economic policies (Al Jazeera, 2011).

The Hashemite Kingdom of Jordan is a constitutional monarchy with two legislative houses – the Senate and the House of Representatives – and a prime minister appointed and dismissed by the monarch. The Hashemite family's lineage to the Prophet Muhammad has been often used to strengthen the monarchy especially during troubled times as, for example, in the June 1967 war, the 1970 civil war, and the 1989 riots against the price increases imposed by the International Monetary Fund (Jordan, 2011).

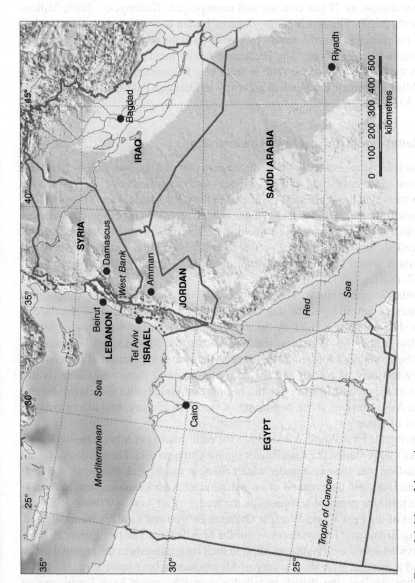

Figure 5.1 Map of the region.

Source: Map by Max Oulton, 2011.

King Hussein and later his son King Abdullah II have tried to restructure Jordan's economic and political system so as to address the difficulties in terms of the liberalisation agenda imposed by international powers. It is argued that the peace dividend following the 1994 treaty with Israel has not filtered down to the population, as 27 per cent are still unemployed (Karatnycky, 2005; Milton-Edwards, 2007). The ethnic composition of Jordan is dominated by a vast majority of Palestinians; thus the monarchy's position in the ongoing Israeli–Palestinian conflict is a sensitive one. The Hashemite family must protect its kingdom and assert the sovereignty of the state in front of a Palestinian population willing to 'establish a national independent authority in liberated Palestine' (Jordan, 2011, para. 83).

Regional geo-historical brief considerations

Jordan is an Arab country in the south-western part of Asia, bordered by Syria and Lebanon in the north, Iraq in the east, Saudi Arabia to the south-east, Egypt to the south-west, and the West Bank and Israel in the west. The location of Jordan is of strategic importance. Historically, it has been the crossroads between the Arabian Peninsula and Syria. For those travelling to the Arabian Peninsula, the territory was called '*masharif al-Hijaz*' – 'the approaches of Hijaz', and if traversing it to Syria it would be called '"masharif al-Sham" – literally, "the approaches of Syria"' (Salibi, 1993, p. 6).[1]

Jordan's capital and its largest city is Amman – named for the Ammonites, the ancient Semitic people that used to inhabit the land east of the Jordan River. For much of its history the ancient land of Jordan was invaded by the Israelite tribes, the Assyrians, the Nabataeans, the Romans, the Persians and then the Ottomans (Jordan, 2011). Due to the strategic position of the contemporary territory of Jordan and the surrounding area, there was fierce rivalry between Rome and Persia over the region that ended with the establishment of the Arab Empire[2] at the beginning of the sixth century, and afterwards the advent of Islam.

During the First World War, in 1916 the emir (leader) of Mecca, Hussein, with Britain's help, started the Arab Revolt against Ottoman rule. The ideology of Arab nationalism was the cause under which Hussein would seek independence from Ottoman rule and the creation of an independent Arab kingdom, thus also seeking to fulfil his personal ambitions as the leader of all Arabs (Wilson, 1987). At the end of the First World War, the Ottoman Empire and its allies were defeated, leaving Britain and France in control of the Middle East. The two European powers divided south-west Asia according to their own interests in the region. Britain gained a mandate over the territory of Mesopotamia, later named Iraq, and over Palestine. In Iraq, the British installed a monarchy under King Faisal, one of Hussein's sons, and in Palestine a direct administration. The British split Palestine into two parts: they formed an Arab emirate, Transjordan, ruled by Abdullah, Faisal's younger brother, and the rest of the territory kept the name Palestine. The same process happened with the Syrian territory, which was divided by France into two republics: Lebanon and Syria. Regarding this process of division of the Middle East, Said comments:

> The two greatest empires were the British and the French; allies and partners in some things, in others they were hostile rivals . . . It was in the Near Orient, the lands of the Arab Near East . . . that the British and the French encountered each other and 'the Orient' with great intensity, familiarity, and complexity. What they shared, however, was not only land or profit or rule; it was the kind of intellectual power I have been calling Orientalism.
>
> (Said, 2003, p. 41)

Between the two world wars, Transjordan was under British mandate, with Abdullah ibn Hussein as emir. In 1946, Transjordan became independent, after the conclusion of the Anglo-Transjordanian Treaty. In 1949, a new constitution was promulgated, Emir Abdullah became king and the name of the state was changed to the Hashemite Kingdom of Jordan (Jordan, 2011). On 14 May 1948, the Jewish community proclaimed its independence as the state of Israel. The existence of Israel was soon recognised by the United States of America and Russia, this leading to a series of conflicts between the rest of the Arab countries (Jordan, Egypt, Lebanon and Syria) in the region and Israel, known as the Arab–Israeli wars. In 1949, an armistice was signed between Jordan and Israel, this being one of the reasons King Abdullah I was murdered on 20 July 1951 by a radical Palestinian at the entrance of the al-Aqsa mosque in Jerusalem Old City. The territory just west of the Jordan River (the West Bank) and East Jerusalem went under Jordanian rule. Eighteen years later, during the third Arab–Israeli war fought between 5–10 June 1967 (also called the 'June War' or the 'Six Day War'), Jordan, now ruled by Abdullah's grandson Hussein, lost the West Bank and East Jerusalem to Israel.

Jordan–Israel–Palestine connections

There are intimate ties between the lands of Jordan, Israel and Palestine (see Figure 5.2), as well as between Jordanians, Israelis and Palestinians. Palestine, as most terms and concepts relating to this region, represents a politically and emotionally charged name. Palestine has changed its geographical and political status over the last three millennia. *Encyclopaedia Britannica* defines the geographic positions of Palestine as the 'area of the eastern Mediterranean region, comprising parts of modern Israel and the Palestinian territories of the Gaza Strip (along the coast of the Mediterranean Sea) and the West Bank (the area west of the Jordan River)' ('Palestine', 2011, para. 1). Palestine has been at the heart of the conflict between Jewish and Arab national movements since the mid-twentieth century. The usage of the term 'Palestine'[3] denotes a traditional region, but there are no agreed-upon boundaries of this region.

In this book, I zoom in on danger-zone tourism in the West Bank of the River Jordan, mostly in cities like Bethlehem, Hebron, Jericho, Nablus and Ramallah (see Figure 5.3). The West Bank, like Palestine, is no less controversial a name.

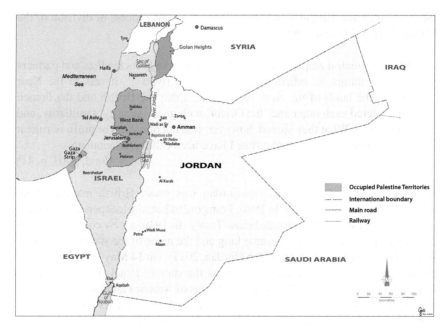

Figure 5.2 Map of some tourist sites in the area.

Source: Map by Max Oulton, 2011.

Figure 5.3 Map of the West Bank.

Source: Map by Max Oulton, 2011.

'West Bank' and 'Palestine' are used here interchangeably not to mean that Palestine is made up of only the West Bank. The West Bank is part of Palestine together with Gaza, but entry into Gaza for any purpose is prohibited, and will remain so, given the recent (beginning in July 2014) violent intensifications of the conflict. Thus, the research that I conducted in Palestine was only in the West Bank. In instances in which statistical data about population in Palestine will be presented, or when geographical and historical data on Palestine will be examined, I will indicate whether it pertains to Gaza or the West Bank.

The West Bank stretches from the west of the Jordan River to the east of Jerusalem (West Bank, 2011). Within Israel, this region is also known according to its biblical names Judaea and Samaria. The social composition of the population in Palestine has been influenced by the ongoing Israeli–Palestinian conflict, where in the early twenty-first century, Israeli Jews made up approximately half of the population west of the Jordan (Palestine, 2011). Arabs, whether Muslims, Christians, or Druze, along with other smaller minorities, accounted for the rest. The Palestinian Central Bureau of Statistics states that the size of the Palestinian population is just under 4 million with nearly 2.4 million in the West Bank, 1.4 million in the Gaza Strip and 400,000 in the Jerusalem Governorate (Visit Palestine, 2011).

Al Quds/Jerusalem represents one of the main points of contention in the ongoing conflict. After the Arab–Israeli war of 1948, the newly proclaimed State of Israel claimed Jerusalem as its capital. As noted above, it was during the Six Day War of 1967 that Israel took the entire city of Jerusalem (Jerusalem, 2011). Its status, however, as Israel's capital is a point of dissension, as Palestinians consider East Jerusalem to be the capital of a future independent Palestinian state. During the period between 1948 and 1967, the West Bank of the River Jordan and East Jerusalem were, therefore, part of the Hashemite Kingdom of Jordan.

The West Bank is in fact central Palestine, Hazbun (2008) argues, and the Hashemite royal family tried to 'suppress or erase all reference to Palestine' and to appropriate 'certain Palestinian symbols, such as the Dome of the Rock and traditional embroidery and [claimed] them as Jordanian' (Brand, cited in Hazbun, 2008, p. 83). While these moves meant to strengthen the Hashemite family's legitimacy in the region, Hazbun (2008) views them as part of Jordan's intentions 'to project its touristic identity as the territory of the biblical Holy Land to Western tourists' (p. 83). The first Jordanian airline was established in the late 1950s with help from the US and was named 'Air Jordan of the Holy Land'. In the 1960s, Jordan implemented for the first time a five-year economic development plan, which also included building state-owned tourist facilities such as an international hotel in Amman, and a rest house in Petra.

The 1967 Arab–Israeli war shaped this territory. The war resulted not only in a total collapse of the emerging Jordanian tourism sector, but it also worsened 'the deprivation of the Palestinians' (Pappe, 2004, p. 188). During this time, approximately one million Palestinians became refugees, having been expelled to the West Bank, the Gaza Strip, Lebanon, Syria and Jordan (Pappe, 2004). About the 1967 war, Ilan Pappe, an Israeli professor of politics at Haifa University writes:

[During the 1967 war] Israel did not occupy just the West Bank. At the end of the six-day campaign, it controlled the Gaza Strip, the Sinai Peninsula and the Golan Heights. In a classical example of blitzkrieg, a highly motivated and professional Israeli army exploited the element of surprise and used its superior Western arms to great advantage, exposing the inferiority of the Arab countries' Eastern bloc military equipment.

(Pappe, 2004, p. 188)

Following the 1967 war, the Palestine Liberation Organisation (PLO) rose to power as a revolutionary force and, dominated by Fatah (the Palestine National Liberation Movement), started launching frequent attacks on Israel ('Palestine', 2011). The late 1970s represented a period of more peaceful dealings between the PLO and Israel. In 1978, the Camp David Accords were negotiated with the provision that a self-governing authority was to be instituted in the West Bank and Gaza. The peace treaty between Egypt and Israel was formally signed a year later on 26 March 1979. The late 1980s saw another wave of increased violence culminating with the first intifada (in Arabic 'shaking off') in December 1987, which was an all-encompassing attempt to end Israeli presence in the West Bank and the Gaza Strip.

The end of 1988 marked a new shift in the Palestinian–Israeli relations. Yasser Arafat proclaimed the independence of Palestine, but without defining its borders, acknowledged the State of Israel and denounced all forms of terrorism. Significant events on the international arena such as the dissolution of the Soviet Union in 1991 and the United States's decision to open dialogue with the PLO led to secret peace talks between the PLO and Israeli officials in Oslo, Norway.

A significant result of the Oslo Accords was the establishment in 1994 of the Palestinian National Authority (PNA) as a governing body for the future autonomous regions in the West Bank and Gaza. The PLO chairman Yasser Arafat was elected president and held his position until his death in 2004, when he was succeeded by the first prime minister of the PNA, Mahmoud Abbas. The Oslo process has been declared dead and irrelevant, thus Pappe writes:

A decade later, it seems to me that the major problem was that the practical consequence of the Declaration of Principles agreed upon by Yasser Arafat, Bill Clinton and Yitzak Rabin on 13 September 1993 on the White House lawn bore little relation to those principles. It was the balance of power tilting dramatically in Israel's favour, which determined how the principles would be translated into reality.

(Pappe, 2004, p. 254)

Said bemoans that:

The Palestinian people are paying the heavy, heavy, unconscionable price of Oslo, which after ten years of negotiating left them with bits of land lacking coherence and continuity, security institutions designed to assure their subservience to Israel, and a life that impoverished them so that the Jewish state can thrive and prosper.

(Said, 2004, p. 165)

Most Israelis also considered that the Oslo process failed to protect their personal security, as acts of violence committed by extremist groups on both sides continued (Pappe, 2008). Against the disappointing background of the failure of the Oslo process, coupled with an unwelcome visit paid by Ariel Sharon to Haram al-Sharif (the Noble Sanctuary), the second intifada started.[4] It is maintained that Ariel Sharon's visit, while heavily guarded by more than a thousand Israeli police and soldiers, to one of the holiest places for Muslims represented 'a gesture designed explicitly to assert his right as an Israeli to visit the Muslim holy place' (Said, 2004, p. 3).

Though the second intifada had officially ended, coexistence between Israelis and Palestinians is still uneasy and marked by bursts of violence. Another peace plan between Israelis and Palestinians is nowhere in sight, but the two Palestinian factions of Hamas and Fatah reconciled in 2011 after a four-year schism. Some, however, fear that the next future peace plans in the region will still tilt the balance of power in disfavour of Palestinians:

> The tragedy of Palestine is that the next peace plan, whenever it appears, will also be based on the false assumption that peace means an Israeli withdrawal to its 1967 borders and the establishment of a Palestinian state next to it. The presence of so many Palestinians in Israel itself and the significance presence of Jewish settlers in what is supposed to be the future Palestine both cast doubt on the feasibility of this idea, which failed to persuade the indigenous population of Palestine in 1947.
>
> (Pappe, 2008, p. 267)

Studying tourism in such a sensitive and troubled spot might seem irrelevant at first, as tourism does not bring any relief to Palestinian refugees. The separation wall[5] is built longer and higher, the number of Israeli settlements increases by the month and the issue of East Jerusalem has not been resolved. Tourism is, however, an important stage where Israelis and Palestinians assert their identities and their claims and tell their stories. Jordan is also shaken by the ongoing conflict and current socio-political developments in the region and the story of tourism in this country is intimately intertwined with the Israeli and Palestinian stories of tourism. International tourists travel to this region and experience these stories through encounters with places of ongoing conflict, with local Israelis, Jordanians and Palestinians.

Notes

1 Geographically speaking – east to west – Jordan has three physiographic regions: the Syro-Arabian desert, the highlands east of the Jordan River and the rift valley of Ghor and Wadi Araba. The rift valley is made up of the Ghor Valley, which in Arabic means 'the sunken land' (Salibi, 1993, p. 3). 'Wadi' of 'Wadi Araba' means valley and 'Araba' is a term that 'seems to derive from a Cannanite and Aramaic [subfamilies of ancient Semitic languages spoken in the region of Canaan between the Jordan River and the Mediterranean] term denoting a steppe or a desert' (p. 4). The Jordan River follows the course of the Ghor Valley from Lake Tiberias (or the Sea of Galilee or Sea of Tiberias

as it appears in the New Testament) up to the point where it flows into the Dead Sea, forming the lowest point on earth – 435 metres below sea level. The Syrian Desert, an extension of the Arabian Desert that covers most of the Arabian Peninsula, represents three-quarters of contemporary Jordan territory and historically was inhabited by Bedouin tribes. The uplands east of the Jordan River consist of the region called 'the Sawad (sawad al-Urdun) meaning "the fertile land"' (p. 4) with Yarmuk and Zarqa as tributaries to the Jordan River. A range of higher hills called Bilad al-Sharat, which have an average elevation of 1,000 metres, are located in the south. Important cities like Amman, Irbid, Karak and Petra can be found in this part of the country.

2 The ruling families of the Ummayad, Abbasid and Fatimid dynasties represent an important aspect in Jordan's history. During the rule of the caliphs (rulers of the Caliphates as the first system of government established in Islam) from the Umayyad family, the capital was located in Damascus, Syria. Under the Ummayads, the territory of Jordan was closer to the centre of power in Damascus and thus more prosperous. The Abbasids, the following ruling family, moved the capital in 750 AD to Baghdad, thus Jordan was farther away from the centre (Jordan, 2011).

The Ummayad and Abbasid, as well as the Fatimid, dynasties are represented on Jordan's flag, which has three horizontal bands of black, white and green corresponding to each respective dynasty. The crimson triangle uniting the three bands stands for the contemporary ruling Hashemite family. The seven-pointed Islamic star represents the seven hills on which Amman was built and the first seven verses of the Qur'an. The flag has its roots in the Arab Revolt of 1916 and reflects Jordan's national identity and the process of state formation.

3 Linguistically speaking, Palestine is a term of Greek origins, 'Philisitia', and means the land of the Philistines who in the twelfth century BC occupied the region between modern Tel-Aviv and Gaza. The Romans in the second century AD used the term 'Syria Palaestina' to refer to the southern part of the Syrian province. The Latin term had later entered Arabic, but until the First World War, the name had no official status. The name was adopted by Britain when it mandated over the region.

4 It is also known as the 'al-Aqsa intifada', after the name of the mosque in the Noble Sanctuary.

5 See Chapter 7 for a discussion about connections between the separation wall/security barrier. For further debates about the separation wall/security barrier, see Buda & McIntosh, 2013; Pallister-Wilkins, 2011; Weizman, 2012.

6 Around Jordan – Switzerland of the Middle East?

> Though a small state, Jordan has frequently found itself at the centre of conflict and crisis in the modern Middle East. It has been a central protagonist in the wars of the region, notably the 1948 and 1967 Arab–Israeli wars.
>
> (Robins, 2004. p. i)

> Jordan is, I call it, Switzerland of Europe, because we are friends with everybody and we don't have any enemies. It's a very safe country. Jordan is the same [as Switzerland] in the Middle East. We are surrounded by crazies, you know, the east is Iraq, west is Palestine, Israel is south, north is Lebanon. See, they are all crazy and they are all trouble makers but if you think about Jordan and the relationship between Jordan and the west it can't be any better, it just cannot be any better.
>
> (Jordanian Tour Guide, interview, 3 October 2010)

The location of Jordan is of strategic importance as also acknowledged in the quotes above. Local tour guides and representatives of tour companies realise the strategic position of their country as 'Switzerland of the Middle East' in a 'troubled region' or as the 'gateway to Iraq', according to another director and co-owner of a Jordanian tourism company.

This chapter focuses on affective tourism in Jordan, as a country in the proximity of areas of ongoing conflict. I argue that the Israeli–Palestinian conflict, as well as other conflicts, which happen near Jordan's borders, are extricated through a complex apparatus that sanitises Jordan of the danger in the conflicts. Since the beginning of the twenty-first century, Jordan has witnessed the al-Aqsa Intifada in 2000–01 in Palestine and Israel; the war in Afghanistan in 2001; in Iraq in 2003; the suicide bombings on three five-star hotels in the capital Amman in 2005; the 2006 Israeli–Hezbollah war in Lebanon; rocket attacks and gunfire exchanges in October 2009 and August 2010 between Lebanon and Israel; 'more minor' rocket attacks in April and August 2010 in Jordan; the Arab Spring of 2011–12; the ongoing Syrian Civil War beginning in early 2011, and more recently, in 2014, the Israel–Gaza conflict (Buda, forthcoming 2015).

In spite of the conflicts that have scarred parts of the Middle East for decades, tourist arrivals increased in 2005 by an estimated 8 per cent (UNWTO, 2006). The United Nations World Tourism Organisation in their *Tourism Highlights 2008* edition describe the Middle East as 'one of the tourism success stories of the decade so far and leads the growth ranking of arrivals in 2007, with an estimated 16% rise to almost 48 million tourists' (p. 9). Jordan itself has experienced a steady increase in tourist arrivals, from 2,383,400 in 2002 to 3,298,900 in 2007, according to documents provided to me by representatives of the Jordan Tourism Board (Euromonitor International, cited in Jordan Tourism Board, 2009). During 2011 and 2012, the Middle Eastern region showed 'mixed results by destination' (UNWTO, 2013, p. 12) with Jordan displaying an increase of 5 per cent in 2012. Along with a rise in tourist arrivals in the Middle East, academic interest in dark tourism to areas of conflict in the region has also increased.

I seek to theorise affective tourism in conflict zones of potential or imagined danger and understand the ways it exists in Jordan. To this end, I analyse the relation between tourism, conflict and danger, as well as its affective and emotional performances. There are two main threads running through this chapter.

The first thread is the sanitation process. Tourism is often understood to exist only if, when and where conflict and danger are absent. Most of those working in the Jordanian tourism industry are too eager to separate and sanitise the country from the Israeli–Palestinian conflict and other troubles in the region. This sanitation process operant in Jordanian tourism is, however, resisted by some tour guides, in particular those working at sites located near the Jordan–Palestine/Israel borders. Unveiling and deconstructing the sanitation process at work in Jordanian tourism, I show how affective tourism is *felt* and *practised* in areas (in the proximity) of conflict by some local industry representatives and tourists.

The second thread weaves emotional and affective geographies of danger-zone tourist subjectivities. Danger-zoners, disrupt and cross peace/war, safety/danger and fun/fear boundaries in Jordan's tourism spaces. The safe-/danger-zone dichotomy enforces a 'tourism–conflict' opposition. This tourism–conflict opposition, although a seemingly strange one, is predicated on the dominant discourse that defines tourism as travel for 'sun, sand, sea and relaxation'. Tourism represents safety and fun, conflict represents danger and fear. Thus the safety/danger and fun/fear binaries translate into tourism–conflict opposition. This dominant dialectic locates tourism as being the opposite of conflict and war. The modern tourism discourse proves how tourists avoid areas of war and ongoing conflicts. My aim is to disrupt the tourism–conflict constructed opposition, and show how danger-zone tourism, tourists and ongoing socio-political conflicts are connected in powerful affective ways.

The strategic position of Jordan, being the 'Switzerland of the Middle East', 'friends with everybody' and 'having no enemies' in a region 'of crazies' allows for an interesting interplay between tourism and conflict. At first blush, this interplay reinforces a safety–danger opposition in tourism. Most tourism industry representatives in Jordan assert that danger can be found in the neighbouring countries, and safety in Jordan. Following this line of reasoning – 'where there is safety there's tourism' and 'where there is danger there is no tourism' – dominant tourism discourses are being reinforced. Drawing on Lisle's (2000, 2007) research, I argue that, it is precisely this reinforcement of the safety–danger opposition that connects conflict and tourism in powerful ways. Such dis/connections actually shape circulations of affect and emotions in Jordanian tourism.

The separation of conflict and tourism is held in place by discourses of safety, political stability and peace, which are all deemed as necessary conditions for tourism (Hall et al., 2003; Pizam & Mansfeld, 1996). Thus, if socio-political conflict is located 'somewhere else', tourism is safe and stable. If the conflict happened 'back then', tourism is the main mechanism to attract tourists to consume 'dark sites' of former conflicts (Lisle, 2000). Understood through this narrative, tourism and conflict are separated in time and space. Thus, the stage for their complete opposition is being reinforced through safety/danger discourses. To disrupt such a construct in Jordan, I unveil the interconnections between tourism, conflict and danger. Rendering visible the existence of conflict and danger in Jordanian tourism means deconstructing the sanitation process undertaken by local tourism industry representatives.

The sanitation of conflicts in Jordan is evident in mass media accounts both foreign and Jordanian. The *Lonely Planet Guide* (2009) also reassures the tourists that:

> Despite being squeezed between the hotspots of Iraq, Saudi Arabia and Israel & the Palestinian Territories, Jordan is probably the safest and most stable country in the region. Regardless of your nationality, you'll be greeted with nothing but courtesy and hospitality in this gem of a country.
>
> (*Lonely Planet Guide*, 2009, para. 3)

In an interview with *Condé Nast Traveler*, the King of Jordan states: 'to have Arabs – whether Iraqis, Lebanese, or others – flooding toward Jordan to escape violence shows that Jordan is secure' (Hack, 2007, p. 2). According to these discourses, danger and conflict are absent in Jordan and the present is being sanitised. In these portrayals of Jordan, safety and friendliness are, supposedly, all one will find in Jordan. The hospitable nature of Jordan and Jordanians is evident in both accounts in the *Lonely Planet Guide* and the *Condé Nast Traveler*. Irrespective of one's nationality, whether from the Arab region or not, one is welcomed with warmth, courtesy and hospitality. The King of Jordan conveniently separates regional conflicts from Jordanian spaces in his assertion that Iraqis, Lebanese and others living in dangerous countries flee towards a safe and stable place, Jordan. Space and time are, thus, being sanitised in Jordan, ready to be marketed for tourists. In order to secure the income of tourists' expenditure, so crucial to some national economies, governments promote safety and stability in their countries (Lisle, 2000). This holds true for Jordan as its economy relies heavily on tourism revenue (Daher, 2007). Thus, the king, the government and local mass media regularly assure tourists that Jordan is safe and stable.

The rockets affair/s

In this section, I examine an incident that took place on 2 August 2010, when several rockets were launched from the Sinai Peninsula in Egypt, supposedly aimed at Eilat in Israel (see Figure 5.2 for the geographical proximity of Eilat in Israel and Aqaba in Jordan). One rocket 'accidentally' fell near the Hotel

Inter Continental in Aqaba and killed a taxi driver stationed in front of the hotel. Competing discourses around the impacts of the incident highlight the conflicts in the region and the sanitation process. The English online edition of the daily newspaper the *Jordan Times* published an article in its 3 August edition: 'Rocket incident unlikely to affect Aqaba tourism', which stated:

> The rocket that hit Aqaba yesterday [2 August] morning does not stand to affect tourism in the Red Sea resort, officials and tourists stressed on Monday. A rocket 'from outside Jordan' struck the coastal city on Monday, killing one Jordanian and injuring four others . . . Although this is the third rocket that has struck Aqaba since 2005, tourism has not been affected, with figures indicating a growth in the number of tourists visiting the city. Two rockets struck Aqaba on April 22 this year causing no casualties, while in 2005, rockets were fired at US warships in Aqaba which killed a Jordanian soldier. According to Aqaba.jo [the official website of the Aqaba Tourist Information Center], around 94,308 overnight tourists visited the port city in the first quarter of 2010. Figures also indicated that the number of overnight visitors reached 896,977 in 2009, up from 812,801 the year before. In 2007, 883,012 tourists visited the city, compared to 802,858 in 2006 and 814,668 in 2005.
>
> (Malkawi & Qatamin, 2010, para. 1, 2, 14–17)

Immediately after the incident, the Jordan Tourism Board also posted on its website assurances that it was an isolated incident that had no effect on tourism. To support this claim, the reporters cited the newly appointed minister assuring them, 'We arrived in Aqaba after the accident and tourists are still there going about their business. Some of them are on the beach and others are in hotels as usual' (Afanah, cited in Malkawi & Qatamin, 2010, para. 4). The Jordan Hotels Association also confirmed there were no cancellations and two tourists were interviewed to express how safe they felt.

I was residing in Jordan when the August rockets affair happened. I witnessed the competing discourses around the negative effect the incident had or did not have on tourism in Jordan. The official stance presented above by the Minister of Tourism clearly stated that 'tourists are going about their business as usual'. The industry perspective, that of the tourism companies, associations and guides, followed the ministerial one. A director of a tourism company based in Amman was slightly more nuanced in his appraisal of the 'rockets affair':

> It impacts us, of course. I mean we lost some bookings because of this but as long as it's not repeated, it's fine. I mean, it's important to explain it to people that the reason why this rocket fell, it is because it missed, I mean we were not the target. We were just next door to the target. That region has a lot of mountains so it is very difficult to hit what you're looking for. So I think that so long as something is done about this problem, I hope the Egyptians will do something about it. People in the back of their minds they are a bit worried yes, we try our best to assure, reassure them that this is not something that happens very often.
>
> (Director Tourism Company, interview, 11 August 2010)

A manager with another Amman based tourism company, confirmed the above appraisal:

Dorina: Last week in Aqaba that rocket fell near InterContinental Hotel.
Manager: This will affect us badly actually, they [tourists] do not forget it easily.
Dorina: And six months ago it was another case of another rocket which hit Aqaba.
Manager: In Aqaba, yeah, that is true [laughter].

                    (Manager Tourism Company, interview, 10 August 2010)

Both respondents above resist, in part, the sanitation process at work in Jordanian tourism. Their discussions of 'the rockets' bad effects' on tourism in Jordan, however limited in time and space, disrupt the image of the country as 'an oasis of stability and peace'. Most other owners and managers of tourism companies, as well as guides that I interviewed, believe that the incident did not negatively affect tourism and experienced no major cancellations. Another manager of a Petra-based tourism business explained so determinedly: 'No, no, no cancellations. You know, now this situation is very weak. It is different now. New York, London this [situation] happens everywhere' (Petra-based Tourism Manager, interview, 14 August 2010).

    The ongoing regional conflict manifested in the rocket incident in Aqaba shifts back and forth in socio-political registers, between 'affecting us badly' to 'this situation is very weak'. It seems to follow the circulation of affect, which is taken to be in flux and reflux to and from conscious experiences (Clough, 2007) as tensions that modify their intensity. The intriguing affective interrelationship between conflict and tourism seems to be part of that 'chaotic cofunctioning of the political, economic and cultural dimensions' (Massumi, 1998, p. 45). Constructing and promoting countries as safe places in order to entice economic profits from the tourism industry, tourism shapes economic and political discourses of global security (Lisle, 2000). Discourses meant to separate conflict and tourism highlight 'the illusion of safety here and now, and danger there and then' (p. 2). In Jordan, the illusion of safety prevails, as danger is understood to be 'there' in Iraq, in Israel/Palestine, even in Lebanon, but not in Jordan. The rockets launched from the Sinai Peninsula in Egypt were aimed at Eilat in Israel, but they 'mistakenly' fell in Aqaba, killing one taxi driver near a hotel. As one tourism company director '*nicely*' put it, 'we were not the target, we were just next door' (Director Tourism Company, interview, 11 August 2010). Discursively insisting on safety and stability is driven by the flourishing tourism industry, which started to prosper following Petra's naming as one of the new seven world wonders on July 2007.[1] Dis/connections between tourism and conflict are so complex and blurred that events relating to tourism or conflicts inadvertently collapse into each other (Lisle, 2000).

    The illusion of safety is so successfully produced and marketed in Jordan that tourists often attest to the country's safety and stability even in the midst of 'rockets raining on resorts' (*Waikato Times*, 2010, para. 1). For their article on the incident, *The New York Times* interviewed a Polish tourist. The tourist said that he had been sleeping on the roof of a hotel in Aqaba when he was awakened by two explosions. He then: 'looked out at the city and I saw the smoke and took two photographs. I went to have a look but I couldn't see anything because of all the soldiers and police' (Polish tourist, cited in Farrell & Kershner, 2010, para. 11).

Regarding the same incident, the *Jordan Times* quotes a Spanish tourist who said that 'I've visited Aqaba more than once and I will not let such accidental happenings spoil my enjoyment. I went shopping and spent good times and I will visit Aqaba again' (Spanish tourist, cited in Malkawi & Qatamin, 2010, para. 7). A Russian tourist is quoted as condemning the attack and naming it an act of terrorism, 'This is a criminal attack, and terrorism incidents are everywhere. [It] will not prevent me from coming back to Aqaba, as I have lots of nice memories in this city' (para. 11).

By positioning tourism alongside incidents illustrative of the ongoing conflict in the region, the safety–danger opposition as the main mechanism for sanitation of the conflict is exposed in its own excesses and impurities (Lisle, 2000). Herein lies a juxtaposition between tourism, danger, death and rockets. Thus, one tourist vouches not to have her enjoyment at the Red Sea in Aqaba spoilt by the rocket that fell close to a hotel and killed one person. Another tourist sleeping on a roof of a hotel was woken up by the loud noise of the exploding rocket and hurried to the place from where the noise came, so as to take pictures.

Tourism and conflict are placed side by side; safety and danger collocate as some tourists report not to be deterred by such 'terrorist attacks'. Through this merging of enjoyment, rockets raining on resorts, photographing a bombed place, and terrorist attacks, affective danger-zone tourism is performed. We are reminded of the tourism puzzle, mentioned in Chapter 3, of tourists 'enjoying' experiences in tourism areas of ongoing turmoil. This enjoyment is reminiscent of a *jouissance*[2] which transgresses the law, seeking total fulfilment in places of rockets launched on resorts. Such instances of *jouissance* are transferred to the Other through the syphoning-off of Lacan's Real into the Symbolic and Imaginary (Fink, 1995). In this transference, *jouissance* and affect overlap in that they both compel and shape actions, such as taking photographs first thing after hearing an explosion. In this context, *jouissance* is the connection between affects and death drives. In its search for fulfilment, the death drive functions beyond pleasure. It originates in Lacan's Real with the imperative to enjoy, which refers to communal union with the Other in blissful transference (MacCannell, 1992).

Accounts of such intrepid tourists are capitalised on by the local mass media and tourism governmental bodies to prove that tourists still perceive Jordan as safe and stable, even after the rocket incident on 2 August 2010. These events disrupt the tourism–conflict opposition, as intrepid tourists are reportedly not being deterred by them, and therefore, by conflict and the danger in the region. They assert and perform their affective danger-zone tourist subjectivities as they vow not to be scared off by 'such accidental happenings' and to 'visit Aqaba again' (Virginia Helth, cited in Malkawi & Qatamin, 2010, para. 7). They seem to obey the Lacanian Real imperative: Enjoy! The boundaries that separate safety/danger and fun/fear are blurred and crossed by danger-zone tourists who consider Aqaba – a city reportedly being the target of rocket attacks in 2005, April and August 2010 – a 'place with lots of nice memories' (Rimo Madochev, cited in para. 11).

Interviews with international tourists that I held for this research project resonate with the above media accounts. Hyun, one tourist in his late twenties from South Korea, decided to go ahead with his plans of diving in the Red Sea six weeks after the rocket incident in Aqaba. The same day that he and I had talked, 16 September 2010, was the day that the United States Embassy in Amman issued a travel warning against Aqaba, which was published on their website and discussed in the English version of the *Jordan Times*. The Jordanian daily newspaper quotes the official travel warning: 'The US embassy recommends that all non-official and personal travel to Aqaba be deferred for at least the next 48 hours. For those citizens resident in Aqaba, the downtown and port areas should be avoided if possible' (US Embassy, cited in Omari, 2010, para. 4).

After reading about the rocket incident and the US travel warning, Hyun said 'I feel more cautious.' He, however, chose not to cancel his plans of travelling to Aqaba, because the adventure of diving in the Red Sea was one of the main purposes of his trip in Jordan. He was one of the tourists who decided to travel to Aqaba and dive in the Red Sea despite the travel warning issued by the US Embassy in Amman. He also informed me that he decided not to tell his family about the rocket incident on 2 August 2010 'because I don't want them to worry about me [mild laugh]' (Hyun, interview, 16 September 2010).

Some Israeli tourists, who, like Hyun, ignored travel warnings, travelled to the Sinai Peninsula in Egypt despite official travel advisories issued by the Israeli government and media accounts of possible terror in the area (Uriely et al., 2007). Uriely and colleagues discuss how these tourists travelled to the Sinai Peninsula within one to seven weeks after multiple terror attacks that occurred on 7 October 2004. The authors' research 'relies on tourism as an adventurous domain of life, in which risk-taking is less threatening and . . . more appealing' (p. 3). They interviewed tourists in their twenties, who were not forthcoming to their parents about their trip and who displayed a relaxed and unafraid attitude, yet were reluctant to talk about their fears. This can be interpreted as part of their desire to be perceived courageous and not '"weak" or cowardly tourists' (p. 5). These Israeli tourists' desire to travel to the Sinai Peninsula a few weeks after several terrorist attacks could have been analysed using the psychoanalytic concept of the death drive. I propose this in Chapter 8 as I discuss in more depth Hyun's decision to dive in the Red Sea just a few weeks after 'rockets [were] raining on resorts'.

Monty, a tourist in his early forties from the United States, travelled to Jordan and the neighbouring Palestine and Israel from 18 June to 2 July 2010. This was one month before the rocket incident on 2 August 2010, but seven weeks after the previous rocket incident on 22 April 2010, when no casualties were recorded. Monty was aware of the volatility of the region, but considered Jordan stable: 'I'd say that Jordan is not volatile itself, but is in a region that can be (Lebanon, Syria, Palestine/Israel, Iraq)' (Monty, online interview, 10 August 2010).

Regarding travel advisories, which did not deter Hyun or the Israeli students interviewed by Uriely and colleagues (2007), Monty explained that he does not 'shy away from countries which my government (US) advises one avoid (e.g.: KSA [Kingdom of Saudi Arabia] . . . and probably most of the Middle East, for that matter)' (Monty, online interview, 10 August 2010). The same holds true for a group of two senior couples from Australia, who visited Jordan eight weeks after the rocket attack on 2 August 2010 in Aqaba. During the interview, they explained that the Australian government issues such travel warnings, but they tend to be ignored by Australians because the warnings are overly cautious and conservative:

Peter: We, in Australia, you can check, and certainly they often have warnings . . .
Bob: They issue travel warnings.
Peter: . . . about Asian ones, particularly Bali, but it doesn't stop the Australians going there.
Bob: They tend to be pretty conservative. They're very cautious. They play it safe.
                    (Four Australian tourists, small group discussion, 5 October 2010)

Regarding the set of attacks in Bali in October 2002 and October 2005, it is maintained that these only have a transitory effect 'on the growth path of tourist arrivals from major markets and . . . Bali's tourism sector is sustainable in the long run' (Smyth et al., 2009, p. 1367). Australian tourists were ready to return to Bali in spite of travel warnings.

Discourses of global security reflected in travel warnings and advisories, such as the travel warning issued by the United States Embassy in Amman for Aqaba, or Australian ones for Bali, for example, are intended to shape tourist activities and further contribute to the division safe/danger-zones. Travel warnings, those 'ominous announcements', meant to alert tourists (Noy & Kohn, 2010, p. 206), have the function of regulating, sanitising and securitising travel and tourism in most societies. If analysed in detail, these warnings 'construct multilayered spatial–visual representations of tourist destinations' (p. 206).

Some tourists, however, choose to travel to places sanctioned by travel warnings as danger-zones. Lakshimi from India travelled to Jordan at the end of September 2010. We had online pre-trip interviews on 28 and 29 August and a joint interview with her travelling companion on 2 October in Petra. On all occasions, she insisted that the ongoing conflict in neighbouring Palestine and Israel was not a factor in her decision to visit Jordan and then Egypt. About the incident in Aqaba she said that 'it does not make me concerned about my trip . . . it sounded like a stray incident or at least in a limited location' (Lakshimi and Rini, interview, 2 October 2010).

David, Marge and their two teenage daughters from the US also travelled to Jordan two weeks after the death of a taxi driver in front of the Hotel InterContinental. When I asked them about places to visit in Jordan, such as Aqaba, they said they were not aware of the rocket incident on 2 August. They were not planning to visit the resort, in any case:

Marge: We weren't planning to go to Aqaba in the first place, but my feeling is that, two things: one is that sometimes it makes a place even more secure, because I know that when I went to Bali, it was right after the bombings in Bali. And it occurred to me, yeah, that there were bombings, but I felt that it was so random that it – because it just happened, it probably wouldn't happen again.

(Marge from the Cheung family, small group
interview, 14 August 2010)

This seems to be the gambler's fallacy, a concept explored in a study on tourist risk perceptions and worries, before and after the 22 July 2011 terrorist attacks in Oslo/Utøya in Norway. The authors 'paradoxically' ask whether terrorism makes tourists feel safer (Wolff & Larsen, 2014). Drawing on the concept of the gambler's fallacy – 'a well-known cognitive bias where people assume that chance is a self-correcting process in which deviation in one direction makes deviations in the opposite direction more likely for the equilibrium to be restored' (p. 206) – the authors find that tourists believe Norway to be a safe destination, probably slightly safer after the attacks.

While Marge and her family did not plan to travel to Aqaba as such, she seems to have negotiated her concerns and emotions while in Jordan, based on presumed increased safety immediately after an attack, called 'inward-oriented rationalisations' in a similar study (Uriely et al., 2007). These inward-oriented rationalisations stress the safety within the visited tourist destination soon after an attack, and 'outward-oriented rationalisations' emphasise terror-related risks that exist in other parts of the world, according to the authors (Uriely et al., 2007). Marge's premise was the presumed slim chances of another rocket incident in Aqaba, or other parts of Jordan, as had been with the bombings in Bali.

Marge's husband, David, talked about the randomness of such an attack and the fact that 'it wouldn't necessarily deter me, because I've been to places before, I mean, where there have been terrorist acts, but that's me. But the other thing I realise is, terrorist acts can be very random' (David from the Cheung family, small group discussion, 14 August 2010). The danger, with this division of inward/outward-oriented rationalisations, is that it enforces dominant binaries in academic knowledge. Binaries, I maintain, need to be problematised and destabilised to forward research in tourism studies based on subjectivities. These subjectivities can be explored and understood through intersecting circulations of affects and death drives. David possibly engages (with) the death drive as he has travelled to places of danger and conflict before. He is not deterred by acts of terrorism, as he has been to places where there were terrorist attacks before. David and his wife resist the tourism–conflict opposition, and cross the safety/ danger boundary, by downplaying the risk of terrorist attacks. Both of them think terrorist attacks are random and cannot be predicted. The couple maintains that they would travel to a region that has been recently bombed 'because it just happened, it probably wouldn't happen again' (David and Marge, small group discussion, 14 August 2010).

All the above-mentioned tourists I interviewed had travelled to Jordan and some of them to Aqaba, one to eight weeks after the rocket incident on 2 August

2010. They willingly took the risk as dangers were negotiated and felt less intense. This is either because it just happened, therefore, the place tends to be 'even more secure' (Marge, small group discussion, 14 August 2010), or because it seemed to be an isolated incident in a limited area (Lakshimi, interview, 2 October 2010); or because the risk taken was a calculated one, as is the case for Mary and John. Mary and John are a couple from Aotearoa New Zealand in their thirties, living in England; they 'are quite keen to travel to troubled places', as they said during our interview:

John: In life, you can't not go where you wanna go. You can't just say, oh, it's too dangerous.
Mary: There's always a calculated risk isn't there? It was the same with Burma. We met people that had travelled through Burma, and Burma was a place where we were quite keen to travel through . . .
John: We were very keen.
Mary: . . . even though we'd read about the troubles and things there, and obviously the military control. We were still quite keen to travel there, and met people that had travelled through there.
John: Yeah, very much so.

(Mary and John, interview, 16 September 2010)

I visited Jordan during March–April 2009, and July–November 2010. In both instances, I have to say I felt safe and secure at a surface level. I felt, like Mary and John, that I took a calculated risk. I even travelled to Aqaba two days after the rocket incident and stayed at the Hotel InterContinental in October for a weekend. The possibility that the Israeli–Palestinian conflict become violently manifest in Jordan was rather dim, but none the less existent. In 2005, three five-star hotels in Amman were bombed and rockets fell on Jordanian soil, as well as in April and August 2010. In spite of this, I did not feel (a conscious) fear for my life. The excitement of travelling in a 'happening' place and collecting information for my research superseded any feelings of doubt or fear I might have had. I even felt like a 'brave' researcher 'having the courage' to be out and about collecting data in a relatively volatile region in close proximity to the ongoing Israeli–Palestinian conflict.

As a tourist in the region, I can vouch for the safety and stability of Jordan; as a tourism researcher, I have tried to unpack the sanitation discourses that present Jordan as an oasis of safety and stability. In doing so, I too might have engaged with the death drive while travelling in a 'dangerous' place. That 'courage' I tried to exhibit as a researcher may very well be the effect of affect. Fear, fun and shame were possibly generated by enticement to, and psychoanalytic enjoyment of, dangers. I too felt like a danger-zoner, blurring and crossing affective and emotional borders.

The process of sanitising Jordan from the conflicts in the region – be they in Iraq, at the Israeli–Lebanon border, or along the Palestinian–Israeli demarcations – is accomplished through the affective workings of a whole apparatus made of mass media, tourism industry representatives and governmental officials, with the concurrence of tourists in the region. The illusion of safety is produced and marketed in Jordan through the enforcement of the safety–danger opposition, which further leads to the demarcation between conflict and tourism. In the next sections, I continue analysing affective workings of the 'sanitation apparatus', as I discuss a present/absent (castrated) peace within a politically un/stable environment.

Wish for peace

> Everybody's wish is for peace . . . it's a dream of [pause] the people living in this part of the world, ever since we are children; we dream of peace all the time because we lived in a conflict area. It was 1948 war, 1967 war, Palestinians, Jordanians and all . . . Don't forget that Jerusalem and Palestine were part of Jordan too at one point before they were separated. Now administratively they are part of the Palestinian state, which is still not complete of course. We are still in a struggle between Palestine and Israel, there's no peace yet. Every day we hear Netanyahu [Prime Minister of Israel], we hear this, we hear that, but nothing really materialised yet. That's why peace is like a hunch . . . Jordanians, Palestinians, all this region you know, even Lebanon and Syria. They're always dreaming of living in peace like other countries in Europe and so forth; like New Zealand [friendly laugh].
>
> (Anwar, interview, 28 July 2010)

Anwar alludes in the above excerpt to Jordan's geographical proximity to Iraq, Lebanon and Syria, and to the ongoing Israeli–Palestinian conflict. Jordan seems to be not only a passive space of spill-overs from the regional turmoil, but also an active place where the conflicts manifest themselves. In this place of socio-political conflict, discourses of peace accentuate a perpetual condition of living with conflict and war. Wishes for peace point to the desire for harmony and agreeable relationships amongst neighbouring countries. Peace is not static and utopian; it is beyond the absence of war, imperfect and permeable. Building peaceful relationships can be achieved through understanding and accepting difference of others, as rebuttal of cultural identities fuels wars and conflicts. Anwar, in the above excerpt, identifies himself as Jordanian, different than Palestinians and Israelis. But since '*we* are still in a struggle between Palestine and Israel, there's *no* peace yet', that is, he feels the absence of peace in the region. Officially, peace is or should be *present* in Jordan, ratified through the 1994 Peace Treaty.

This present/absent peace I call a *castrated* peace, a stealth peace. The psychoanalytical concept of castration is not only useful to explain the ambiguity in 'Middle Eastern peace', but also to explore, understand and eventually address issues of national and regional identities, fears and anxieties. Castration refers to prohibitions and differences that uphold the illusion of identity (Bronfen, 1992). It points to disharmonies and asymmetries emerging in fear of separations. Castration anxiety in this context refers to amoral and social anxieties, generated by traumatic experiences of loss (Freud, 1978 [1964], Vol. XXII, p. 125). In the neighbouring region of Palestine/Israel, peace is frequently lost. In Jordan, the 'present absence of peace' is more poignant. Jordan signed a peace treaty with Israel, together with Egypt being the only countries in the region to have done so. Peace is, therefore, present, at least in official Jordanian discourses. But the continuous 'dreaming of living in peace like other countries in Europe and so forth; like New Zealand', shows an absence of a (putative) peace, negotiated in the 1994 Treaty. It reflects a peace-envy, in a Freudian sense.

Regarding peace and the conflict that has tainted the region for over six decades, Arfan, a Jordanian tour guide, expresses his opinion:

> Jordan first of all is a separate country from Palestine, we have a lot of Palestinians living in Jordan. I don't know if you know that there is about 40–50 per cent of the population in Jordan are Palestinians, but they are Jordanian citizens so they live in Jordan, as Jordanians they have every right we have. I say, we support two different countries, Israel and Palestine, but we are not going to get ourselves involved, that's two different countries. I think they can solve their problems between each other if they want to, but we will not allow them to bring their troubles here to Jordan because Jordan's completely separated from Palestine, completely separated from Israel and it's their lives. In my personal opinion I really don't care, if they want to fix the thing they can fix it, if they want to keep fighting for the rest of their lives they can, that's their choice. As long as they don't bring their problems to Jordan, we're cool you know, they are good, we are good, everybody's happy. But it will never be fixed, that's just my opinion, they all started it then, they will never finish it, you know why? Because none of them wants peace, they are both, Israelis and Palestinians, stubborn; they both want it all, no one is willing to give up. If you don't give up something, you're not going to gain anything that's just my whole point, so it's going to be something that's going to go [on] forever, that's just my personal opinion.
>
> (Arfan, interview, 3 October 2010)

At a first read, Arfan's opinion on the Israeli–Palestinian conflict is a straightforward one. Jordan is a country 'completely separated' from Israel and Palestine. The troubled area, Palestine/Israel, is castrated from Jordan in Arfan's discourse. While Jordanians support both countries, they will not allow either of them to bring their troubles to Jordan. As Arfan asserts the 'complete separation' of Jordan from Palestine and Israel, he himself undoes this separation. He states that '40–50 per cent of the population in Jordan are Palestinians', who hold Jordanian citizenship and have all the rights that Jordanians have. With half of Jordanians being of Palestinian descent, Arfan's feelings and emotions for the Palestinian cause seem to be intertwined with the need for a distinct Jordanian identity. The illusion of identity mentioned above is underwritten by differences between Palestinians and Jordanians, which Arfan asserts 'we [Jordanians] are not going to get ourselves involved' (Arfan, interview, 3 October 2010).

In the context of the Israeli–Palestinian conflict, it is argued that a Palestinian identity is denied. Aspirations for a nationalist territory, emotionally connected to ancestral memories of an inherited geographical identity, are curtailed (Curti,

2008). It is maintained that 'the renaming of Palestine as Israel by the European Jewish settler colonists was not only of symbolic value; it also involved (and still involves) a geographic overhauling of the entire country' (p. 112). In this transformation of the land of Palestine/Israel, 'the Palestinians became a disease, a virus, an impurity', tainting the land represented as a body; thus a separation wall has been built to contain 'this infection and its growing anatomical threats' (p. 111). Peace is compared to a state of health and demonstrates that to understand health, one must understand disease; thus to understand peace, one must understand the conflict (Moufakkir & Kelly, 2010, p. xix). A number of authors have argued that tourism is a vital force for peace (D'Amore, 1988; Jafari, 1989), or could be used as a tool to promote peace (Kim et al., 2007). It is also noted that conflict is part of the peace concept and for tourism to be a force for peace, it needs to include considerations of conflict in the debate (Askjellrud, 2003; Hall et al., 2003).

In Jordan, tourism industry representatives disavow the pervasive regional conflicts. As Arfan points out, Israel and Palestine are two countries and Jordan will not get involved. The complexity and sensitivity of peace and conflicts, however, make Jordanian neutrality a Sisyphean task. The desire for peace is reflected in the narratives of tourism industry representatives I interviewed, but also in the material culture of the place, in the naming of hotels and restaurants (see Figure 6.1) and shops (see Figures 6.2, 6.3 and 6.4).

Nazmi, a director of a large tourism company in Jordan and a former minister of tourism, explains that the fashion of including 'peace' in naming a lot of shops and hotels started in 1994, when the peace treaty with Israel was signed (Nazmi, interview, 1 August 2010). The ubiquitous use of the word 'peace' in many English names of hotels and souvenir shops is meant to invoke *good, peaceful feelings.* These are underlined by images of the calm desert, of the Treasury in Petra Park, or the narghile (water pipe), amongst others. This tense insistence of 'it's peaceful here' coexisting with 'wishes for real peace' underlines the castration aspect. Mohib, a manager with a multinational tourism company, explains the need to emphasise peace in Jordan:

> In a sense it's [peace] still our . . . [dream/wish]. Now for people who are still in the US or in the UK or in Australia even, when you tell them to travel to the Middle East they think of the Middle East as a troubled area. So that's why I think, we want to stress the point that we are a peaceful country. We do love peace and we want to give them peace, and I think everybody wants to live in peace; not only Jordan, any country in the world wants to live in peace. But we do keep stress on this because of all the political issues that we have in this area. We want to have them [tourists] thinking 'Now, this is a peaceful country, it is peaceful.' You have to understand, okay Jordan as a country is peaceful, but the problem is that we had separate wars in the past; so we were involved in wars in the past. So this means that we have to keep on stressing that we are a peaceful country [now].
>
> (Mohib, interview, 29 July 2010)

The temporal castration of the 'separate wars in the past' from the peaceful present reveals itself as a powerful sanitation practice at work in the conflict–tourism

Figure 6.1 Peace Way Hotel in Petra.

Source: Dorina Buda, 2010.

Figure 6.2 Land of Peace gift and coffee shop in Petra.

Source: Dorina Buda, 2010.

Figure 6.3 Peace Shop in Petra.
Source: Dorina Buda, 2010.

opposition. Jordan is now a peaceful country, temporally secure from the dangers of past wars; it is safe for the 'Western tourist gaze'. Mohib alludes to the 'Western' ('US, UK or even Australia') tourist gaze, which treats the Middle East as a unified, troublesome region, a gaze which, in his opinion, needs to be corrected by stressing

Figure 6.4 For Ever Love & Peace Shop in Madaba.
Source: Dorina Buda, 2010.

the peacefulness of Jordan. It has been argued that the tourist gaze should be problematised since it stresses the privileged and extraordinary position of the tourist
(MacCannell, 2001). A version of the gaze is proposed to include understandings
and feelings, '*conscious or not*, that visibility presupposes invisibility; that in every
seeing there is an unseen; a backside, a dark side' (p. 23, my emphasis). In the
excerpt above, Mohib explains that (the wish for) peace has to be made visible by
'stressing that Jordan is a peaceful country'. The unseen, the backside, has to make
its way to the 'Western tourist gaze', which should not be a gaze upon an unsafe
country, but a gaze informed by feelings of peace: 'now this is a peaceful country,
it is peaceful'. Tourism and tourists can play an important role in promoting peace
and bringing about '"dialogue for peace" to unmask the dialectical and reciprocal negotiations involved in intercultural communication' (Blanchard & Higgins-
Desbiolles, 2013, p. 4). In this respect, tourism in relation to peace is envisioned in
the context of human rights, justice and international citizenship and addresses tourism efforts to connect the personal or individual to the cultural and multicultural.

Safety and political stability

Jordan has always been a safe destination. It has been an oasis of peace and
stability. These days when an incident happens anywhere in the world, you

cannot stop it, but you can try to prevent as much [as possible] – and the government [in Jordan] at least has taken all the measures to make sure that unfortunate incidents do not happen. And this is not only for Jordan; this is for a lot of European countries, North America, Asia, anywhere you go, there's the same thing . . . Jordan is definitely safe. Jordan is a safe destination.

(Nawfal, interview, 26 October 2010)

Nawfal, former director of the Jordan Tourism Board and a Minister of Tourism and Antiquities (MoTA), presents Jordan as a safe and stable country in the context of an unstable world where 'you cannot stop an unfortunate event from happening', 'but you can try to prevent it'. Safi, owner of a tourism company also talks about safety in Jordanian tourism:

Jordanians as people are very welcoming. But of course in the back of their [tourists'] heads they are always, you know they think they are coming to somewhere that's not completely safe . . . Most people travel a lot nowadays and most people have been to Europe, the States and so on. They want to see something different. We offer that, I mean as far as the countries [in the Middle East] involved, the quality of the sites are world class, so I think that the moment they feel that this area is safe they'll come here even more than they do now. It's more about them wanting to experience something different, something new.

(Safi, interview, 11 August 2010)

The dominant discourse is that political instability is disastrous for tourism, that it is only safety and stability – socio-political homeostasis – which can provide a proper background for the workings of tourism. As Nawfal expresses in the excerpt above, for Jordan to be a safe destination it must emphasise that the country has *always* been an oasis of peace and stability. Safety and stability are interrelated concepts, powerful enough to shape tourism practices, that is, 'only safe places that have achieved a certain level of peace and stability can guarantee the continuation of tourism in an environment unimpeded by the disruptions of war' (Lisle, 2000, p. 2), or of an ongoing conflict, I would add. A colonel with the Jordanian Tourism Police (JTP) declares that the 'political effect on the area is finished, it's obsolete'. His assertion that the political instability effect is obsolete points to the same mainstream discourse that political instability can never coexist with tourism practices. The colonel further adds that tourism 'is taking its chances of development because the [current favourable] political situation is helping the development' (JTP Colonel, interview, 26 July 2010) in the country.

The regulation of safety and stability, connected to tourism, is achieved by annihilating, separating, or sanitising the opposite – 'political instability is obsolete'. Sanitation of the Israeli–Palestinian conflict in Jordan is achieved by proclaiming a strong political stability in Jordan, which sustains tourism development. In countries unsettled by ongoing conflicts or located in the proximity of one, the promotion of mass tourism depends on these practices of sanitation. Images of pristine beaches by the Red Sea, of wellness and spa pools by the Dead Sea, as well as historical, archaeological and religious sites, tend to erase proofs of instability, generated by the ongoing nature of the conflict. This sanitation process reinforces the safety/ stability/peaceful versus danger/instability/conflict oppositions.

These discourses, instead, trouble and confuse the above dichotomies. Political instability in tourism refers to a situation whereby political legitimacy of a regime is challenged by forces outside of the accepted parameters of the political system, and the basic functional prerequisites for social and political order are periodically disrupted (Hall & O'Sullivan, 1996; Sönmez, 1998). Following these definitions, Jordan seemed to have been largely stable between 2006 and 2011. In January 2011 Jordanians started protesting on the streets of the capital, Amman, and other large cities and demanded that Prime Minister Samir Rifai step down and the new prime minister be elected, rather than appointed by the King (Al Jazeera, 2011; BBC, 2011). These demonstrations came after protests in Tunisia and were followed by the Arab Spring revolutions in Egypt, Syria, Yemen and Libya.

The concept of political in/stability has been re-evaluated, taking into consideration the idea of change as vital to political stability: 'a crucial and paradoxical element in stability: [is] change' (Wilson, 2002, p. 203). Logically thinking, change is the opposite of stability, some change, however, appears to be necessary to maintain political stability. Thus, following the protests in 2011, the Jordanian king accepted the resignation of Samir Rifai and named another Prime Minister, Marouf Bakhit, who held the position from 2005–07. The Ministry of Tourism and Antiquities (MoTA) does not seem to be on more stable political grounds either, with frequent changes of ministers.[3]

In our interview, Safi continues 'It's a region that has problems, has issues but Jordan, I think that as a country we're looked upon favourably by the Europeans and the Americans' (Safi, interview, 11 August 2010). He even downplays any danger, saying that there's 'nowhere in the world that is completely safe, you know? Be it London or Madrid, whatever. Anywhere it is a bit dangerous.'

Indeed, in a growing number of places, the orbits of security and tourism collide in explicit ways supported by the pre- and post-contextuality of affect (Massumi, 2002a). Terrorists, tourists and soldiers occupy the same space (Lisle, 2007). In its trans-situational character affect is '*an autonomy of event-connection*' (Massumi, 2002a, p. 217, emphasis in original). In Amman, and other cities and tourist sites in Jordan, the dis/continuity of security is the affective thread that brings together tourists, tourist activities with tourist police and soldiers. Continuity entails discontinuity; their interconnection 'is operative, not metaphysical or definitional' (p. 217). Affect's excess continuity is the transparent glue that binds and dis/connects the worlds of tourism. About the soldiers roaming around in plain sight in Jordanian tourist places, Anwar explains:

> tourist police are well educated into the tourism hospitality business; meaning that it can help people. It's all there to support them [tourists] and make them feel secure . . . they help in a way to complement the safety and security of our guests.
> (Anwar, interview, 28 July 2010)

This spatial collocation of tourists and police people, as well as soldiers orbiting the same space, implies a temporal collapse as well. The ongoing nature of the conflict has turned the region into an enticing danger-zone where tourists travel, lured by imageries of exotic difference, safety and conflict. Spatial collocation and temporal diminution are 'well-known indicators' that define the postmodern and post-structural. Such aspects are useful in explaining the continuity of affect, or as Massumi (2002a, p. 217) writes '[s]elf-continuity across the gaps'. The ever-increasing intensification of time–space compression – the phenomenon of reducing the relative affective and spatial distance between people and places – is generated by social dynamics and ever-changing technologies. The juxtaposition of time, space and affect seems to facilitate 'the ease of travel . . . [and] makes it possible for war zones to immediately re-enter the orbit of the tourist gaze as the next hotspot' (Lisle, 2007, p. 340).

Politics and emotions over the Aqaba/Arava border

> We are very upset of the way they [Israel] advertise it [Jordan]. We are not talking about politics but because we are tour guides we feel that it affects our work. They advertise Jordan this way: two weeks in Israel and get one free day in Petra; so when the groups come to Petra at the end of their visit in Israel after two weeks' time, they bought everything, they did their shopping, so they do not spend any money in Jordan. You know they do it as [a] one-day trip so everything is booked, [thus] the locals, the hotels, the restaurants in Jordan do not get any profits. So that's why, you know, we feel that. What kind of tourism is this [that Israel in promoting about Jordan]?
>
> (Four Jordanian tour guides, group interview, 4 October 2010)

In the above excerpt from a small group discussion with four licensed Jordanian tour guides, in their late twenties to late forties, Mohammed, quoted above, as well as the other three guides in the interview showed discontentment, if not anger, about the way Petra is advertised in neighbouring Israel, that is, as a free gift if one visits Israel for two weeks. These day-trip tourists crossing the Arava/Aqaba border from Israel create much anger amongst Jordanian tour guides. They feel that tourists visiting Jordan, namely Aqaba and Petra, for only one day, do not generate enough profits for the local tourism industry.

Anger can be understood in several ways, as legitimate if connected to injustice; wrong when it is in excess and towards wrong things and wrong people; full of information and energy; as a mirror of past relations, or as a vision for the future (Ahmed, 2004b; Ngai, 2005). When the four Jordanian guides say they 'are *very* upset', but do not want to enter any political debates, they actually mobilise the political correctness of anger, its justifiability: 'it is because Israeli's actions affect our work that we are angry, not because of politics'. Overtly, anger here is nuanced as 'very upset' in relation to threatening someone's livelihood through interference with work and earnings. An in-depth reading points to a traumatic anger, collective and embedded in archaic memories. Anger here is defined by the relationship to a past of wars and conflicts between Palestinians, Israelis, Jordanians and others in the region. The emphasis on good proportionality and socio-political correctness in the guides' discussion, brings forth the potential for 'correct anger', that is, anger balanced between 'two equally negative extremes, one an excess anger, the other a defect' (Fisher, 2002, p. 173).

Thus, both in retaliation to Israel's actions and so that Jordan does gain some more profit, new entry fees in Petra Park were implemented in the second half of 2010. All visitors who spend less than 24 hours in Jordan are charged an entrance fee of 90 Jordanian dinars (JD), approximately €100. Tourists who stay longer than 24 hours are charged JD50 (€56) for a one-day pass, JD57 (€64) for a two-day pass and JD60 (€66) for a three-day pass (Petra National Trust, 2011). This represents a steep increase from JD21 (€24) for one-day entry, JD26 (€29) for a two-day pass and JD31 (€35) for a three-day pass. Almost everyone is asked to justify their stay in Jordan, either by showing their passport or by evidence of a hotel stay. One of the Commissioners for the Petra National Trust (PNT) explained:

> Petra is a cultural site and you have carrying capacity for the site. So normally the day visitors, whether coming through sea by ship or on land by bus, because Aqaba it's a gate, you see [mild laugh] for Jordan, so there are those coming from Saudi Arabia, coming from Egypt, coming from Israel – not only from Israel. The problem, suppose that you have those coming through cruises and you have normally, a package tour come to Petra around 50 maximum, the bus has 44, maximum 50, people. But if you have the cruise, then you have one thousand. And those people make pressure over the site, the infrastructure, the services, the toilets, the water, etc., etc., etc. And it was a kind of management of a flow of tourist[s] . . . you have to pay the difference between [the] normal tourist who comes to see Jordan and to spend one week, five days in Jordan, and the one who comes just for a couple of hours in Jordan. This is the difference.
>
> (PNT commissioner, interview, 16 August 2010)

The situation presents itself as much more complex politically and emotionally for those Jordanian tour guides who work with Israeli tourism companies which send tourists over the Arava/Aqaba border point for a short one-day tour of Petra. It is not just a matter of distribution of profits, but also a matter of feelings and emotions, as these are the catalyst for action. During the same group discussion, Abbas, another Jordanian tour guide shared his emotional opinions on this matter:

> To be honest with you, we have conflicts with Israel about tourism: they don't want tourists coming to Jordan and they don't want our economy to grow. I have several stories about this. I swear to God that one day an American [from the United States of America] guy . . . when we finished the tour he told me at the border 'I am really so sorry about what I heard in Israel. They tell me that Jordanians are rubbish people, they are thieves, they are killers, they are not good people and to be careful there, don't give them your money. But I know the truth now.' So many groups come here to Jordan without money because they tell them in Israel: 'It is a prepaid package trip so you don't have to carry money, everything's included: transportation, tour guides, food, and water, so you don't have to take any money, they will steal from you, they steal every day. Fuck [lowering voice] Israel, they told us not to bring any money.'
>
> (Four Jordanian Tour Guides, group interview, 4 October 2010)

This excerpt from the same discussion with the group of guides is loaded with energy and passion. It is anger expressed towards allegedly unfair tourism practices encouraged by their Israeli counterparts. Being *against* something implies being *for* something else, for a vision of the future, even if it is not yet articulated. Crucially, anger ought to be aired, ought to be voiced, striking a socially correct and acceptable balance, as I mentioned above. Anger should not be allowed to transform into silence, because this would mean turning away from the future, or repressing its potential for advancements. These accounts seem, at first, to contradict the debate on how the conflict is sanitised in Jordan. Local tour guides' stories annihilate the absence of the Israeli–Palestinian conflict in Jordan. Such are the workings of emotion and affect, paradoxical at first blush, yet intense and signalling profound socio-political tumult.

It has been argued so far in this chapter that most representatives of the tourism industry in Jordan, be they company managers or owners, tour guides, or tourism governmental officials, concur in presenting Jordan as a stable country, as an oasis of peace impervious to the neighbouring conflict. A more in-depth reading of these accounts and the ones I will continue to discuss in this chapter, lead further to unveiling the workings and doings of affect and emotion in Jordanian tourism. In Jordan, manifestations of the ongoing regional conflict are present/absent, or castrated like 'Middle Eastern peace', and they become more evident as one travels closer to the borders, especially the border with Israel/Palestine.

Relations between Jordan and Israel 'have been traditionally hostile to each other' (Pizam et al., 2002, p. 177), assert the authors in a study on the role of tourism as an agent of change. Following the 1994 peace treaty between the two countries, relations improved with the opening of the borders for tourism exchange, as well as other types of economic cooperation. However, in 2000–01, the second Palestinian uprising, also called the Al-Aqsa Intifada, brought tourism between Israel and Jordan, as well as other Arab neighbours 'to a standstill. Shooting and bombing are a daily occurrence, and anecdotal evidence suggests that friendly relations and positive attitudes toward Jordan and the Jordanian people have been replaced by distrust and dislike' (p. 177). While the second intifada represented a rather violent outburst of the Israeli–Palestinian conflict, it has certainly been followed by other periods of strong animosities as mentioned earlier. As I sit and write this chapter [September/October 2014] more news circulates of violent clashes between the Israeli Defence Force and Palestinians in Gaza.

In this hostile political context, tourism is an emotional affair. Strong emotions are inflicted on Jordanian tour guides when they interact with tourists coming from Israel, whether Israelis or of other nationalities. In an individual interview Abbas emotionally recounts:

> I hate it when someone says bad things about Jordan and Jordanians . . . I care about Jordan, I swear one of the reasons why I work as a tour guide is to change your [tourists'] opinions about Arabs about Islam . . . to show them we're something else, we're not what you hear about us in your countries.
>
> (Abbas, interview, 4 October 2010)

Hate, an excess of anger at times, slides between and among people and things. Hate is argued not to '*reside* in a given subject or object . . . it circulates between signifiers in relationships of difference and displacement' (Ahmed, 2004b, p. 44, emphasis in original). Hate comes forth in Abbas's account, not only in its direct naming, but also through the defensive use of 'care' – 'I care about Jordan.' This is a form of justification and persuasion for the Jordanian guide who feels threatened and victimised; hate does not simply tell the story of unfair tourism practices, but makes the story affective by mobilising collective fellow feelings. Hate and other such emotions are organised in the unconscious when 'an affective impulse is perceived but misconstrued, and which becomes attached to another idea' (p. 44). So, what is repressed in the unconscious is not the emotion as such, but the idea to which it may have been initially and briefly attached. Ahmed opines, that psychoanalysis presents useful routes to understanding hate and anger as processes of movement and/or dis/association.

Associating himself with Islam and Arabs, and hating when someone discredits him through his associations, Abbas feels moved to share his unfortunate stories of tour guiding groups from Israel. Emotions such as anger, hate and love, drive Abbas to work in the tourism industry and he aims to improve tourists' impressions about and behaviour towards Arabs and Islam. The Islamophobic discourse in the 'Western' world has become extremely vocal after the 9/11 incident in the United States. Even before, Said argued that 'there is an unquestioned assumption that Islam can be characterized limitlessly by means of a handful of recklessly general and repeatedly deployed clichés' (1997, p. li). These clichés have led to an increase in anti-Arab racism, Islamophobic discourses, intensifications of the Israeli–Palestinian conflict, all of which seem to have the effect of stripping Arab peoples of their dignity (Jamoul, 2004). It is this dignity that Abbas seeks to restore and recapture by being a tour guide and showing tourists 'we're something else, we're not what you hear about us in your countries' (Abbas, interview, 4 October 2010). This is his justifiability for feeling anger and hatred.

The same experiences, feelings and emotions were shared by Abdul. He is a Jordanian guide in his thirties, who tours one-day Russian visitors coming from Israel through the Arava/Aqaba border:

Abdul: I'm telling you the truth, the tourists who come from Israel are not usual tourists. They are not useful for our country. Why? Because they are spending all the money in Israel and the Israelis telling my tourists that everything in Jordan is from China and from India, not to buy anything in Jordan and to be careful in Jordan because it's an Arabic country. I'm hearing this everyday.

Dorina: From whom, who tells you?

Abed: From the tourists.

Dorina: They tell you?!

Abed: Because when I'm speaking with my people [Russian tourist groups] they are feeling that they are speaking with a Russian, because I know their language very well, perfect. I studied in Ukraine about six years.

(Abdul, interview, 20 October 2010)

Another aspect that did not sit well with Abdul was the collection from tourists of Jordanian visa fees by Israeli tour guides. Abed was informed by some groups of tourists that they were charged US$60 for a Jordanian entry visa, when a Jordanian visa issued at the Aqaba border point is free for tourists. He brought this matter to the attention of tourism companies in Aqaba and to border officials, he even proposed to post a sign at the border in Russian with a free visa notice. Abdul's frustration increased when Jordanian border officials would not support such a decision: 'he [border official] told me don't do it, don't try even, we will not do anything, we can't do anything, what happens in Israel it's in Israel' (Abdul, interview, 20 October 2010).

I crossed the Jordanian–Israeli/Palestinian border a few times by air and by land, but never through the Arava/Aqaba border point, so at the time of these interviews I was not fully aware of the official entry and exit fees at all border crossing points. The Jordanian Tourism Board (2011) explains on their website that:

> Arrivals at Aqaba, either through the seaport, the airport or at the crossing from Israel or Saudi Arabia, are granted a free visa to Jordan. There is no obligation associated with this visa, provided that they leave the country within 1 month of arrival, and that they do not need to renew their visa.
>
> (Jordanian Tourism Board, 2011, para. 4)

Browsing online websites of some Israeli tourism agencies I noticed some disclaimers included information about Jordanian entry and exit visas:

General information: The tour is conducted in English with a Jordanian guide in air-conditioned buses.

Included: Entrance fees and lunch.

Not included: Israeli border tax. Jordanian border exit tax. Tips. Visa for Jordan. Drinks.

(Israel Guide: Hotels, Apartments, Car Rent, Touring, 2011, para. 2)

Price does not include:
Border Tax + tips = $55.00 per person

Drinks purchased

Camel/donkey/horse rides in Petra.

(Petra Israel, One-day tour of Petra from Israel, 2011, para. 8)

The [Petra day] tour includes:

> Transportation in an air-conditioned coach
> Guide
> Tour of the Lost City of Petra
> Buffet lunch
> Wadi Musa
> Tour of the city of Akaba (time permitting)

Not included:

Drinks. Border Tax and Gratuities approximately $60 p.p. payable locally.

(Travel Link The True Israel Specialists, 2015, para. 3–4)

The exit visa from Israel through the Arava border costs Israeli shekels (ILS) 96 (€20) according to the official website of the Israeli Airports Authority. I found no information on the exit visa from Jordan through Aqaba. The only official information is the one cited above from the Jordan Tourism Board, which states that entry visas into Jordan through Aqaba are free of charge. When I crossed the King Hussein/Allenby Bridge border point, located about one hour's drive north of Amman, to travel to Al Quds/Jerusalem, I remember having paid a Jordanian exit visa fee of JD8 (€9).

Emotions are brought forth by dissensions and misunderstandings between Israeli and Jordanian tour guides. Such hostile relations impact tourism and tourists in the area. Abbas, for example, has refused to work with Israeli tour guides and tourists coming from Israel as he himself attested:

> With Israel, now even if they pay me 3,000 dinars a day to guide from the border to Petra I will not do it. The groups, they look at you like this [taking a disgusted and defying pose]. Inside themselves they know that there is something wrong, it's just a rubbish person guiding them in Jordan, or they believe what they [Israeli tour guides] told them there [Israel]. Groups that come from Egypt are completely different, so there's a big difference between groups who are coming from Egypt than those coming from Israel, a big difference.
>
> (Abbas, interview, 4 October 2011)

Abdul lost work with some Jordanian tourism companies because the tour agencies in Israel complained to their Jordanian counterparts that 'this guide is telling all the tourists [long pause – sighing] [they said] "he is a trouble maker." So, I lost about two or three companies because of that (telling the truth about the visa situation) but I'm still doing it' (Abed, interview, 20 October 2010). These accounts of Jordanian tourism companies and guides working strenuously with their Israeli counterparts disrupt the sanitised image that the tourism apparatus promotes of

Jordan. Circulations of affect and emotions linked to regional conflicts are imbued in Jordanian tour guides' accounts and disrupt the peace/war opposition. As noted before, there is a signed peace treaty between Jordan and Israel; strong animosities, however, dominate tourism interactions over the border between tour guides from both countries.

In Aqaba, the conflict seems to be more evident than tourism industry representatives and officials in Amman represent it to be, or are willing to accept. Jordan's image as an oasis of peace and stability is challenged by tour guides' narratives loaded with affect and emotion. These stories emphasise that 'the conflict between Israel and Jordan is not about water or about the Dead Sea, it's about tourism itself' (Abbas, interview, 4 October 2011). The conflict is not located only in Palestine and Israel, as '"Jordan the oasis of peace" postcard-like image' would have us believe, but also at the borders. The temporal argument collapses as well, since 'wars and conflicts', which happened in the past seem to be a contemporaneous matter with impacts on tourism in Jordan.

Guiding at the Jordan River/border: the Baptismal Site

Tourism in Jordan and especially near the borders, where tensions feel more palpable and affect intensifies, becomes a space of shared emotions. The Jordan River is, along some of its stretches, the border with Palestine/Israel. In this section, I focus on how emotions further trouble the peace/war and safety/danger binaries, a defining characteristic of affective danger-zone tourism. This contributes to further presenting ways in which affect troubles interconnections between tourism/conflict/danger, and how affective tourism is performed in places in close proximity to ongoing conflicts.

Abbas recounts another of his stories about a group of British tourists he guided, an incident he thought illustrative of the dissensions between tourism in Jordan and tourism in Israel:

> About the peace, we don't have peace. It's just for the economy, they [Israelis] don't respect the peace. We have conflicts about the Dead Sea, about the Baptism Site. I was guiding a British group one day, they came from [visiting] Egypt when I showed them the Baptism Site that's just 20 minutes before the Dead Sea, they were laughing and telling me 'we have seen this in Israel the Baptism site in Israel, what are you talking about?'
>
> (Abbas, interview, 4 October 2011)

Abbas' very passionate, almost extreme declarations – 'we have no peace', 'they do not respect peace', 'we have conflicts about the Dead Sea, about the Baptism Site' – point to the competitive nature between tourism in Jordan and tourism in Israel. It also alludes to the ongoing conflict in the region, which made Jordan 'lose' Jerusalem and the West Bank in the 1967 War. In this context of past wars, conflicts and peace, tourism sites become entangled with politics, and the conflict is *felt*. 'Bethany Beyond the Jordan – the Baptismal Site' represents such an example. The site is located about 50 kilometres west of Amman and ten kilometres north of the Dead Sea. It is on the River Jordan, which acts as a natural border between Jordan and Palestine/Israel. The site is managed by the Baptism Site Commission under the patronage of His Royal Highness Prince Ghazi bin Mohammad, head of the board of directors. I had on-site interviews with the Director of the Baptismal Site Commission and assistant director Engineer Rostum Mkhjian, as well as with tourist escorts and international tourists.

I visited Bethany Beyond the Jordan – the Baptismal Site for the first time on 14 April 2009. I remember the small parking lot, buying a ticket for JD7, and waiting. About half an hour later, the handful of people gathered by the ticket counter was invited into a large, covered pick-up truck with around ten seats. What seemed to be our guide introduced himself as being our escort into the Baptism Site area, which, as he said, was a military zone; hence we needed not to stray from the main path indicated by him. As we walked along the path, we reached a panoramic spot where the escort stopped to share some historical and religious facts with us. We continued until we reached a Greek Orthodox church with a golden dome situated right on the bank of the River Jordan. Across the river, we could see Israeli flags. A person next to me, with whom I was conversing while walking, looked in the distance at the flags. He said '*Es tut mir weh*! [It hurts!]' He is a Jordanian citizen of Palestinian origin who spent a lot of time in Germany and, as I had studied in Germany for a while, we exchanged opinions about the country. This person's words, his facial expression, exuded feelings of pain and sorrow. That image will always stay with me, perhaps because of a whirl of emotions that overwhelmed me as I saw his face and heard his words.

The following year in 2010, I spent considerably more time at Bethany, from 15–24 September. As part of my research fieldwork, I decided to conduct participant observation, recruiting tourists and tour escorts, as well as Baptism Site officials as participants in my research. One of my informants, an army colonel and director of the Tourist Police Department at the time, introduced me to the two directors of the site and promised to help me with whatever research needs I might have. It was, however, challenging to connect with the team of ten tourist escorts, all men aged between 30–40 years. My diary entry for 17 September, two days after arriving at the site, reads:

> I am quite uncomfortable with their hesitancy to the point where I am almost wanting to leave. I want to cancel my interview plans with these guides. The most frequent explanation they are giving me 'I am not afraid, but we are in a military zone, we are working for the government.'
>
> (Dorina, diary note, 17 September 2010)

I consider that understanding the workings of affect in tourism at the border area between Jordan and Palestine/Israel contributes to unveiling the tourism sanitation process. Examining these sanitation discourses render emotional and affective connections between tourism and conflict more visible. The tourist escorts working at the site have a different status than licensed tour guides in Jordan, who work freelance on a daily basis with tourism agencies. The escorts at the Baptism Site have no such license and are government employees. Their reluctance to be interviewed by me was obvious both because of their caution not to stray from official narratives, and also because they wanted to avoid being seen in the company of a young, single, Christian Orthodox, eastern European and unaccompanied female like myself. Personal information about me was easily obtainable from director and assistant director of the site, who were contacted by some escorts as they intended to become respondents in my project.

I visited the Baptism Site, keeping in mind the information I had learned from the previous year, of the site being a military area, which was reinforced by the escorts' refusals to have interviews with me 'because we are in a military area'. The official stance, however, is that the site is no longer a military area, as it was de-mined and demilitarised after the peace treaty was signed. Yet, intelligence personnel are present at the site, as well as two teams of soldiers – one team is located at the entrance into the actual site and one right by the river. During the week spent in Bethany, I would take daily at least three or four one-hour-long tours into the site. I noticed that the casual presentations of tourist escorts almost always include the expression 'military area/zone'. Official discourses present Bethany as a tourist, archaeological and religious site, which developed following the Peace Treaty of 1994, as Director of the Baptismal Site Commission explains:

At the beginning, before signing the treaty, it was a strict zone. It was a military zone. After signing the treaty, this is very important, one of the agreements was to develop this area – the eastern part of the Dead Sea as well as the Baptism Site. We consider it is a part of the fruit of the peace. This is one of the benefits of the peace, to develop something that was a closed area, military zone, restricted area, now became as touristic area, a religious site. So at the beginning, even after the Treaty, when we come at the beginning here, there were some difficulties because the site is located on the border between Jordan and the West Bank, you know? It's a border – first it's a border. Wherever you go in the world, a border must be guarded by patrols, by military, by police, whatever you call it – but it's a border you know.

(Director of the Baptismal Site Commission, interview, 16 September 2010)

The interviewee insists on the concept of border as reflecting a division of territory and establishment of authority and responsibility over it. Depending on relations between countries that share a border, the degree of permeability ranges from open borders with no checkpoints to completely closed borders, which nobody is allowed to cross (Timothy, 2001). This particular border zone between Jordan and Palestine/Israel is a closed one, as no one is allowed to cross it. Border patrols, military, or police personnel are present when border permeability is restricted by political problems or conflicts between actors.

Globalisation has engendered great changes in government policies towards borders, which in many cases have become more open to traffic, instead of remaining closed and guarded (Gelbman & Timothy, 2010). Such policies have contributed to liberalising economic cooperation. This can, in some cases, lead to border-crossing agreements and development of international tourism (Gelbman & Timothy, 2010). While Jordanian–Israeli relations have eased after the Peace Treaty and borders have opened, tight control over the borders as well as heavy presence of border military is still common.

The Baptismal Site, located at the border between Jordan and Palestine/Israel, is different from the Aqaba/Arava border in the south of Jordan, discussed previously. The tourist resort of Aqaba is distant from the border crossing, as is Petra, the site tourists cross from Israel to visit. The Baptismal Site is a 10-square-kilometre archaeological, religious and tourist park situated adjacent to the border, but without being an actual crossing point. Owing to its geographical location within the border zone, developing a tourist site at Bethany Beyond the Jordan was a highly complex political and military matter, as one director of the Baptism Site Commission (BSC) continues to explain:

> So, when we came, the first time inside [the border zone] we had some difficulties concerning how to match security issues with tourism. Actually this took us a few months you know to sit together, to talk together . . . to settle everything, duties and specificities. We put an action plan down actually, at the beginning, because it's a border first, still most of the site is located in the border. As well, it is very important, we must recognise this; frankly speaking, this is occupied territory in front of us, on the other side of the Jordan River in front of the Baptism Site. The Israelis consider this site [on the other side] is under their military control. Sorry, it's also now up till now . . . [On the Jordanian side] today the army only has to take care of the security of the border between the two countries, as any country in the world. For the management, operation, for visiting, it is the Baptism Site Commission, which handles all that.
>
> (Director BSC, interview, 16 September 2010)

There seems to be a shifting discourse of the Baptismal Site being and/or not being a military zone: military personnel are present at the site 'to take care of the security of the border between the two countries'. On the one hand, the danger of the conflict needs to be obfuscated for a tourist and religious site to be developed. Thus, the growing numbers of tourists visiting the site stand testimony to how safe the location is. Indeed marrying tourism, politics and the military within a border zone between two countries with not-so-friendly relations, presents itself as a challenging prospect. The Baptism Site Commission manages more than 100,000 visitors a year: 92,900 in 2007; 141,179 in 2008; 134,274 in 2009 and by August 2010 the statistics provided by the Assistant Manager of the site showed 90,798 visitors at Bethany Beyond the Jordan – the Baptismal Site (Baptism Site Commission, 2010).

On the other hand, as the director of the BSC noted, 'we must recognize this, frankly speaking, this is occupied territory in front of us . . . under Israeli military control'. The site with most of its archaeological and religious assets on the Jordanian side, and only a part of the Jordan River on the Israeli/Palestinian side has been asymmetrically developed. In Jordan, the site is a tourist and religious place with military personnel, to ensure the safety of the borders. On the Israeli side, the site is closed and under tight military control:

> They [Israel] declare it as a restricted military zone. They do not allow for the people to come in their site, only once a year during the Epiphany [Christian celebration beginning of January]. I hear – it's not official, but I hear from some of the Israelis, they told me in their last meeting with them, through the office of liaison, that they have in mind to open the site for the public. They told me that. I don't know [anything more]. Up till now it's not open.
>
> (Director BSC, interview, 16 September 2010)

The interviewee's information proved to be valid, as less than one year after the interview Israeli officials have made it public that they have started de-mining the area and plan to turn it into a tourist zone. It is reported that $2.9 million had been invested so far, and Lieutenant Colonel Ofer Mey-tal from the Israeli Department of Civil Administration heads a project of removing the land mines 'that were placed by Israel in the 1970s under threat from Jordanian incursions. For now, other land mines will remain behind clearly marked barbed wired fencing' (Sudilovski, 2011, para. 6). Regarding the mines at the Baptismal Site on the Israeli/Palestinian side, one of the local tourist escorts pointed to me the ones visible with the naked eye from the Jordanian side (see Figures 6.5 and 6.6).

The same tourist escort agreed to keep a photo diary for one day and take pictures of areas and signs in the site that he, as a Jordanian local guide, finds interesting and also what he has witnessed over the seven years of working at the Baptismal Site as being photographed a lot by tourists. Wonderful pictures were taken by Habbab to showcase the archaeological importance of the place, and also of the natural landscape to emphasise another theme of the Baptismal Site, that is, the wilderness of John the Baptist. He photographed the Israeli flags (see Figure 6.7) on the other side of the river-border, because tourists are fascinated about 'how close they are to the border' (Habbab, interview, 19 September 2010).

In the same task of keeping a diary, Adel, another escort at the site, photographed the Jordanian flag (see Figure 6.8) as he noted that was important for him. With a slightly disappointed voice, he said that most tourists took pictures of the Israeli flags as they wondered at the proximity of the Israeli/Palestinian border, and forgot to photograph the Jordanian flag. Adel continued, as if he wanted to rectify his words, that he always advised tourists to take pictures of the Israeli flags 'to show tourists we are good brothers' (Adel, interview, 20 September 2010). Another important aspect of a tour inside the Baptismal Site is the first view of the river where tourists marvel: 'this is the border'.

Features of the border landscape such as flags, panoramic views, signs with different messages spark tourists' interest and fascination. Borders seem to carry not only a certain fascination, but also a mystique and ineffability. Borders make the transition from life lived in one place to life lived in another place and connect different realms of experiences and states of being (Timothy, 2001). As interfaces between different languages, cultures, social, economic and political systems, borders have become attractions in and of themselves (Timothy, 2001). A great

Figure 6.5 Flags and landmines on the Israeli side of the Baptismal Site.
Source: Dorina Buda, 2010.

Figure 6.6 Tourists on the Jordanian side of the Baptismal Site.
Source: Dorina Buda, 2010.

Figure 6.7 Israeli flags on the Israeli side of the Baptismal Site.

Source: Habbab, 2010, used with permission.

example is the Finnish-USSR frontier, which would be visited by many Finns and foreign tourists alike 'to *feel* the mystique of the place, take photos of the prohibitory sign, or even to step into the restricted border zone to experience a geopolitical thrill' (Medvedev, cited in Timothy, 2001, p. 44, my emphasis).

I remember, in a small group discussion with two Australian couples in their sixties, Bob offered to take a picture of his wife, Diane, at the Baptismal Site but only to catch the small military camp on the side of the Greek Orthodox church. Bob was moved into action by his danger-zone fascination when he only pretended to photograph his wife and then moved the photo camera lenses to zoom in on the military station. He has not emailed me any pictures of their trip, but I took a similar one myself (see Figure 6.9). Bob, as well as I, inhabited our danger-zone tourist subjectivities as we decided to photograph a 'forbidden' and 'dangerous' object (the small military base in Figure 6.9). In doing so, both of us crossed the safety/danger and fun/fear boundaries. I also noticed that one picture taken by Adel for this project's photo diary was one of a tourist group he guided and the soldier standing by the group (see Figure 6.10), further demonstrating that orbits of security and tourism collide in affective ways that connect tourism to conflict.

This crossing of boundaries represents the ways in which affect transgresses tourism registers. When travelling in a conflict zone, people move across different and multiple tourist experiences. Discourses of affective tourism support

Figure 6.8 Jordanian flag on the Jordanian side of the Baptismal Site.
Source: Adel, 2010, used with permission.

compromising and fluid statements and encompass a wide range of tourism performances, unlike the modern system of knowledge that stressed more polemic,
exclusive and authoritative modes of theorising tourism. Danger-zone tourist subjectivities perform affect and emotion as multiple borders are asserted, resisted
and crossed in Jordan tourism spaces.

Figure 6.9 Small military base at the Baptismal Site.

Source: Dorina Buda, 2009.

Figure 6.10 Tourist group on the Jordanian side of the Baptismal Site.

Source: Adel, 2010, used with permission.

Israeli–Jordanian tourism affairs

In July 2010, Moses, an Israeli tourist, travelled with his German girlfriend around Jordan. This was Moses's sixth visit to Jordan over the years, but this time he decided to 'play it safe' and not identify himself as an Israeli:

Moses: There [in Jordan] it is advisable to not identify as an Israeli. Me and my girlfriend told them that I'm from Estonia.
Dorina: When was that?
Moses: Last July [2010].
Dorina: Why did you think there was the need to hide your nationality?
Moses: Because the area is full of Palestinians, including actual refugee camps.
Dorina: Why Estonia of all countries?
Moses: Less likely that any Jordanian will speak Estonian. We did run into one who could speak German in the bus to Jerash from Amman. At the hotel I told them that I was Israeli and I think that they probably reported that to the police. That guy in the bus to Jerash who spoke German talked with my girlfriend in German and Arabic, then the bus broke down and we went outside. He wanted to say something nice about Germany. He told her that it was nice that Germany was good at football and (in Arabic which every Israeli will understand) '*Itbach al Yahud*', which means slaughtering Jews. And I stood there and smiled like an idiot. My girlfriend told me 'I'll translate for you later' I told her 'thanks' and since we were very embarrassed we decided to hitchhike to Jerash.

(Moses, online interview, 31 August 2010)

Fears of anti-Semitism might have driven Moses to hide his Jewish Israeli identity while travelling with his girlfriend in Jordan. '*Itbach al Yahud*' which means in Arabic, as Moses pointed out, 'slaughter the Jews' is tantamount to a call for genocide. It represents a very racist opinion expressed by the Jordanian person with whom Moses and his girlfriend interacted. Anti-Semitism and Islamophobia have common roots, but with two distinct discourses, 'Islam had been defined by its absences (legal rationality, autonomous cities, asceticism and citizenship), Judaism had been defined by the contradictory nature of its religious injunctions' (Turner, 2004, p. 175). These two very complex and politically loaded concepts do not represent major points in my argument in this section, or this volume as a whole. I mention them just to point to another possible route into understanding the way the ongoing Israeli–Palestinian conflict shapes tourism in Jordan. However, I find Judith Butler's debate on and distinction between anti-Semitism and criticism of the state of Israel illuminating:

> every progressive person ought to challenge anti-semitism vigorously wherever it occurs. It seems, though, that historically we have now reached a position in which Jews cannot legitimately be understood always and only as presumptive victims. Sometimes we surely are, but sometimes we surely are not. No political ethics can start from the assumption that Jews monopolise the position of victim. 'Victim' is a quickly transposable term: it can shift from minute to

minute, from the Jew killed by suicide bombers on a bus to the Palestinian child killed by Israeli gunfire. The public sphere needs to be one in which both kinds of violence are challenged insistently and in the name of justice.

(Butler, 2003, para. 2)

Returning to Moses, his experience renders the tensions that circulate in Jordan and is performed in a tourism context while inhabiting the position of 'victim' 'hiding away in plain sight' from Palestinians, including refugees. As Butler (2003) argues 'victim' is a quickly transposable term that can shift rapidly; in Moses's case, his feelings and emotions as 'victim' shifted from visit to visit. His feelings of 'victimhood' shape and define his danger-zone tourist subjectivity. He travelled six times to Jordan and I asked if on all occasions in Jordan he hid his Israeli citizenship. I found it quite telling that on all previous five occasions he stated his Israeli citizenship, yet on his sixth visit he decided to 'be Estonian'. His decision seemed to have been motivated by him feeling 'a victim' due to the geography of Jordan and demographics of the Palestinian population. The northern parts of Jordan have a denser Palestinian population and he tried to avoid this region on previous trips, especially since there are 'actual refugee camps'.

Dorina: Was it the first time you did this [hide your citizenship]?
Moses: First time – yes, but it was interesting to pretend to be from elsewhere away from regional politics.
Dorina: So, you decided on your sixth visit to hide the fact that you were Israeli, why have you not done this on your prior visits, especially the first one which you said was a bit intimidating?
Moses: Prior visits were for hiking in the south (except the visit to Petra). We hardly came in contact with locals.
Dorina: So, from your five prior visits you decided that if you ever visit other parts of Jordan it is not safe to tell people you are Israeli?
Moses: No, I got to that conclusion before, but never went up north. In my first visit to Jordan me and a friend took his car over the border and we stopped not far from Wadi Ram to take an old man [who was hitch-hiking] and we told him we're from Israel. It quite frightened him. He wanted to get out of the car [pause] and the look in his eyes.

(Moses, online interview, 31 August 2010)

Moses perceives danger in Jordan and his own state of 'victim' as linked to the number of Palestinians living in the northern parts of Jordan, yet he performed his danger-zoner status by deciding to travel there with his girlfriend. He did not disclose his citizenship so as to protect himself and his girlfriend from possible incidents. For him, Jordan, and especially the northern part, seems to be as much of a danger-zone as Palestine is or Israel, for that matter. Even within a single country, there are 'safer' versus 'more dangerous' areas, which further destabilises the safety/danger opposition underlying the intensification of circulation of affect. Jordan cannot be understood as the 'safe' destination in opposition to Israel/Palestine as 'dangerous' places. As Moses pointed out, in Jordan there are nuances of safety and danger that one can feel depending on the area within the country one travels to. Equally, in Israel, there are regions that some feel are safer and others more dangerous.

It is argued that Israeli tourists perceive Israel to be more dangerous than certain places in neighbouring countries, such as Sinai in Egypt, for example (Uriely et al., 2007). Several tourists are cited to attest feeling more scared in places in Israel than when travelling in Sinai. An Israeli woman gave this account: 'in Tel Aviv I'm more afraid. I don't take buses anymore, and I also don't go to big malls . . . I haven't visited Jerusalem in years . . . Israel in general is scary' (p. 6). Regarding Jordan, Israelis visit it in large numbers. Tourism between Jordan and Israel has never been symmetric. Since October 1994, when the Peace Treaty was signed, Israelis have increasingly visited Jordan in comparison to Jordanian tourists, who have visited Israel mainly for 'visiting friends and relatives' (Pizam et al., 2002).

This is also my observation. From more than 35 Jordanian interviewees, only two persons had travelled to Israel and Palestine. Discussing this with local Jordanians working in the tourism industry, I was told that a lot of Jordanians would like to travel to Palestine and especially Jerusalem which, along with other parts of the Holy Land in Israel and Palestine, is sacrosanct to the three mono-theistic religions: Christianity, Islam and Judaism. However, Muslim tourists to the Holy Land have been virtually non-existent since the Six Day War of 1967 (Bowman, 1995). There exists no 'distinct market segment of Muslim pilgrim tourists to Israel . . . Only 1–5 per cent of all the tourists to Israel are Muslim' (Collins-Kreiner & Mansfeld, 2005, p. 115). It is thought that 'There might also be a political factor that avoids portraying sites or elements of Muslim deriva-tion' (p. 115). With the exception of Jordan and Egypt, Israel, which controls all the borders of the Occupied Palestinian Territories, does not have peace accords signed with Arab countries in the region, thus making it impossible for regional Muslim pilgrims to travel to the Holy Land.

A lot of Jordanians choose not to go to Israel and Palestine because of the unfair visa system. That is, Jordanian citizens need to apply for a visa at the Israeli Embassy prior to their travel to Israel and the Occupied Palestinian Territories, while Israeli citizens get a visa upon arrival at the border crossing. This represents another mani-festation of this conflictual situation that problematises the peace/war dichotomy. There is no physical and declared war between Israel and Jordan, but there seems to be a bureaucratic one. Jordanians whom I interviewed feel that the visa issue is another way for Israel to insist on its superiority, its ability to impose its hegemony over Arab countries; this is a rather humiliating position for the Arabs, one that fuels resentment. Mahdy, a Jordanian tour guide, expressed his frustration over this matter:

Not a lot of Jordanians go to Jerusalem, unfortunately, because the reason is from Israel. To go there it's too difficult, but the Israeli people they get the visa upon arrival, but as a Jordanian when we are going to their country they don't allow it for us. For example, if I was living in Aqaba or in Petra I have to go to the Israeli Embassy [in Amman] to stand in the lines for I don't know how many hours and I don't like it, so I don't want to go . . . It's not fair.

(Mahdy, interview, 21 October 2010)

Another, more political and deeply emotional reason for Jordanians not to travel to Jerusalem, Palestine, or Israel is their refusal to recognise the state of Israel. A local Jordanian newspaper in English, *The Star*, published in its late August 2010 edition an article entitled 'Jerusalem visits sparks debate', in which the issue of Jordanians travelling to Jerusalem is discussed. Sheikh Ikrima Sabri , the imam [person who leads prayers in a mosque] of Al-Aqsa Mosque, and also the president of the Islamic Higher Committee in Jerusalem, does not wholly approve of Arabs and Muslims visiting the occupied city of Jerusalem. Such visits, he considers, are 'a form of normalizing relations with the Israeli occupation' (cited in Abu Tarboush, 2010). However, the imam approves of 'Palestinians and Muslims who live abroad and hold a foreign nationality – which already maintains relations with Israel' to travel to Palestine/Israel so as to 'stay connected with their people and land' (cited in Abu Tarboush, 2010). The president of the Jordanian Anti-Normalisation Committee has voiced the same opinion: 'we would love to visit Jerusalem but only when it is liberated from the Israeli occupation' (as cited in Abu Tarboush, 2010).

Emotions of love as in 'we would love to visit Jerusalem', and of hate – 'I hate it when someone says bad things about Jordan' (Abbas, interview, 4 October 2011) – influence the politics of tourism in Jordan, and at the same time raise the necessity to discuss conflict, affect and emotion as eventfully ingressive in the tourism context (Massumi, 2002). Emotions are disorienting. Love and hate are 'something besides what they are' (Massumi, 2002, p. 36), they are affect and its perceptions of it – emotion. In that intense and contracted capture of affect, there is something about emotion that is still not actualised and separable from, yet unable to be attached to 'any *particular*, functionally anchored perspective (Massumi, 1995, p. 35, emphasis in the original). The circulation of affect and emotion in conflict tourism moves the discourse of Jordan as 'an oasis of peace, safety and stability' beyond rigid exclusion of conflict from tourism. A sanitising of the conflict is useful inasmuch as it brings some immediate tourist income for Jordan. Without debates on the ways the conflict shapes tourism in Jordan, the feelings and emotions of Jordanians employed in the tourism sector will vacillate between the extremes of hatred and love. This could see tourism leading to intensifications of the regional conflict, instead of alleviating it. Scholars need to recognise the importance of affect, emotion and feeling as they powerfully connect tourism and conflict in Jordan.

Notes

1 Petra has been designated a UNESCO heritage site since 1985. The new seven world wonders was a project organised by the New7Wonders Foundation, a body regulated by the Swiss Federal Foundation Authority, which attempted to update the seven wonders of the ancient world. After a popularity poll of about 100 million votes cast over the Internet or over the phone, the following were named as new world wonders: the Great Wall of China, Petra in Jordan, Chichén Itzá in Mexico, the Statue of Christ Redeemer in Brazil, the Colosseum in Italy, Machu Picchu in Peru and the Taj Mahal in India (New Open World Corporation, 2011).
2 For a discussion on psychoanalytic terms such as *jouissance*, and the Real, Symbolic, and Imaginary in tourism studies, see Chapter 3 'Psychoanalysing Tourism'.
3 Between 2010–2011, for example, there have been five ministers in charge of MoTA: Maha Al Khatib, Suzanne Afanah, Zeid Goussous, Haifa Abu Ghazaleh and Nayef Al Fayez (*Jordan Times*, 2011).

7 Crossing into the West Bank
It's all political and emotional in Israel/Palestine

Emotions are mobile, fluid, touching bodies and places. This makes it difficult to pin down what we feel, as well as find the right emotion-label to express or represent subjective emotional experiences (Richards, 2005). However important representation might be in analysing emotions (Gouk & Hills, 2005), we are reminded that we have insufficient cultural-theoretical vocabulary specific to emotion and affect (Massumi, 2002a). Tourist encounters are mediated through feelings and emotions. Likewise emotions and feelings, with their specific cultural dimensions, can be accessed when travelling. Subjective emotional experiences, resistant as they may be to representation and verbal expression, refer to people's feelings and emotions for one another, and for places, spaces and objects.

In this chapter, I discuss the ways affective tourism, with a focus on emotions, is performed in Palestine through encounters imbued with fascination, frustration, anger and shock, while touring places in conflict. The aim is to further examine circulations of affect and emotion in places of danger and conflict. Such circulations assert, disrupt and pervade fun/fear and safety/danger binaries. I continue unveiling the ways tourism and conflict intermingle beyond the superficial antithetical connection that dominates mainstream tourism research.

This chapter is divided into two parts. In the first part, 'It's all political', I present a brief historical overview of tourism in Palestine (Bar & Cohen-Hattab, 2003; Cohen-Hattab 2004a, 2004b; Cohen-Hattab & Katz, 2001). I argue that the Palestinian and Israeli ways of practising tourism in the area have been affectively, politically and socio-economically intermingled for decades. Further, I maintain that there are more than just two sides, Palestinian and Israeli, to the story of tourism in this politically contested place. The several nuanced 'in-between' positions can potentially disrupt borders between Palestinian and Israeli tourism representatives. The argument is that the Israeli–Palestinian conflict and its political discourses (Gregory, 2004a, 2004b; Said, 1993, 1997, 2003, 2004) are interwoven in tourism activities in Palestine/Israel.

In the second part, I discuss the separation wall and its checkpoints as tourist attractions. The distinctions between different types of tourists – danger-zoners, religious, cultural and historic, for example – 'their' specific motivations and experiences are blurred and infused with the area's affective and emotional intensity. These tourist attractions, the separation wall, checkpoints and refugee camps are so pervasive and present in the Palestinian landscape that they attract most tourists to Palestine irrespective of their primary motivations, be it religion, culture, nature, or history. I maintain that tourists often perceive life in Palestine as 'life in prison' for the locals (Bornstein, 2008; Bowman, 2007a).

The argument that 'a body of walls rests on a wall of bodies' (Curti, 2008) is useful to unveil the mix of fear, frustration and fascination experienced in Palestine. Further, I map anger, fear and shock which many tour guides attest that some tourists feel while touring the West Bank. I engage with geographical theories on the haptic sense to show how touching that which some tourists in Palestine may fear can disrupt safety/danger and fun/fear binaries. As I discuss some characteristics of affective tourism in Palestine, I continue to maintain that tourism and conflict mingle and 'hang together', glued by affect. Within this coexistence between tourism and conflict, binaries are asserted and disrupted by danger-zone tourists who touch places, places that touch tourists and tourists who touch each other, local Palestinians and Israeli soldiers.

I mainly focus on the current Palestinian narrative of attracting tourists to sympathise with their cause. My decision has mostly been taken on logistical, rather than political, grounds, as I had more means available to collect data in the West Bank in Palestine, than in Israel proper. My position, though, is a political one, but rather than rallying with one extreme or the other, I aim to present the complexity of tourism and emotions in Palestine as evidenced by tour guides and tourists that I interviewed.

It's all political

'It's all political' is an expression I often heard in Palestine/Israel, either during interviews with tourism industry representatives, or while casually talking with other locals and tourists. It seems that it has been 'all political' in the region for a long time. Tourism represents a stage on the Israeli–Palestinian arena where the 'all political' is acted out. In the Occupied Palestinian Territories during the last six decades, tourism has been predicated on the political way of doing pilgrimage. This political way has become alternative to the traditional pilgrimage practised prior to the British Mandate (1917–48). The Palestinian socio-political discourse in tourism is also alternative to the Israeli way, the latter having become the dominant and mainstream one. Israeli and Palestinian views of 'doing tourism' are contested and intimately entangled with the politics of the conflict between the 'two sides'. In this complex entanglement, tourism and conflict connect in ways that further disrupt binaries peace/war, safety/danger and fun/fear.

Traditional religious pilgrimage used to be mainstream tourism prior to the British Mandate in Palestine. During the British Mandate, Palestine became more 'Westernised', more democratic and attracted more secular western European tourists and also more politically oriented tourists (Bar & Cohen-Hattab, 2003; Cohen-Hattab, 2004a, 2004b; Cohen-Hattab & Katz, 2001). On the one hand, infrastructure was improved, hotels and resorts were built, and historical and religious as well as cultural sites and monuments were preserved and even restored.

On the other hand, the ideological battle between Zionists and Arab Palestinians started to be articulated. 'Jewish tourism to Palestine' (Cohen-Hattab & Katz, 2001, p. 170) started off under the British Mandate, with Tel Aviv being promoted as 'the first Hebrew city' and the setting up of guest houses in new Jewish settlements: 'This Jewish tourism was mainly brought about and developed by Zionist publicity following the flowering of Jewish nationalism' (p. 171).

The Arab–Palestinian population opposed the institution of a Jewish/Israeli state on their own Palestinian homeland. This opposition was taken onto the streets as well as in the political and economic arenas in which tourism was an ideological tool to present tourists with their own vision of Palestine. Political tourism, as it is practised today in the Occupied Palestinian Territories, has its roots in this shift from traditional mainstream pilgrimage to politically and ideologically infused tourism during and after the British Mandate.

During the British Mandate in Palestine, tourism became the battleground for economic and political superiority between Jews and local Arabs (Cohen-Hattab, 2004b). Tourists in Jerusalem had at that time more interactions with local Arabs since 'Arabs made detailed preparations to prevent anyone but themselves from profiting economically [from tourism]' (p. 65). Citing information from the Zionist Trade and Industry Department based in Jerusalem, it is further contended that Arab tour guides only directed tourists to non-Jewish stores and hotels, moreover 'the Arabs exploited the country's burgeoning tourist industry in order to spread anti-Semitic propaganda by distributing invidious anti-Jewish leaflets among their foreign charges' (p. 66). The friction between Arabs and Israelis was growing, and in the need to gain international recognition 'the Zionists were convinced of the need to try and capture the country's tourist trade for themselves' (p. 66).

Due to historical events, most notably the establishment of the state of Israel in 1948 and the 1967 War, Israel was in the position to make their narrative the mainstream tourism discourse, whereas the Palestinian narrative was relegated to 'the alternative' side. The tables seem to have turned. Some make a case for the injustices Palestinian tourism is suffering because of 'the supremacy and domination of the Israeli establishment over land, and people' (Isaac, 2010, p. 21), which prevents the Palestinian people from rightfully reaping the benefits of a land with so many cultural, natural, historic and religious sites. To counteract this trend, Palestinian tourism organisations have in turn begun to use tourism as a socio-political tool to make tourists aware of the '*realities on the ground*', a phrase one often hears when in Palestine.

Alternative Tourism Group (ATG), the Siraj Center for Holy Land Studies (Siraj Center) and Holy Land Trust (HLT) are organisations located in Beit Sahour and Bethlehem in Palestine. For them, tourism is a socio-political means to carve a move away from traditional pilgrimage, controlled in great parts by Israel (ATG, 2010; Bowman, 1995; Isaac, 2010). These Palestinian tourism organisations adopt a political, advocacy and activist approach to tourism. I maintain that activities carried out by these organisations connect tourism and conflict through their political discourse. In doing so, these organisations enact, stage and perform emotion, affect and conflict in tourism.

ATG was founded in 1995 as Palestinian culture and its socio-political realities 'did not find adequate expression in conventional pilgrim-oriented tourism'; the organisation's main aim is to 'present a critical look at the history, culture and politics of Palestine and its complex relationship with Israel' (ATG, 2010, para. 1). Siraj Center is officially licensed by the Palestinian Ministry of Tourism and Antiquities as a tourism company owned by the Palestinian Center for Rapprochement Between People. One of the points on the Siraj Center's (2011) agenda is to:

> organize fact finding missions to Palestine in order for people all over the world to have first hand experience of the ongoing Israeli occupation by meeting with Palestinians and Israelis and meet face to face with the real issues of illegal settlements, the Israeli Wall, water issues, borders and refugees.
>
> (Siraj Center, 2011, para. 5)

The separation wall, discussed in more detail in the following section of this chapter, has a wide range of names: security fence, separation barrier, segregation wall and apartheid wall. Siraj Center seems to be narrowing the scope by calling it 'the Israeli Wall'. While the decision to build the wall was taken by the Israeli Defence Ministry, it can be argued that the erection of the wall does not represent the will of all Israeli citizens in the country or in diasporas. It is indeed easy, if not simplistic and superficial, to recognise just two sides to a debate or even of a conflict, when there are so many nuanced stances in between.

B'Tselem, an Israeli information centre for human rights in the Occupied Palestinian Territories documents the Israeli public and policy makers about human rights violations in Palestine. It attempts to 'combat the phenomenon of denial prevalent among the Israeli public, and help create a human rights culture in Israel' (B'Tselem, 2011, para. 1). Another example of interstitial discourses is represented by the 500 Israeli reserve soldiers, who have refused to serve beyond the Green Line[1] since February 2002 (Gregory, 2004a). On the grounds of conscience and moral reasons, some of them petitioned the Israeli Supreme Court. While the court accepted their claims as moral ones, it still maintained the soldiers' prison sentences.

In tourism, one example of the 'in-between' positions Israelis and Palestinians take regarding the conflict is Green Olive Tours, a social enterprise owned and managed by a Jewish Israeli man, named Fred Schlomka. Green Olive Tours organises tours to the West Bank employing Palestinian guides in a move to decry perpetrated injustices. The tours are 'informative and analytical, covering the history, culture, and political geography of Palestine (West Bank) and Israel' (Schlomka, 2011, para. 1). This is evident in its mission statement to provide tourists 'ongoing commentary, interpretation, and critical analysis of the situation on the ground' so as to understand 'The "icons" of the Israeli Occupation . . . : The Separation Barrier, checkpoints, segregated roads, settlements, and walled Palestinian ghettos' (para. 4). This discourse of Israeli occupation, of the shocking realities on the ground, as well as the need for justice and peace, is overtly and boldly woven in narratives of Green Olive Tours. These stand testimony to affects and emotions arisen out of such complex and sensitive events of conflict, which do not seem to deter, but perhaps entice, tourists into the region. Green Olive Tours' vocabulary of 'occupation, separation, segregation, walling' expresses stirring emotions, and deprivation of power – castration.

Two sides?

Fred Schlomka explains that approximately 80 per cent of tourists to Israel and the Occupied Palestinian Territories are on package group tours, and most of them are Christians and Jews on heritage tours:

> We [in Israel/Palestine] have a Christian Disneyland, we have a Jewish Disneyland. You come here on the Jewish heritage tour, we show you all the Jewish stuff. You come here on a Holy Land tour, pilgrim tour, you get all the Christian stuff, and you rarely step out of it. So you have this view of the country that's just a partial view. And most of the package tours are like that.
> (Fred Schlomka, interview, 19 July 2010)

An alternative to the 'Holy Land – Disneyland' tours, Fred and Green Olive Tours offer a different type of tourism, not one that presents 'just a partial view', but one that encompasses discussions about the harsh realities on the ground. Fred, however, feels that the majority of tourists in Israel take 'Christian or Jewish Disneyland' tours and remain oblivious to the rest of the regional stories. Tourists are disadvantaged, as they do not step outside of the 'Disneyland' story. Fred bemoans that the number of those that do is limited – 'last year maybe 2,000 people I had on my tours' (Fred Schlomka, interview, 19 July 2010).

Higher demand of such tours is, on the contrary, reported by the Palestinian ATG. A Palestinian manager with ATG, Sadid, explains how this organisation is committed to showing both the Israeli and the Palestinian perspectives:

> The good at ATG is that we are not one-sided. We've never been one-sided. We are just focusing on the attitude on the ground. So, we show the Palestinian side and the Israeli side. We show people the reality on the ground of what's happening . . . For example, I arrange meetings with the settlers from a farther settlement, which is in the West Bank. It's like 20 minutes from Bethlehem. And I call him and I tell him that I have a group who would like to meet with him. They meet with him and he says his point of view, which I don't agree totally with him about what he says, but as a tourist when you come to the country, you have the right to listen to both sides and then you can decide. You listen to me, you listen to him, you walk on the ground, you look what's happening – then you can decide what's right and what's wrong. So when I show both sides not to be like just one-sided. And that's why we have very good credibility and we have a lot of demand.
> (Sadid, interview, 12 October 2010)

It is argued that ordinary Israelis and Palestinians are locked into binary structures of alterity such as Islam/Judaism, Arab/West, Zionist/Palestinian. Seemingly, both have denied each other and themselves, entrapped by dichotomic monologisms to which almost everybody has actively or passively succumbed (Ashcroft, 2004). Fred's and Sadid's accounts, however, show that the rhetoric of denial of both Arabs and Israelis are changing, shifting and intermingling. These binaries should not be taken as oppositions, but resonating into each other, with affect being their commonality. These constructed binary structures of Palestinian–Israeli otherness constitute the point of emergence of affect 'in their actual specificity, and it is their vanishing point, in singularity, in their virtual coexistence and interconnection – that critical point shadowing every image/expression-event' (Massumi, 2002a, p. 33).

The two 'Disneylands', Christian and Jewish, resonate with each other, since a great part of religious and tourist sites are the same. In his company's case, Fred employs Palestinian guides and tour escorts, pointing to the overlapping of the binaries mentioned above. Fred, however, does not mention a Muslim 'Disneyland'. This is partly because Muslim tourists, whether from Jordan, Egypt or from diasporas across the world, encounter insurmountable challenges to enter Palestine/Israel.

Sadid's account also shows willingness to, at least, acknowledge the stories of the Israeli side by arranging meetings between tourists and Jewish settlers. Settlers present their own points of view, which Sadid does not 'agree with totally, but as a tourist when you come to the country, you have the right to listen to both sides'. I would add, listen to as many sides as possible. The interview I had with Sadid further proves that Israelis and Palestinians do not remain separated into binary oppositions, but that some cooperate, albeit cautiously.

ATG and other Palestinian organisations mentioned above, such as Siraj Center and the Holy Land Trust, cooperate with Green Olive Tours so as to offer critical tours around the West Bank about Palestinian culture and 'life under Occupation' (Green Olive Tours, 2011, para. 2). Depending on the length of one's stay, tours in the West Bank are tailored to give an overview of (three-day Palestine Village tours), an introduction to (four-day Introduction to Palestine tour), an experience of (seven-day Palestine Experience tour), or immersion in (ten-day Palestine Immersion tour) Palestinian culture. The number of days spent in Palestine quantifies the type and depth of experience one can have, the more days the more comprehensive and intense is the 'Palestinian experience'. It might seem overly simplistic to claim a full ten-day stay in Palestine can offer an in-depth understanding of the critical issues in Palestine, moreover that the region has 'too much history' of biblical and post-biblical pasts (Bowman, 2007b, p. 28).

Sean, a British tourist in his early forties, took a four-day tour in the West Bank and lived with a Christian Palestinian family in Beit Sahour. About his experience in Palestine, Sean says: 'By the end of my stay, I had the *feeling* that I had been in the West Bank for *considerably longer* than the four days I had actually spent there, such was the *intensity* of what I experienced every day' (Sean, personal communication, 18 October 2010, my emphasis)

While it is argued that affect is ineffable and inexpressible, its intensity is immediately embodied in autonomic reactions manifested in and through the body at the interface between affect and things (Massumi, 2002a). This affective intensity of experiences in the West Bank seems to expand (perception of) time and slow it down in Palestine. It makes Sean feel he has been in the region for considerably longer that just four days. Before going on this four-day trip in the West Bank, Sean toured the Holy Land with an Israeli tour guide, thus having the opportunity to hear one of the Israeli stances as well:

> He [the tour guide] was obviously very very pro-Israeli. Having seen what I've seen in the last 48 hours, I can see the many things that he told us simply aren't true. He made it sound as if Israel is generously giving water in unlimited supply to the West Bank, and that clearly is not true, according to what we've seen and heard. I could have chosen to be confrontational in challenging some of the things I was being told, but I chose not to for several reasons. I didn't come here to provoke an argument.
>
> (Sean, interview, 20 July 2010)

Sometimes, tour guides dismiss one discourse in favour of another. These discourses, even if seemingly antithetical, complement each other in many ways, as Sean reflects:

> I've read a lot about the Palestinian–Israeli conflict, but I don't really feel I understand it. I'm not sure I do even now, after ten days touring around, but it's certainly helping me to put things into perspective and trying to at least remain impartial, which is very difficult when you're hearing both sides of an argument and they're both extremely different . . . I'd come to hear both sides of the argument really – although that's probably simplistic in saying that. I don't think there are two sides to this argument; I think there are probably far, far more than that. There seems to be a huge discrepancy among Jewish people as to what they believe, either politically or religiously, and I imagine the situation is very similar with the Palestinians. It's a fascinating place to come and try and understand what's happening here.
>
> (Sean, interview, 20 July 2010)

Monty, like Sean, was on a seven-day tour in the West Bank living with a Palestinian family. He also went on a tour of the Old City of Jerusalem with a guide who presented the situation through an Israeli prism:

> I went on an 'underground/tunnel' tour [in the Old City of Jerusalem], which isn't really tunnels, but like many cities that are over 2,000 years old, the street level has gotten higher. Anyway, the tour ends in the Muslim Quarter and the tour guide announces that there will be an armed guard at the front and at the back of the group. I quietly questioned the tour guide (who was

from the States) about the wisdom of doing this and saying this because it just made people freak out about being in 'the Muslim Quarter' and that this was somehow unsafe, when I had been up and down all sorts of streets at all hours of the day and night in the various quarters of the Old City and found it to be absolutely and completely safe. She agreed that she'd seen people be relaxed when she said that they were going to the Muslim Quarter and then only get nervous when she said that they had guards. People were comfy with the Muslim Quarter until they heard that they needed a guard and that made them feel unsafe. She retreated into legal liability and that the tour company needed to do it to cover themselves, just in case something ever happened. I wondered if there was also the agenda of scaring western tourists (probably Jews and Christians) about Muslims being in Jerusalem.

(Monty, online interview, 10 August 2010)

These tours organised and conducted either by Israeli tourism companies or Palestinian ones inhabit the same space, even though they are divided physically by fences, barriers and walls. Through the prism of their respective political ideology, they present a different place. The reasoning behind these contested tourism agendas is a call for solidarity with one or the other cause, even though pro-Palestinian solidarity tourism is argued to be much rarer than its Israeli equivalent (Brin, 2006). The focus in Brin's approach is on the ways tourism is used as political propaganda since 'the two main parties of the conflict – namely, the Israelis and Palestinians – are only too willing to exploit tourism as an opportunity to persuade tourists with their political agendas' (p. 226). About pro-Palestinian tourism, Brin writes:

> Pro-Palestinian tours take visitors through East Jerusalem neighborhoods and adjacent Jewish settlements and Palestinian refugee camps in order to illustrate alleged injustices done by Israel as well as Palestinian political and religious institutions, some of which have been shut down by Israeli authorities over the years.
>
> (Brin, 2006, p. 230)

Most of these tours are conducted by Palestinian organisations together with 'a few East Jerusalem hotels and hostels', 'though some are conducted by leftist Israeli/Jewish bodies as well' (p. 231). Brin does not delve into this aspect of Israeli/Jewish organisations conducting pro-Palestinian tours. He does allude to the nuanced in-between stances that mediate the two sides by discussing the story of some Jewish tourists on a 'Birthright Israel' trip who decided to '"turn their backs" on their Israeli hosts and join pro-Palestinian rallies and activities while in Israel' (p. 229). These 'Birthright Israel' trips are organised by the Israeli government, the Jewish Agency and the Jewish Federations of North America to bring young Jewish people (18–26 years old) from around the world to visit Israel, for free, for a fortnight. In summer 2004, a group of Jewish participants, after taking part in their programme, 'joined the activities of the International Solidarity Movement, a radical organization protesting against Israeli occupation and construction of the Separation Barrier' (p. 228). This is considered so rare and ironic as 'some participants of "Birthright" have been reported to have used their "free ticket" to Israel to participate in pro-Palestinian activities in the West Bank' (p. 228). As 'ironic' and 'rare' as they may be, these instances stand proof to the nuanced stances Israelis and Palestinians take in regards to the ongoing conflict.

In Al-Khalīl/Hebron

Tourism as a political tool is skilfully used by Palestinians to rally international tourists to voice solidarity for life under occupation, such is the case of the city of al-Khalīl/Hebron. Hebron is one of the important Jewish holy places, but also a major Palestinian city (Bowman, 2001; Clarke, 2000), which lies about 20 kilometres south of Bethlehem (Bayt Laḥm in Arabic, Bet Leḥem in Hebrew) and 20 kilometres south of Al Quds/Jerusalem. The city used to be part of the Hashemite Kingdom of Jordan from 1948 after the end of the British Mandate in Palestine, and went under Israeli control following the 1967 war.

In Hebron, tourists visit the Tomb of the Matriarchs and Patriarchs called the Ibrahimi Mosque by Muslims, and the Cave of Macphelah by Jews (Paine, 1995). This site is on the majority of pilgrimage routes, as it is holy to the three mono-theistic religions. Abraham, the father of the three religions, is buried there. As a result of the February 1994 massacre, when Baruch Goldstein opened fire and killed 30 Muslim worshippers in the Ibrahimi Mosque, the uneasy sharing of the site was replaced by an enforced separation of the building (Clarke, 2000). There are now two entrances, one for Jewish and one for Muslim worshippers, each entrance being guarded by Israeli Border Guards.

ATG organises tours to Hebron, which combine religious pilgrimages with political tourism, a combination they call 'tourism for justice' or 'pilgrimage for justice'. Ashraf, a tour guide with ATG explains the importance of Hebron and the high demand for these tours, since 'a majority of our clients have Christian backgrounds, pilgrims, who also want to learn; they want to meet [locals], they want to understand [the conflict]':

> Hebron, a lot of people say it's dangerous there; it's a lot of soldiers, and tension. But we say it's good to visit Hebron for two reasons you know: [Firstly,] Hebron is a very old biblical town, but it's not promoted by Israel because it's very scandalising. Secondly, it's a very good place to explain the political situation. So you can have like a lecture [about religion and politics] – you know when you go to visit the shrine of the tombs of Abraham there, Sarah, all the patriarchs and matriarchs. It fits into the pilgrimage programme, but at the same time you see realities there. You see settlers in the old city, you see occupation which is very visible. It's not like here, in Bethlehem for example, where you have settlements around, but in Hebron

there are settlements in the centre of the city. So it's a good example to show occupation in a visible and direct way.

(Ashraf, interview, 13 October 2010)

Daily life in Hebron is uneasy and fraught with violence (Clarke, 2000; Paine, 1995), which is *feel-able* to those living there and those visiting it. Monty shared with me his photos taken in Hebron. As explained to him by the Palestinian guide, the Israelis who live in homes above the street of what used to be a popular and crowded souk, 'throw all sorts of disgusting trash, including dirty diapers/nappies onto the street below, so the Palestinians put a chain-link fence up as a sort of net to catch some of the garbage before it reached the street' (see Figure 7.1) (Monty, personal communication, 30 August 2010). Yusuf, the Palestinian tourist escort working with Green Olive Tours, opines that the fence does not help in all situations:

> It might protect from the trash, garbage, rocks, wood you know, big heavy things but [not] when they [Israeli settlers] throw a lot of shit like dirty water, urine, eggs. One day I was there on Saturday and it was demonstrations against the settlements in the Hebron [area] and the settlers' kids, they start throwing eggs from the roof of their house and dirty water. So the fence doesn't protect all the time.

(Yusuf, interview, 16 October 2010)

The Palestinian story of Hebron is interwoven with the Israeli narrative. The interlacing does not always highlight peaceful cohabitation in the city. There are instances where the story of Hebron is constructed by annihilating the Israeli discourse, by making it appear monstrous. Inside the Ibrahimi Mosque, Sadid, the ATG guide, told our tour group about the horrible massacre of 1994, but no reference was made to the killing of about 700 unarmed Jews in 1929 (Paine, 1995) or the incident in 1980 when seven Yeshiva students were ambushed and killed on a Shabbat in May (Clarke, 2000). These political pilgrimages or pilgrimages for peace with a pro-Palestinian bent are carefully choreographed political and ideological events. Being practice-based, these are arguably different from more classical ideological and propagandistic models (Clarke, 2000).

These tours allow tourists to visit and appropriate the Palestinian realities on the ground, to see the wire fence that holds back only larger pieces of rubbish thrown onto the Palestinian community below (see Figure 7.2), to see Israeli soldiers body-checking tourists at the entrance in the Jewish part of the site (see Figure 7.3), or guarding the entrance into the Muslim mosque (see Figure 7.4). Tourists at such a site of religious sacrality, like Hebron, are aware that they will not be presented with a 'well-balanced' view. Often, when tourists want to hear one of the Israeli perspectives they would book through an Israeli tour company.

Figure 7.1 Israeli settlers dump rubbish on Palestinians.

Source: Monty, 2010, used with permission.

Figure 7.2 Fence covering to keep larger rubbish items from falling into the street below.

Source: Monty, 2010, used with permission.

Figure 7.3 Group of tourists visiting the Cave of Macphelah in Hebron.

Source: Dorina Buda, October, 2010.

Figure 7.4 Israeli soldiers at the entrance of Ibrahimi Mosque in Hebron.

Source: Dorina Buda, October, 2010.

The separation wall and checkpoints: sites of frustration and fascination

The wall annexed a lot of agricultural fields, olive groves, and it is still not finished. If you go to the southwest of Bethlehem the wall is not finished, but this is the agricultural land of Bethlehem so it's a big catastrophe and this is what Israel is trying to do, annex all the south-west of Bethlehem to create a Jerusalem area. And this really is the agricultural land. The wall impacted tourism as well. If you go anytime in the morning to the checkpoint, you see this line of buses waiting to cross or to exit from that [checkpoint]. Sometimes you are fed up to wait on a checkpoint or the entrance to the wall because of control. Many times also the Israeli guides they say, oh there's a lot of traffic, let's forget about Bethlehem and then they [tourists] accept . . . We sometimes take our tourists on foot to cross the wall, you understand – this is part of the programme . . . we tell the groups, you walk how Palestinians walk. We want them to experience this, to feel how it's happening, to have the experience. And of course when they see checkpoints many times we will stand on a checkpoint with a group and it's three hours on the checkpoint, just because of the soldiers.

(Ashraf, interview, 13 October 2010)

Visits to the separation wall, as well as crossing checkpoints, have become the *pièce de résistance* of Palestinian tourism. Whether in Palestine to visit heritage, cultural, history, religious, or nature sites, tourists cross checkpoints, pay visits to refugee camps and walk along the wall. It is argued that 'Visitors coming to Jerusalem *for*, rather than despite, the potential tension and violence are rather difficult to isolate and define, for a number of reasons' (Brin, 2006, p. 225, emphasis in original). One of the reasons is that tourists' curiosity about the socio-political climate in the region represents only a part of the multifold tourism experiences. Such curiosities are rarely straightforward and easy to identify (Brin, 2006). The boundaries between tourist typologies and activities are blurred due to the intensity and pervasiveness of affects and emotions felt, experienced and performed in such a contested place.

In this part of the chapter, I delve into fear and touch to capture the emotional and sensuous nature of tourism in a place of ongoing conflict. I argue that checkpoints and the separation wall are places that may generate fear, anger and shock. In these places, the fear/fun and safety/danger dichotomies collocate in the haptic, that is, by engaging the sense of touch beyond the cutaneous experience. Touching objects, things (like the separation wall and checkpoints), or persons (armed soldiers) that may provoke fear, or are perceived as dangerous, becomes fascinating.

Checkpoints increased in number, once the separation wall started to be built.[2] According to the United Nations Office for the Coordination of Humanitarian Affairs in the Occupied Palestinian Territories (UNOCHA), there are 505 obstacles blocking mainly Palestinian movement, but also delaying tourists' access in and throughout the West Bank. These obstacles include permanently or temporarily staffed checkpoints, roadblocks, earth mounds, earth walls, road gates, road barriers and trenches. Out of all these obstacles, 87 are checkpoints, with 36 of them located along the wall to control access to East Jerusalem and Israel (UNOCHA, 2010). There is specific, rich and precise terminology to show ways in which movement in Palestine is curtailed, vocabulary especially employed by Israeli military 'checkpoints, crossings, terminals, roadblocks, inspection points' (Braverman, 2011, p. 271). For Palestinians, checkpoints 'are spaces where the Zionist/Israeli colonialist project is palpable in all its might and ugliness and where Palestinians are physically reminded of their subjugated position' (Tawil-Souri, 2011, p. 5). In Israeli military terminology, checkpoints are actually border crossings endowed with modern technological devices such as 'sensor machines and scanners . . . advanced computer systems and biometric cards' (Braverman, 2011, p. 266). Checkpoints carry a deep irony as they symbolise restricted mobility mainly for Palestinians, yet they were born out of the 1990s peace processes. These have become a characteristic in/of the Palestinian landscape being facilitated by the ideological discourse of 'safeguarding Israel against terror attacks' (Tawil-Souri, 2011, p. 6).

As Ashraf, a Palestinian tour guide in his late thirties, bemoaned in the above excerpt from our interview, the wall annexes a great part of the Palestinian fertile land; this resonates with Gregory's explanation: 'Thousands of hectares of some of the most highly productive Palestinian land will be on the Israeli side too, with implications not only for the beleaguered Palestinian economy but also for the subsistence of the Palestinian population' (2004a, p. 122). Checkpoints and the wall have become the norm in the Palestinian landscape. These restrain movement for Palestinians and tourists in, out of and throughout the West Bank, since 'the wall is not an immobile line on the map; it shifts and moves in multiple registers' (Gregory, 2004b, p. 603).

Checkpoints control access into Palestine; they delay and sometimes deny entry, for tourists and locals alike, often provoking fear and anger. It should be noted that locals and tourists must cross not only a couple, but countless, checkpoints 'to get on the other side, walled in and/or walled out'. To move in and around the West Bank from Bethlehem to Ramallah, from Jericho to Hebron and so on, one must pass through countless checkpoints and filters. For some tourists, the wall and accompanying checkpoints are a curiosity, an anomaly, which may intrigue and fascinate, an aspect which is defining for affective tourism more so in danger-zones of socio-political conflict. Those travelling in Palestine engage in 'alternative tourist experiences', that is, alternative to the traditional religious pilgrimages to the Church of Nativity in Bethlehem, or the Tomb of the Patriarchs and Matriarchs in Hebron. Tourists witness the Palestinians' plight, cross checkpoints, see the wall, and move around places of potential and/or imagined danger. In this movement around places of conflict in the West Bank, fear and anger blur into intrigue and fascination. For most tourists, these are *extra*-ordinary encounters, *outside* of the everyday experiences in their/our respective home countries. There is the feeling and knowledge of a return to a more secure and stable daily existence.

Figure 7.5 'USA Supports You' graffiti on separation wall in Bethlehem.
Source: Dorina Buda, 2010.

The first time that I crossed the wall through Bethlehem Checkpoint in July 2010 I was fascinated and intrigued. I had heard of the Berlin Wall, I had visited the Great Wall of China, but this separation wall was rather puzzling. It was a Tuesday morning. I was part of a one-day tour in Bethlehem with Green Olive Tours. The tour began in Al Quds/Jerusalem and when we reached Bethlehem Checkpoint I saw the wall grey and tall. I felt it cold. As I crossed the checkpoint, the wall changed its visual register as it was covered in vivid colours with messages of all sorts, such as 'USA supports you' (see Figure 7.5), 'with love and kisses' (see Figure 7.6) and others.

At the end of the tour, crossing back into Jerusalem I felt a mix of contradictory emotions: fascination, anger, fear and frustration. As I was in the queue trying to stay patient and composed I wrote the following in my diary:

Tuesday 20th July 2010, Jerusalem

16.15 hours, Bethlehem checkpoint finishing the tour in Bethlehem, West Bank returning to Jerusalem.

A huge crowd of people waiting to cross the checkpoint, both Palestinians and foreign visitors. We have been here for more than 20 minutes, the queue is huge, moving so slowly. It is not a linear queue of people calmly and quietly waiting to cross to the other side, but an unnerving mass of sweaty bodies (outside temperature is about 33°C) devoid of patience and confidence. I am completely disgusted at the procedures people need to go through. It reminds me of similar experiences we would have in Romania during the 1990s when crossing the border to Hungary. Early morning cars would line up at the border and wait for days to travel to Hungary, some would not return, some would go further to western European countries and try to settle there, some would drive back and forth with small goods for sale to make a living. Then and now, there in eastern Europe and here in the Middle East I feel it's a disgusting and humiliating experience of abject misery.

(Dorina, diary note, 20 July 2010)

It has been over five years since I wrote this. Upon reflection, these feelings seem too harsh, somehow too raw. Such an experience brought back some childhood memories. My feelings, reactions and senses aroused during that day might point to some repressed anger at the restricted mobility I felt as a Romanian wanting to travel in western Europe after the fall of the Iron Curtain. I remember we had to queue for hours on end to travel to Hungary to buy goods for our house and then to return to Romania. I must have been 12 or 13 years old when we travelled with my mother to buy new carpets, curtains and the like for our apartment. On another occasion, when I first travelled to Germany by myself I was 20 years old.

Figure 7.6 'With Love and Kisses' graffiti on separation wall in Bethlehem

Source: Dorina Buda, 2010.

I was awarded a scholarship from the German Academic Exchange Programme. Months before my scholarship in Bremen I had to take a ten-hour return trip to another city in Romania to have my German visa glued in the passport. I took a bus to travel to Bremen and we had to wait for at least five hours at each border crossing between Romania and Germany for all sorts of checking procedures. Travelling on a Romanian passport then was not easy, not that conditions have improved considerably since. One could argue that these accounts of my childhood memories of restricted mobility might position me as middle class, even though I have to confess I do not exactly know how this concept fits a Romanian communist and post-communist setting, whereby everyone had to conform with the imposed socio-cultural uniformity. I felt anger at Romanians not being welcomed to travel as freely as others in western Europe. Anger at the long and tedious border procedures we had to go through because of the stigma attached to being a Romanian.

Archaic anger helped me empathise with the Palestinians in the queue, for anger can address perceived injustices through action and re-action. All those memories, feelings and emotions, some of which are not easy to articulate, I thought long gone, or did not *feel/know* they resided in me. Perhaps I would not have felt the same anger in Bethlehem had I not experienced border-crossing procedures during the post-communist regime in Romania. The separation wall and its checkpoints are constructions, which bring about macabre feelings with the potential to unveil repressed memories. Sean, the British tourist mentioned in the previous sections, relived memories of past visits in Belfast and Berlin:

> I regret to say that it evoked memories of past visits to West Belfast in darker days, as well as my first trip to East and West Berlin in 1986. However, it is significant that the separation barrier in the West Bank is twice as high as the Berlin Wall ever was. Likewise its effects are far more subtle. It does considerably more than just offer a protective barrier against terrorists as the Israeli authorities claim, by effectively enabling the Israeli government to dictate where different categories of people can live, work and travel. It became apparent to me on this trip that the Palestinians are severely disadvantaged in every case.
>
> (Sean, personal communication, 18 October 2010)

To be sure, these complex memories and emotions were not brought forth 'just' by seeing the wall. Haptic engagements with the whole system of occupation in Palestine – such as walking along the wall, reacting to the colourful messages on it, touching the cold turnstile at checkpoints, being pushed around queuing at checkpoints, body checks at religious and heritage sites – prompt feelings of anger, fear, frustration, fun and fascination. My fear and anger merged with fun and excitement as I touched the wall or the turnstiles, signs and fences at checkpoints. I felt I was on the border between safety and danger. It is precisely with blurring of these boundaries: fun/fear and safety/danger brought about by haptic geographies at checkpoints and at the wall that the next section deals. As I argued so far in this chapter, most tourists in Palestine engage affectively and emotionally in and with places of ongoing conflict. It is, however, a defining trait for affective tourist subjectivities to have fear and fun merge when travelling in places of conflict and danger.

Haptic geographies at the wall and checkpoints

Ashraf confirms that indeed 'when they [tourists] see the things by their own eyes, I mean when they touch the things physically, it's a totally different experience' (Ashraf, interview, 13 October 2010). Ashraf alludes to the scopic regime of touch and the visuo-haptic collocation. The merging of 'see, eyes, touch and physicality' is facilitated by the synaesthetic register of affect, that is 'a participation of the senses in each other . . . an ability to transform the effects of one sensory mode into those of another' (Massumi, 2002a, p. 35). The 'visuo-haptic collocation' refers to a combination of visual representations and haptic sensations (Paterson, 2006) whereby the physicality of touch is accentuated by intimate proximities of objects, bodies and places in turmoil. The scopic regime of touch is emphasised on the Palestinian side of the wall by the sight of colourful images on a painfully grey concrete body of walls. The kinaesthetic aspect in the haptic system is brought forth while walking along the wall, counting the cameras posted at regular intervals on top of the wall, touching the wall and even drawing graffiti on the wall.

Tourists see and touch the wall, the visual and kinaesthetic are juxtaposed, forming the haptic system. Haptic tourism geographies – bodies touching places, places touching bodies, and bodies that touch one other – are useful in exploring in more depth experiences at the wall. Haptic engagements – not only with and at the wall, but also with numerous checkpoints surrounding the wall in Palestine/Israel – involve standing in the queue along with many other jostling human bodies, touching the turnstile, pushing it to move forward, passing through metal detectors, and handing in your travel documents (see Figures 7.7 and 7.8).

The wall has become a complex tourist attraction, which poses some difficulties for Palestinian tour guides when they are asked about it. Rafiq explains that it is always complicated to respond to tourists' questions regarding the rationale behind the building of the wall:

> They [tourists] ask lots of questions about the wall, and I explain the difference between the wall and the fence. But they also ask about why the wall was built, why the wall exists. And this leads to other questions like, they will start getting into issues like suicide bombers. They'll start driving you into these issues of refugee suicide bombers and so on. So it gets very complicated.
>
> (Rafiq, interview, 14 October 2010)

Monty's interest in travelling to Palestine and Israel 'was more to see things first hand, like the separation barrier, a refugee camp, and then typical tourist stuff, like museums and places holy to one, two, or all three Abrahamic religions'

Figure 7.7 Through the metal detector at a checkpoint in Palestine.

Source: Dorina Buda, 2010.

Figure 7.8 Gazing at and touching the turnstile at the checkpoint in Palestine.

Source: Dorina Buda, 2010.

(Monty, interview, 10 August 2010). As frustrating as it may be to cross check-points, to visit and walk along the wall, fascination with the wall has transformed these realities of the occupation in Palestine into tourist attractions. Tourists marvel at its sight, are fascinated by the colourful messages on the wall, and ask their tour guides a number of questions. Yussuf, the Palestinian tourist escort with Green Olive Tours, explains that

> most of the writing things on the wall are done by international people – 99 per cent is done by international [tourists] and volunteers, not local people – and in different languages. Not all English. Spanish, a lot of Italians, Koreans and so on.
>
> (Yussuf, interview, 16 October 2010)

Yussuf says that some people, mostly tourists, like the messages on the wall, but some, especially locals, are against 'making the wall pretty':

> An old man once told me 'we don't need people to make the wall pretty, to make nice graffiti on the wall, so the people [tourists] will come to literally [just] see the nice graffiti, and they will forget about the wall and what affect [it has on Palestinian lives]' – you know what I mean? So, that old man was sad, and he said, 'tell your group [of tourists] or tell the people we don't need more people to do some graffiti on the wall – on the ugly wall. Leave it ugly.' We don't want to make it look pretty with nice graffiti. People they come here – 'wow, it's nice', and they will forget about what the wall's effects are. So, we need people to just destroy the wall not make it pretty.
>
> (Yussuf, interview, 16 October 2010)

Most of the messages that I saw drawn on the wall represent signs of protest against the occupation, signs of resistance, encouragement and hope. Partly because of these messages, the wall has become a tourist attraction in Palestine. The colourful graffiti make the wall enticing and fascinating for tourists. This may be why the old Palestinian man in Yussuf's story considers that foreigners are attracted by and to the wall, while forgetting the real story within the wall.

The body's kinaesthetic abilities, and scopic and tactile bodily registers forge affective and emotional relations with places. Such engagements with places allude to 'a something' that can be called an *affective praesentia*, that is, feeling one's way in the world, knowing the world from inside-out and outside-in; or as Hetherington calls it 'knowing the world that is both inside and outside knowledge' (2003, p. 1937). Praesentia of checkpoints in the West Bank, then, is performed affectively through haptic encounters. Such encounters can be with material objects such as the turnstile, the metal detector, or the window of the cubicle through which you slip your documents. Haptic encounters can also be with other bodies, who push, jostle your own bodily space forward, closer to the exit.

Touch may be unwelcome and intrusive. It can feel like a source of violation of the private and intimate bodily space, especially when touched in unwelcome ways so as to generate disdain, and or even pain (Hetherington, 2003; Johnston, 2012). I remember that I felt uncomfortable being jostled by other impatient tourist bodies in the queue at a checkpoint. I was more understanding with locals skipping the line and pushing past me to get closer to the metal detector and the turnstile:

> A local woman in her late fifties asked if she could pass us (a group of tourists) to go in front of the queue. I did not mind as she started to explain she had her senior mother with her and four children. Another tourist, with a German-sounding accent complained and was vocal about not agreeing that the woman and her party went in front of the queue. 'Are you better that us, why should you go before us, stay in the queue like the rest of us. Stop pushing' he said in a loud voice. I interfered and explained that we carried EU/USA passports and were doing this as a tourist experience, rather the woman had to go through that ordeal on a daily basis.
>
> (Dorina, diary note, 20 July 2010)

The new border administration in Israel entails modern micro-mechanics such as turnstiles, fences and signs. These are implemented by Israel to 'promote orderliness' and 'decrease human friction' (Braverman, 2011, p. 279). The environment formed at checkpoints, lining up in front of turnstiles, however, results in facilitating and increasing other forms of unwanted and violent touches, even generating chaos. A Palestinian person is reported to have broken one of his ribs while queuing at a checkpoint as he was pressed between the entrance and the turnstile (Braverman, 2011). This violent form of touch can only build more resentment amongst Palestinians, who feel the walled-in life in Palestine is a prison.

Visiting 'within walls'

> I remember – you know I'm 41 now, I'm not young. I remember when I was a kid, we used to go to Jerusalem by public bus – of course from Beit Sahour to Jerusalem, half shekel you're in Jerusalem. And things were very cheap there. Villagers, they just sit in the street there and they sell fruit, clothes, whatever. Now, most people they cannot sell their products. The market here in Bethlehem for example, there is not enough for people. That's number one. Because they don't have permit to go to Israel and to sell. Number two: the wall took all the Palestinian agricultural land, so we don't have even lands enough to make food and vegetables for the Palestinians. Number three: many people lost their jobs. They can't apply for jobs. The bus company in Beit Sahour, they used to go to work in Israel everywhere. They cannot work anymore. So now actually they have increasing crisis with the bank, because they bought the new buses, when Oslo happened and they believed that it's peace and things, and then they couldn't pay for the loans of the buses, the payments of the buses, and they are suffering now. After the wall, they [Israel] started something called permission, and if you want to go to Israel, you need

a permit. If you don't have it then you don't go. Now for travel agencies it's easier to book one bus for the whole country instead of changing guides and drivers all the time for people. So I prefer to have a bus that can access both places, which is an Israeli bus – even [a] Palestinian-owned company, but Israeli plates. I will not have Palestinian plates, because the tour leader doesn't want one bus in the West Bank and another bus in Israel – he wants one bus, one guide, one driver all the time. So now those buses, they are still without any work. So the wall has 100 per cent affected the economy.

(Sadid, interview, 12 October 2010)

The above title 'Visiting "within walls"' could seem provocative at first. I continue, however, with my argument that affect is raw intensity. Such intensities circulate between tourists and local tourism industry representatives moving in, between and within walled-in and walled-out places of conflict and danger. This has the potential to blur the dichotomies of fun/fear, safety/danger and even peace/war.

Local Palestinian guides that I interviewed compared life in the West Bank to life in prison, where one needs permits 'to leave the walls', the 'walled-in space'. Such is Sadid's account presented above, who describes the limitations of life in Palestine, especially after the construction of the wall; a life that is regulated by the Israeli government who chooses to give (or not give) permits to Palestinians to access places outside the walled-in space. Bornstein argues that 'the Israeli Occupation has created an increasingly prison-like society for Palestinians' (2008, p. 108). He maintains that checkpoints and walls, 'despite the military's explanation that the structures were being built to contain danger, these forms of control are an assault, widely perceived as collective punishment, and an attempt to encourage Palestinian acquiescence or emigration' (p. 108). Exit from and re/entry in the walled-in space, for however long or short a period of time, proves to be oppressively regulated and dangerous. Thus, some tourists might feel that they cross into the 'dangerous' and 'fearful' 'walled-in space' when they travel in the West Bank. The wall and its checkpoints as symbols of the conflict might bring about fear, but can also arouse some of the tourists' curiosity, intrigue and fascination.

A comparison between occupation in Palestine and life in prison breaks down, for the dispersed Palestinian places are more that of a camp rather a prison (Gregory, 2004a). The concept of a cyst has been proposed instead, to understand Palestinian life within walls, as it relates better to the Palestinian plight and suffering (Bowman, 2007a). Within the walled area, one can understand the 'logic of "encystation"'(p. 129), which is entrapment of Palestinian communities on land over which Israel claims sovereignty. A cyst is defined as 'a closed cavity or sac of a morbid or abnormal character, containing liquid or semi-solid matter' (Oxford English Dictionary, 2011). Another comparison between the body and the nation state in general is also put forth. In this case it is about the land of Palestine/Israel, in which the Palestinians are treated as 'a disease, a virus, an impurity tainting it' (Curti, 2008, p. 111). The function of the wall, then, is to contain 'this infection and its growing anatomical threats' from poisoning the healthy whole (p. 111). To create a hermetic and healthy place, the wall is being built in spite of several United Nations Security Council resolutions, in spite of the Advisory of the International Court of Justice, and in spite of the decision of the Fourth Geneva Council.

Within the walls, life is being made almost impossible 'by intentional crippling of the economy, the strangling of access to food, water, medicine, and education, and the imposition of a sense of isolation and political impotence' (Bowman, 2007a, p. 129). Anger, fear, frustration with the wall are all felt by the Palestinian tour guides whom I met and interviewed. Rafiq, who has worked as a tour guide in Palestine since 2003, explains that 'there is no justification for why the wall was built' (Rafiq, interview, 14 October 2010). Farouk does not understand 'the need for this humiliation. There is no need for all that they [Israel] are doing.' He tells his tourists that 'The wall is not a border. Now Israeli guides talk about it as like border between Israel and the West Bank – but that's not true. It's a lie' (Farouk, interview, 14 October 2010). According to the academic community and international law, the wall is not a border since it diverts considerably from the Green Line. Said (2004) explains:

> the wall doesn't simply divide Israel from a putative Palestinian state on the basis of the 1967 borders: it actually takes in new tracts of Palestinian land, sometimes five or six kilometers at a stretch. It is surrounded by trenches, electric wire, and moats; there are watchtowers at regular intervals. Almost a decade after the end of the South African apartheid, this ghastly racist wall is going up with scarcely a peep from the majority of Israelis and of their American allies.
>
> (Said, 2004, p. 281)

Fred Schlomka of Green Olive Tours also calls the wall 'the apartheid wall' and explains that in Hebrew the separation wall is called '*Gader Ha Hafrada*':

> Now it's interesting to note that the word 'separation' in Afrikaans is *apartheid*. It's the same word. *Hafrada* in Hebrew – *apartheid* in Afrikaans. And the government has a policy of *hafrada*. You hear the word used by politicians, journalists and so on in Hebrew. So, although they don't like the word 'apartheid' they actually use the same word in Hebrew to describe policies and the physical barriers and so on.
>
> (Fred Schlomka, interview, 19 July 2010)

As a tourist in Palestine I remember I first felt fear 'what if soldiers will not allow me to enter the West Bank?' 'What if they arrest me?' I drafted all sorts of scenarios in my head while queuing at checkpoints. As I crossed into the West Bank without major problems I started feeling angry listening to the stories shared by the Palestinian guiding our group. How can something like this happen? How can the wall happen? The humiliation! The shame! Anger and frustration raged inside me, moved me into action. I decided to stay longer in Bethlehem, which exacerbated my confusion. I then did not know what to feel, what to think, it was all 'a bit much' for me. I was intrigued by life 'within walls'. Was I fascinated? Was it a mixture of fear, anger, fun with a tinge of excitement that I started to feel? Was I 'just' in shock?

Feeling the 'total shock'

> Some people know a little, but maybe some of them have read a lot about it [the Israeli–Palestinian conflict], you know, but it's totally different when they come here, you understand? And yesterday I had friends, you know, from France . . . they were first timers, first time here, it was a total shock for them, *on dit en français le choc total* [we say in French the total shock], it is like a big shock for them, they discovered different things.
>
> (Ashraf, interview, 13 October 2010)

The same idea, of tourists to Palestine perceiving what they see on the ground so shockingly different than what they might expect, is shared by Fred Schlomka of the Green Olive Tours. His view is more nuanced, saying that tourists' shock depends on their level of knowledge about the place:

> It depends how much background knowledge they bring. If they have little or no knowledge they are often very shocked by what they see and the analysis I provide to them. If they already have some knowledge they are coming on the tours to get more information and so on, so they are usually less shocked about what they see.
>
> (Fred Schlomka, interview, 19 July 2010)

The shock, that Ashraf and Fred talk about, makes me think of shock which prompts us to search for new emotional responses to situations perceived as *extra*-ordinary, outside of everyday experiences. Shock is a strategy that 'confronts us with the limitations of our capacity for responding in general' (Ngai, 2005, p. 262). Shock as emotional response connects to *escapes of affect*, which are always perceived. These perceived escapes of affect localised in a sudden event, in a sudden realisation and described in negative terms is typically a form of shock (Massumi, 2002a, p. 36). Shock, as localised sudden affect, points to a sudden realisation of something *extra*-ordinary which accompanies the system of sensory values, touch, smell, hear, see (amongst others). Such a system is rarely articulated through language, but it is practised, perceived and experienced.

The sensory and emotional experience generated *in* and *by* the toured place is socially constructed and permeated with cultural values. In Palestine, tourists engage their senses, feel shock and shocking emotions in nuanced ways. Experiences of places are necessarily multi-sensual and multi-emotional, as more than one sense or emotion is prompted, and because emotions and senses work together. In areas of turmoil and conflict, tourist subjectivities feel shock – that mixture of fun and fear, which engages the senses. Shock, I argue, is a blend of feelings, emotions, perceptions and sensations prompted when crossing the fun/fear, safety/danger and peace/war boundaries.

Shock is haptic when touching the cold steel of the turnstiles at numerous checkpoints. For me touching the turnstile, pushing it to move forward made me feel fearful 'what will the soldier ask me?' Shock is aural when listening to the noise of the bulldozers, operating cranes and other such construction equipment at various sites where new settlements are erected. Shock involves the visual when gazing at the imposing separation wall. Shock responds to the olfactory when smelling the olive trees and tasting traditional hummus. The realities of Palestine shock tourists with a blend of such sensations, feelings and emotions. Thus, I maintain that as emotions, feelings and senses 'make' Palestine, Palestine makes sense for tourists.

Monty felt 'somewhat steeled for the experience [of visiting a refugee camp in Palestine]. I wasn't shocked because I knew that it was going to be bad' (Monty, interview, 30 August 2010). Some tourists prepare beforehand for the shock expected when travelling. There is a wide range of resources on the Internet, as well as in the print media (for example, the *Culture Shock!* series) with numerous cultural instructions and travel guidelines for international tourists (Hottola, 2004). These are meant to mediate feelings of frustration and anxiety when tourists enter a different culture. The term 'culture shock' has come to be used as a common language signifier of everyday difficulties tourists meet while travelling in a foreign country (Chen et al., 2011; Furnham, 1984; Hottola, 2004). It is argued that while culture shock may be part of tourism, it is incorrectly and loosely used to denote generic linguistic misunderstandings in intercultural situations such as 'language shock' or 'environmental/ecological shock' (Hottola, 2004).

My own body felt a 'temperature shock' as thermometers showed 40–50°C during the summer days of July and August 2010 and 30–35°C during the night, especially in the area surrounding Jericho and the Dead Sea. This 'temperature shock' is part of an emotional and sensuous haptic system, whereby the skin is touched by the hot air. Hot air shocks! Being touched by the hot desert air of the lowest geographical point on earth, my body, my senses dilated to feel the texture, temperature, motion of the wind and air. Being touched by the heat is an awareness of temperature, pressure and motion – a haptic shock, which plays an important role when *in* a place, when affectively and emotionally engaging with place.

Another layer of the 'total shock' is an 'emotional shock', prompted by direct exposure to realities in Palestine, a country torn by ongoing conflicts for more than six decades. Lack of water, the everyday presence of armed soldiers on the streets, and standing in never-ending queues at checkpoints to visit family members just several kilometres away, are just a few daily situations in Palestine. These make up for an emotional reality witnessed by tourists. Sean had the 'privilege' of entering the West Bank in an Israeli car, about which he reflects below:

> As a foreigner, it was a very strange feeling indeed to pass unchallenged in an Israeli car through the checkpoints at such settlements, knowing that Palestinians are forcibly prevented from doing the same, thereby rendering them unable to drive across their own land in their own cars. The sight of the countless irrigation pipes sprinkling unlimited freshwater supplies onto the numerous flowerbeds adjoining the roads right across the 35,000-strong settlement of Ma'aleh Adumim was poignant when considering the fact that all Palestinian homes in the nearby area of Bethlehem had been without water of any kind for the previous two weeks due to a so-called 'shortage' which had led the Israeli authorities to cut off the supply there.
>
> (Sean, personal communication, 18 October 2010)

Following the Oslo Accords, the Palestinian Authority was given control over isolated territorial 'islands', but Israel retained control over the airspace and the sub-terrain (Gregory, 2004a). The sub-terrain has a network of aquifers, which is drained by Israeli underground pipes. During frequent water shortages, as witnessed by Sean, commercial tank trucks sell water to Palestinians at prohibitively high prices (Bowman, 2007a). Like Sean, I felt an overload of emotions at life under occupation while briefly living in Palestine. I also found the experience emotionally humbling, as Monty reflects:

> [I felt] sympathy, of course – not pain, as it would've probably been fleeting cheap sentiment, as I don't live that life . . . if I were to have felt pain for the experience of another just because I was seeing them and then an hour later and a day later and a month later, because I wasn't seeing them, I felt no pain, I'd say that such could be accurately described as cheap sentiment.
> (Monty, interview, 30 August 2010)

In the context of Palestine, shock is an affective and emotional response to sudden situations. It is a combination of autonomous unformed potential – affect, and qualified intense capturing – emotion. Such responses follow from being in a place where what will happen next cannot be easily understood, controlled and predicted. Sympathy might seem like a less ceremonious and prestigious feeling compared to anger, for example. Monty's response, however, is no less empathetic, showing deeper affective and possibly cathartic engagements. At a surface level, he disavows feeling others' pain – '[I felt] sympathy, of course not pain.' None the less he felt 'somewhat steeled' in a Palestinian refugee camp (as I point out above), perhaps because he indeed sympathised with others' pain. Such emotions do not position Monty, as a tourist, on an equal footing with those in the refugee camp, but entail potentials for reflection and retaliation.

Touring places in Palestine and often meeting armed soldiers at checkpoints can be an unnerving experience whereby fear, danger and conflict can be asserted. Senses may be overloaded because releasing anger and frustration is almost prohibited. Yussuf and Ashraf, both Palestinian tour guides, shared stories of tourists feeling angry and frustrated. Exteriorising, as in the inside-out model (Ahmed, 2004b), and communicating these feelings are not encouraged in the context of the Israeli–Palestinian conflict. Thus, binaries like danger/safety, fun/fear and peace/conflict are in such cases reinforced, but then transgressed:

> So one day we get pulled over [at one checkpoint] by [an Israeli] soldier – I was driving – and there was an American woman sitting right beside me, and two Italians. I had three people: one American, two Italians. We were on the way to Ramallah. So she [US tourist] didn't take any photos [of the checkpoint]; she was just holding her camera. And he asked her: 'Where are you going?' And I said right away, 'We're going to Jericho.' And he said: 'No. I'm asking her, where's she going?' She said, 'Yeah, Jericho.' He said: 'Okay. Can I just see your camera?' So he went through almost all her pictures, and he made her delete like half of the pictures . . . And she said: 'No. Why you want me to delete them?' so they almost started to fight. But I

told her, they have their rules, so just please delete them. She almost wanted to fight . . . She is like 50, 55 years old. She said this was the first time – 'I have never been through this before. People ask me to delete my photos? Who the hell are you [to ask me something like this]?'

(Yussuf, interview, 16 October 2010)

The shock of having an armed soldier invade the bodily space of the tourist to take her camera and further violate the privacy of her pictures, memories, and souvenirs generates anger and disdain. Danger is reasserted in the interaction between soldier, tour escort and tourist, but the woman's feelings of 'Who the hell are you?' challenged the danger that the soldier tried to convey.

This haptic bodily interaction, mediated through the handling of the photo camera, brings about anger as a response to perceived injustice (Henderson, 2008). The hostility of this soldier–tourist encounter was manifested in the soldier's touching the tourist's camera, flicking through her pictures and making her delete most of them. This resembles the haptic experience at the checkpoints where bodies are jostled around while in line to show an Israeli soldier travel and identity documents. In those situations and places, anger and fear are mobilised. This particular interaction between the man soldier–woman tourist seems to reassert not only the safety/danger boundary, but also the bodily gendered boundaries, their hegemonic and patriarchal impositions, whereby the man constrains the woman to delete her pictures. The complexity of this interaction can be understood through the soldier–tourist and man–woman encounter, but also through the lens of the political relationship between Israel and the US, this last aspect being beyond the scope of this project.

Ashraf recounts the story of a Swedish group of tourists, which in many ways resembles Youssuf's and the US tourist's encounter with the soldier:

A Swedish group, lawyers with the international court of justice. Once we'd been to Hebron and we crossed the checkpoints – all checkpoints in Hebron, so police stopped us: 'Your passports.' So we give the passports to the police. They check – no problem. Five minutes later, another police car came, they asked for the passports. To those policemen, we said: 'We have just been checked. We have just given our passports to the police, why you ask [again].' They refused to give. Now you imagine, they refuse to give again the passports to the police, because they are not used – why do it, in five minutes to show our passports two times. For Palestinians, we sometimes show it ten times [laughs] a day. But for the Swedes, they refuse to show their passports again. So, they kept us like half an hour and they really, there were ten people [in the group], we won't show our passports – all of them. And the police finally, after half an hour, they left, I mean fortunately. It was not normal [for the tourists], because they are not used that all these people ask for their passports again and again. So for them, they get angry from these experiences.

(Ayaman, interview, 13 October 2010)

'Getting angry from these experiences' is something one can be sympathetic about when travelling in a locale of ongoing conflict. The Swedish tourists asserted their anger by refusing to show their passports and be complacent with the soldiers' requests. The idea that anger should necessarily be avoided because it leads to negative socio-political outcomes has been challenged (Henderson, 2008). Anger can sometimes be the main, and handiest, response to perceiving and witnessing injustice. Due attention should be paid to anger – in this haptic encounter of handling identity documents – since affronts to common human dignity is something to be angry about (Henderson, 2008). Anger in this story represents a position taken towards a somehow humiliating situation of being subjected to frequent passport handlings, identity checks, questions about purpose of travel and about associations with one cause or the other involved in the ongoing regional conflict.

There are cases when defying a soldier's request can lead to imprisonment. The case of Ghazi-Walid Falah, a Canadian geographer, is now well known in the academic community and beyond. He was detained by the Israeli Security Police while travelling in northern Palestine in July 2006 for 23 days 'placed under severe conditions, and subjected to maltreatment, abuse and humiliation' (Falah, 2007, p. 749). Another case was that of the three women from Minnesota, in the US, who were denied entry into Israel in July 2009. As they refused to leave the country they were taken into custody, 'treated as criminals, while their only goal was to learn about the reality of life for the Palestinian people' (FightBack! News, 2009, para. 1). This was not the case with the Swedish tourists. However, the Swedes took that risk when they directly defied the soldier, thus breaking down the fear and danger factors.

Notes

1 The Green Line has been set out in the Armistice Agreements (1949) between Israel and its neighbours (Egypt, Jordan, Lebanon and Syria). These agreements ended the official hostilities of the Arab–Israeli War. The Green Line, also known as the '1967 border', is used to mark the line between Israel and the territories captured in the Six Day War. The name derives from the green ink that was used to draw the line on the map.
2 On 23 July 2001, the Israeli government decided to build the security fence to protect its citizens from the 'wave of suicide bombings' emanating from the West Bank (Israeli Ministry of Defence, 2007). The 'security fence', as it is known in Israeli terminology, was established 'in order to reduce the number of terrorist attacks whether in the form of explosive-rigged vehicles or in the form of suicide bombers who enter into Israel with the intention of murdering innocent babies, children, women and men' (para. 1). In international law parlance, the Israeli security fence is termed 'wall' as it is a complex, operational system that cannot be understood in the limited physical sense of fence (International Court of Justice, 9 July 2004). In July 2004, the International Court of Justice located in The Hague decided by 14 votes to 1 that the separation wall was illegal and the Court ordered that the wall be dismantled. The court added that 'Israel is under an obligation to make reparation for all damage caused by the construction of the wall in the Occupied Palestinian Territory, including in and around East Jerusalem' (International Court of Justice, 2004, p. 55). In 2004, the Secretary-General submitted a report for consideration by the International Court of Justice. At this time, 180 kilometres of the wall complex, with a width of 50–70 metres, increasing to as much as 100 metres in some places, were completed or under construction. Ignoring the advisory of the International Court of Justice, Israel went on to build more than 500 kilometres. By 2010, it had reached 709 kilometres, which is a distance twice as long as the Green Line, according to B'Tselem, an Israeli information centre for human rights in the Occupied Territories.

8   'Between a rock and a hard place'

A brief detour to Iraq

Jon Stewart:	Jordan is, I would think, in a difficult position in terms of the natural resources. I mean, I think you discovered uranium, but you do not have the oil resources. You have a tremendous Palestinian population there. I imagine Israel looks to you for a little bit of security as well on that border. What can Jordan do? And what can't you do?
King Abdullah II of Jordan:	Well, we describe ourselves between Iraq and a hard place, and this is to us a normal day's work.[1]

(Stewart, 2010)

The extract above is from an interview with King Abdullah II of Jordan. The king alludes to Iraq as a rock, and Jordan's neighbours, Israel and the Occupied Palestinian Territories, as the hard place. Such a description illustrates the complex, contested and affective relationships in that part of the Middle East, which pervade any socio-economic and political endeavours, including tourism.

In this chapter, affective routes in 'Middle Eastern' tourism are furthered. I continue visiting the same destinations, Jordan and Palestine/Israel, with a detour to Iraq. The focus here is on death drives and the overlaps with affect, in what regards the binary opposition – life/death. The death drive is located at the junction between life and death and some danger-zone tourists engage it in places of ongoing conflicts. When accessed, the death drive does not generate the end of life, but a renewed sense of life and vitality. In my analysis, the death drive is mostly connected to fear; together they make the body 'feel alive'. The death drive resides primarily in the Lacanian order of the Real, or the unconscious. So does affect. Having psychoanalytical and psychological nuances, affects connect and overlap with death drives through the Real. Both affects and death drives escape and syphon off into Lacan's Symbolic and Imaginary, impacting more conscious ways of knowing and experiencing the world. Affect is a concept 'with a distinctly psychological pedigree' (Thien, 2005, p. 451). It is maintained that in Freud's earliest writings on the unconscious, he mentioned 'an affective or emotional impulse' (cited in Thien, 2005, p. 451) to explain instincts and drives. Drawing on Freud's work, it is argued that affect is a matrix, which contains both feelings and emotions. Compared to drives, affects have more freedom in regards to time, aim and object and can be attached to ideas, institutions, people, places and sensations amongst others.

It is contended in the theoretical beginnings of this book that death drives and affects cannot be entirely attributed to the register of the intangible Real. They escape from the Real and become interlaced in the Symbolic and Imaginary, which makes them amenable to analysis. The Symbolic represents our desires and feelings through language:

> Through the word – already a presence made of absence – absence itself gives itself a name in that moment of origin . . . And from this pair of sounds modulated on presence and absence there is born the world of meaning of a particular language in which the world of things will come to be arranged.
>
> (Sarup, 1992, p. 65)

By this I do not mean to focus on the structurality of language as the basis of understanding a world through the structuralist discourse, but to render the idea that death drives and affects can and do escape, thus being able to find expression at a language (the Symbolic) level.

'Why would humans be motivated by death and not life?' asks Ragland-Sullivan (1995, p. 85), in her analysis of Lacan's concept of the death drive. In her attempt to answer this seemingly paradoxical question, I might find the answer to my query: why are some tourists travelling to areas of ongoing conflict? What do these tourists feel? What emotions are negotiated with others and themselves when in a place of conflict? Are these tourists, even partly, engaging the death drive when travelling in a conflict zone? These questions might seem nonsensical at first. I feel compelled to restate, yet again, that the death drive does not oppose life, does not refer to 'destroying the physical body', but brings together life and death. At the centre of this togetherness lies a traumatic element: 'the irreducibility of loss taken as positive factor . . . Thus, it is loss that drives life' (p. 87).

As I argued in Chapter 4, there has been a recent upsurge in academic interest in dark tourism. Notwithstanding this increased attention, the motivations and emotions felt by those who visit, as well as those who live and/or work at dark sites remain under-examined. Indeed, there is much potential to critically explore affective and emotional implications in regards to dark tourism. This chapter and the book as a whole add to the literature on the broad phenomenon of dark tourism. The focus is on affects, emotions and senses felt and performed by 'those in vanguard of "dark tourism"' (Lennon & Foley, 2000, p. 9). These tourists visit dangerous places of ongoing conflict and seem to have an interest in 'presumed fascination in death and dying' (Sharpley, 2009, p. 7). They cross boundaries between fun and fear, safety and danger, peace and war, life and death.

Crossing boundaries: fun/fear and life/death

Dorina: Are you in a way seeking adventure and adrenaline rush in your trips? Do you experience adventure here in Jordan?

Hyun: Yes! Yes! That's why I contacted adventure tourism company in Jordan, to do scuba diving, to have these adventures in the canyon, in the desert.

(Hyun, interview, 16 September 2010)

Hyun, the South Korean tourist introduced in previous chapters decided to travel to Jordan in spite of his friends and family members advising him not to. He took the trip even in spite of his own views about the region: 'I had some prejudice, like anybody else, that it's the Middle East and it's a very dangerous place, you should not go. [My friends and family told me] never go there! You might get killed [mild laugh].' Deciding to travel alone, as he did, to 'a very dangerous country' points to the death drive escaping or bursting into the conscious, or in Lacan's Imaginary order, as desirable vitality by 'trying something new that I cannot try in Korea' (Hyun, interview, 16 September 2010).

Hyun had a more 'acceptable' and 'fun' explanation for travelling to a country in the middle of an area of conflict, namely that he wanted to scuba dive in the Red Sea, to go on canyon trips, to experience the desert, which he cannot do in Korea. Hyun might not be able to engage in such fun activities in Korea, but he surely can in other 'calmer and safer' regions. He, however, chose Jordan of all places, in spite of warnings from friends and family, and Korea's cautionary government travel warning for Jordan 'travel at your own risk' (Hyun, interview, 16 September 2010). Hyun travelled to Jordan as an adventure tourist interested in scuba diving and canyon trips. Seemingly, he plays with adventure and fun seeking a *sense of aliveness* in a place of conflict and danger. I openly asked Hyun about his feelings regarding the neighbouring Israeli–Palestinian conflict, and about him being in a 'political hotspot', possibly dangerous. He replied that South Korea was still at war with North Korea even though it seemed to be on halt for the moment. Witnessing armed soldiers or police wo/men at certain tourist sites, being stopped at checkpoints on Jordanian highways, for example, was not much of a disturbance to him as he sees soldiers at tourist sites in his home country too:

> I feel nothing, because I always experience that kind of news in Korea and that news is much bigger news . . . [I always see soldiers] on the opposite side of the beach; there are so-called guard posts, like in Jordan . . . And coast lines, they always have soldiers, in case of North Korea coming down with the submarines. But no one feels anything about that kind of like military base, because we got used to it, even if there are some gun shots from North Korea.
>
> (Hyun, interview, 16 September 2010)

Hyun admitted that he never travelled to North Korea even though he would like to, because there is a ban on free travel to the North. Desire for the Other is where desire finds form, desire is '*désir de l'Autre*' (the desire of the Other)' Lacan argued (trans. 1997a, p. 312). Communist North Korea is the Other for democratic South Korea. Through this prism, Hyun desires to travel to North Korea and witness the conflict presented daily in the news in South Korea, such as: the North's nuclear testing, the threat of shootings and submarines invading the South's coastal regions (Hyun, interview, 16 September 2010). The ban on travel to North Korea represents the forbidden desire for Hyun. 'Desire by definition marks a structural lack' (Ragland-Sullivan, 1995, p. 156), and the lack is realised in the ban to visit North Korea due to the conflict with South Korea.

Travelling to another destination in the proximity of a conflict such as Jordan arguably alludes to this desire for the forbidden conflict present in Hyun's life through mass media, soldiers on beaches and the like, but absent through the ban on travel to the other side. In Jordan, Hyun can experience the fun of scuba diving, canyon and desert trips. He can also engage in the 'dangerous adventure' of the Israeli–Palestinian conflict – a *castrated conflict* (just like peace in this region), present-absent, in Jordan as the North–South conflict is in South Korea. The fact that he does not cross into Palestine from Jordan to witness the 'heart' of the conflict speaks of the repetition that gives so much comfort. Hyun repeats the scenario of his experience in South Korea staying on the safer side of the conflict, but fears to transgress it, he fears to challenge the fixity of his life.

The death drive, arguably, operates in Hyun's case through the Freudian repetition principle, explained as compulsion to repeat. Through compulsion to repeat, the aim is to re-experience something identical, which Freud thought was in and of itself a clear a source of pleasure. The main condition for enjoyment, however, is novelty, also according to Freud. Thus, travelling to a country that has similar ways of handling a decades-long conflict suggests that the repetition principle is linked to the escapes of death drives in the conscious life (Ragland-Sullivan, 1995, p. 68).

Like Hyun, Lakshimi and Rini, two Indian women in their forties, travelled to the region for the adventure, in their case, the adventure of collecting places of world wonders, such as Petra in Jordan and Alexandria in Egypt. In our interview, both of them agreed that the presence of armed soldiers, police people and checkpoints was normal for them:

> border disputes is something in India we're very familiar with . . . In India also there are quite a few places you cross the military zone and they say, 'No photography allowed', some tunnels and we'll see soldiers with guns. So it's quite common, in India too.
>
> (Lakshimi, interview, 2 October 2010)

It can be argued that Lakshimi and Rini's experiences in India with military zones, prohibitions, denied access, and so on, are experienced as a 'normal' part of everyday life. Hence their visit to Jordan offers a repeat of the same 'normalcy' or familiarity, a death drive engaged through compulsion to repeat. If the death drive is understood to unsettle the life/death boundaries, then Lakshimi and Rini have asserted and disturbed this binary along with the fun/fear one. Living in a country with 'a few places as military zones', the boundaries of lived normalcy, ordinary, out-of the ordinary and extra-ordinary have been blurred. This may have led to them becoming desensitised to conflict. Consequently, feeling no fear when visiting another conflict zone, or feeling fear as something acceptable, the fun/fear dichotomy is disrupted and the death drive engaged. Amongst the first pictures Lakshimi took in Jordan, as part of a photo diary for this research project was of two tourist policewomen (see Figure 8.1).

In the diary entry for 29 September 2010, two days after her arrival in Jordan, and after having visited the Baptismal Site at the border with Palestine/Israel, Lakshimi wrote: 'For the first time since arriving we realised that the Israeli border is so near, and saw all the armed guards. One does not realise it in Madaba'[2] (Lakshimi, diary

Figure 8.1 Jordanian tourist policewomen.
Source: Lakshimi, 2010, used with permission.

notes, 29 September 2010). The familiarity of the landscape marked by the neighbouring conflict through the presence of tourist policewomen and armed soldiers
made them 'immediately [feel] at home – not at all like a foreigner' (Lakshimi, diary
note, 27 September 2010).

Also collecting world wonders and travelling in politically troubled areas, like
Lakshimi and Rini, was the New Zealand couple Mary and John. Having spent
ten days on holiday in Jordan in October 2010, they did not express any worry
with the checkpoints or the armed soldiers. They found their presence acceptable: 'there's an armed guard on the Israeli side [and one on the Jordanian side
at Bethany Beyond the Jordan – the Baptismal Site]. That's the minimum you'd
expect. Really' (Mary and John, interview, 16 September 2010).

I, too, am at home with the presence of police and soldiers. My parents are
both military officers, my extended family is employed either in the army or in
the police force. I grew up in communist Romania with a well-endowed army and
intelligence personnel, which pervaded every aspect of our lives. Soldiers and
guns are not all that new to me, but witnessing active presence of armed soldiers
in plain sight, almost parading, at tourist sites (see Figures 8.2a and 8.2b) is indeed
something that intrigues if not fascinates me. I took the photograph in Figure 8.2a
on my first visit to Petra in 2009, and admittedly I had mixed feelings about the

armed policeman guarding tourists at the main entrance into Petra Park. His presence symbolises to me an imminent danger that the tourists in the queue must be protected against. The soldier, his gun, tourists and their backpacks inhabit the entrance to one of the world's wonders. It is through this entanglement of soldiers, tourists, guns and backpacks that fun/fear, safety/danger, peace/war and life/death binaries are asserted and transgressed.

Figure 8.2a Tourists and armed Jordanian policeman at the main entrance in Petra.

Figure 8.2b Armed policeman at the main Entrance in Petra.
Source: Dorina Buda, 2009.

Paul is a British tourist from England in his late twenties travelling together with his girlfriend in Jordan. He too had mixed feelings regarding tourist places securitised through checkpoints peopled by both armed soldiers and tourists. Regarding his visit at the Baptismal Site and the Dead Sea, Paul says:

When we got to Bethany [Beyond Jordan – the Baptismal Site], obviously you had the guided tour. And someone said, 'oh, why can't we just walk?' And the guide just said, 'You must all stay together at all times.' And the guide sort of just said, 'it's just what we do here.' He didn't explain why, and obviously I realised it was because of the security, 'cos of the proximity to the border with Occupied Palestinian Territories. But in general that was fine. At one point, and we were just down by the river, on the Jordanian side, and some tourists on the Palestinian side, Israelis, came down. And so you had – I glanced behind me and there was the Jordanian guard with his machine gun, then across the river there was the Israeli guard with his machine gun, and at that point you realise how close you are to the danger-zone and the trouble zone, and that was – just that one small moment was probably the most disconcerting of the entire, my entire two months away, so . . . I can still picture the image, and I can actually remember thinking, I should take a picture of this, but maybe I shouldn't. I wasn't sure how the soldiers would react, so I didn't take a picture, but I can still picture – if I was a good artist, I could draw the picture exactly how it was and where people were. I can remember what some of the tourists looked like, and kept themselves clearly behind an Israeli flag in the background fluttering. And then just to that side, the Jordanian side, the Jordanian soldier. So yes, it's very, very clear. One of the clearest images I think, of my visit to Jordan is that particular moment, just that one moment in – for maybe half a minute of eight/nine days in Jordan, and I can remember that very, very clearly.

(Paul, interview, 6 September 2010)

The Baptismal Site, discussed in the previous chapter, is on the tourist circuit for its religious, historical and archaeological importance. It gained its prominence in the media when the late Pope John Paul II visited it during the bi-millenary event of the year 2000 and designated it as the unique place where John baptised Jesus Christ. The site itself is 10 square kilometres and is geostrategically located right on the border between Jordan and Palestine/Israel and is guarded at all times by armed soldiers on both sides.

On the one hand, Paul had disconcerting feelings to see soldiers with machine guns at a tourist site/border area. On the other hand, he immediately felt like taking a picture of the whole situation as a souvenir of the moment, but he knew he could not, or should not. Those moments of felt tensions, of wanting to capture the moment in a photograph, point to the workings of the death drive overlapping with affect. Paul alludes to the circulation of death drives and affects in 'this danger-zone and the trouble zone', whereby disconcerting feelings move between 'some tourists on the Palestinian side', 'the Israeli guard with his machine gun' and 'the Jordanian guard with his machine gun'. This circulation of drives and raw affect creates emotional connections, divisions and attachments. At first, Paul does not name it as dangerous or fearful, because affect is inexpressible and ineffable, but it is felt: 'I glanced behind me and . . . then across the river . . . you realise how close you are to the danger.' The strength and duration of that image's effect were intense enough to remain impressed into Paul's mind and body in such a way that he felt he 'could even draw the picture exactly how it was and where people were'. Paul thinks the whole situation of half a minute of intense tension rather disconcerting.

It is, actually, half a second that is 'the minimum perceivable lapse' (Massumi, 1995, p. 89) between outside stimulation and bodily reaction. In this half-second, affect shows its autonomy. This half-second – 'between the beginning of a bodily event and its completion in an outwardly directed, active expression' (Massumi, 1995, p. 90) – cannot be explained or measured through medical cortical electrodes and/or electro-encephalograph (EEG) machines. Massumi's explanations of the *autonomous half-second* can be translated to understand Paul's half-minute of clearly felt yet ineffable intensity.

Feeling disconcerted, unsettled, or disturbed at the sight of gunned soldiers, on both sides of the Jordan River, was counteracted by the fun thought of possibly taking a picture of the whole situation. Seemingly, fun and fear mingle in Paul's account as, later that day and later on his tour around Jordan, he took several pictures of checkpoints, soldiers, police and tourists. Upon his return to England he emailed me some of his photos, one of which can be seen in Figure 8.3, similar to a photo I took around Jordan (see Figure 8.4). Both photos I find illustrative of enjoyment (reminiscent of Lacan's *jouissance*) crossing boundaries: fun/fear, safety/danger and even peace/war. About his photograph, Paul made the following comments:

> I love this picture and the contrast between the checkpoint, the soldier and the nice hilly landscape distinguishable through the window. This is actually at the checkpoint on the road to the Dead Sea from the Baptismal Site. I took the picture as we had been waiting for five minutes behind the rented car full of tourists. There were four of us in our car (one guide and three tourists). The reaction of the others was one of amusement/bewilderment as to why I would want such a photo, but I am with you, I like the contrasts!
>
> (Paul, personal communication, 30 September 2010)

Love, amusement, bewilderment and contrasts point to a psychoanalytic language of *jouissance* and death drives. *Jouissance* is beyond satisfaction: it is satisfaction of the death drive. The aim of the drive is not to reach a goal and obtain satisfaction, but to trace a contour and on the arch of its way back, it accomplishes the task. It is like the itinerary one must take on an assigned mission (Braunstein, 2003). The felt intense encounter by the border at the Baptismal Site repeated itself in the 'safer' space of the car with fellow tourists and a local taxi driver. This time in the car, the initial disconcerting feelings at the Baptismal Site, were nuanced with amusement, bewilderment and eventually love. The disconcerting feelings experienced at the Baptismal Site might have arguably acted as motivation or perpetrator for the rest of holiday activities in Jordan, hence booking a tourist taxi to drive around Jordan and to the Dead Sea. Humans are, after all, motivated by the death drive and not driven by the pleasure principle.

Figure 8.3 Checkpoint on the road to the Dead Sea from the Baptismal Site.

Source: Paul, 2010, used with permission.

Figure 8.4 Armed policeman near a tourist police booth.

Source: Dorina Buda, 2010.

Noel, a tourist from Switzerland in his mid-twenties also visited the Baptismal Site in October 2010. He talked to me about his experience at the site, about the 'very interesting', but also 'very strange' feelings one has in tourist places with military checkpoints where something can happen at any time:

> Well it was a military checkpoint, which are pretty striking . . . you see you are approaching the West Bank and you see they are on the high [alert] – they're probably, they don't look like they'd be on heightened alert, but they signal that something can happen. But like twenty years ago we had the same thing in Germany, when you approached Checkpoint Charlie I guess . . . it's a very strange feeling that in such a small place, you have so many things which influence the whole world. So I found it [the experience at the Baptismal Site] very interesting.
>
> (Noel, interview, 23 September 2010)

These 'pretty striking checkpoints' on 'heightened alert' signalling possible dangers generate mixed feelings of fun and fear for some tourists like Noel, or Paul above, or me (see Figure 8.5). There seem to be elements of purging embedded collective traumas through the Berlin Wall signifier, but also individual, personal and familial. Noel grew up with stories about Checkpoint Charlie and the Berlin Wall.

Figure 8.5 Checkpoint at Bethany Beyond the Jordan – the Baptismal Site.
Source: Dorina Buda, 2010.

Since the age of twelve, he had wanted to travel to the Middle East. His travels in Jordan seem to be felt through the shared archaic trauma of the Second World War and the Cold War, since 'twenty years ago *we* had the same thing in Germany' (Noel, interview, 23 September 2010, my emphasis). I asked him whether the complex, unstable and sometimes violent nature of the political situation in the region represents a source of fear or concern. His answer was that he received support from home because 'my father travels a lot on business' and 'probably from when I was 12, 13 years old I wanted to go to the Middle East.'

The compulsion to repeat 'unpleasurable' experiences was initially observed by Freud in children's play. This would happen 'for the additional reason that they can master a powerful impression . . . Each fresh repetition seems to strengthen the mastery they are in search of' (Freud, 1974, p. 35). This character trait, Freud argues, disappears in adult life as enjoyment is then reached through novelty. Compulsion to repeat unpleasurable childhood memories seem to be motivated by that *daemonic power*, at the heart of Freudian death drive. Experiencing the heightened alert of the Jordanian checkpoints at the Baptismal Site, Noel not only had the opportunity to reflect on the collective war trauma, but also to experience fun and fear connected to an ongoing conflict. Noel, therefore, can be argued to have engaged the death drive and *jouissance* through the felt tension at the checkpoint.

Sense (of) fear!

> When I arrive somewhere where I don't know anything, I don't talk. Just that everything is open – eyes, ears, the smell and everything. So it's like finding the, how can I say it, [pause] it's a rebirth. Everything is new. I just have to open all the senses of my body . . . my eyes, my ears, my smell – everything, so I feel more comfortable after, with people that I meet. I don't feel as if there's a fear [that blocks me] because fear is everywhere. So you just have to be confident enough with yourself and travelling helps me in that.
>
> (Gaston, interview, 19 September 2010)

Gaston, a tourist from France in his early forties travelled to Jordan. I met him while visiting the Baptismal Site. Gaston feels the 'fear that is everywhere' and considers it can be negotiated while travelling if one opens up one's bodily senses. Through viscerality, an introceptive sensibility or 'gut feeling', the body registers excitations, which are first 'gathered by the five "exteroceptive" senses even before they are fully processed by the brain' (Massumi, 2002a, p. 60). An intensive quality, subtracted from these sensuous excitations, through gut visceral feelings, Massumi argues, is registered affect.

Affect is pervasive, it is not blocking; it is autonomous through its openness. Likewise, fear is infinite and open, it is everywhere and of the everyday. Fear is felt and sensed viscerally, in the gut, making you feel alive, feel renewed and reborn. This renewed vitality or sense of aliveness is sought after when travelling to an area of conflict and danger. Sensing fear with all one's bodily senses, borders between fun/fear and life/death are crossed and made fluid. Gaston's explicit quest for a 'reborn feeling through bodily senses' allows for a more critical and deeper interpretation of danger-zone tourist subjectivities, which involves notions of reflexivity, embodiment and affect. Engaging sensuously with places while travelling in Jordan disrupts mainstream interpretations of dark tourism to sites of ongoing conflict as being morbid and ghoulish. It shows that danger-zone tourist subjectivities can be more than 'abnormal' and 'deviant'. Such pejorative readings of deviance and morbidity ignore discursive complexities of places and suggest that tourism 'closes down the possibility for reflection and simply encourages passive subjects to reproduce prevailing norms, values and attitudes' (Lisle, 2004, p. 5).

For Gaston, travelling to a place connected to the Israeli–Palestinian conflict opened up opportunities to reflect on his father's personal stories from the Algerian War:

> It's very personal because of the stories of my dad, he did the Algerian War and I can see the result fifty years later . . . He was 20 years old when he left his [home] country, left the countryside, arrived in another country and was given a gun to save his life. I'm sure that the man who is my dad now is not the same one than before the war. So, I'm sad for them [the Israeli soldiers at the border with Jordan as seen in the Baptismal Site]. Seeing the weapons, okay, it's not [a big deal] – I'm sad for them because I can't say that most of them have a choice. And it will change their life. I'm very lucky because there's no war in France, what would I do if there was one? But definitely, war changes people, because of what they see, of what they do . . . With my dad it's what he told me. I just asked him one day 'Do you become *méchant* [mean, malicious], bad afterwards?' And he just told me, 'Yes, because you have no choice.' Fifty years later, he started to talk about it. So he's lived with it, every day. 'I'm not for war, I'm sorry' is what I told him. I say, if there's one war one day, I won't go. I'd rather shoot myself than kill anyone. Never. Become the . . . so I'm seeing this situation today [at the Baptismal Site]. I'm sad for them [Israeli soldiers].
>
> (Gaston, interview, 19 September 2010)

Through his experience at the Baptismal Site, Gaston reflected on and accessed the potential to reshape those embedded family memories. In Jordan, he felt that existential fear, sense of aliveness, while confronting his own family histories connected to wars, more specifically the Algerian War. He vowed to shoot himself rather than fight in a war and kill people. The father's decision to start talking about the Algerian War after fifty years seems to be poignantly felt by the son. Lacan's paternal metaphor can be quite literally employed to understand Gaston's experience. The Name-of-the-Father (*nom du père*) at the foundation of the paternal metaphor was put forward by Lacan to explain the role of the father in the Symbolic order, not necessarily biological or de facto father. In his usual fashion, Lacan plays with words and sounds '*le nom dupère*' (the name-of-the-father) and '*le non du père*' (the no-of-the-father) to explain the father being and having legislative and prohibitive function.

This function is the Law in Lacan's work, a law that is not judicial legislation, but represents a set of fundamental principles at the basis of social interactions. The legislative nature of the father figure imposes constraints, generates lacks and sorrows for Gaston and the rest of the family. It seems as if Gaston accesses the death drive at the Baptismal Site while gazing at the armed soldiers, and feeling sad for them. In that time-space, the allegedly malicious soldiers perform the paternal function. There is a *jouissance* in Gaston's sadness: 'I'm sad for them because I can't say that most of them have a choice. And it will change their life' (military service is compulsory in Israel for both women and men). He reflected on his own and soldiers' feelings through his paternal traumas and vouched not to ever fight any war and kill people. This seemingly voiced *jouissance* of 'rather killing myself' is illustrative of the ways in which the death drive may be operant in a Jordanian tourist locale reminiscent of family traumas. Freudian and Lacanian concepts are intimately linked and 'function in dynamic cadence' (Ragland-Sullivan, 1992, p. 10), thus *jouissance*, the name-of-the-father and the death drive are all interconnected. Gaston's 'very personal paternal stories' are relived and renegotiated while accessing the death drive and making him feel alive.

I, too, wanted to feel alive when on 2 August 2010 I travelled to Aqaba, the seaside resort by the Red Sea at the border between Jordan, Israel, Egypt and Saudi Arabia (see Chapter 6). I was curious and driven as could be about the 'rockets incident'. At that time, I was in the capital, in Amman, lodged at the American Center for Oriental Research. Within minutes of the rocket incident, the director of the centre informed everyone that the US embassy advised people to refrain from travelling to Aqaba. The following day, online and print newspapers reported the story of the five rockets launched from the Sinai Peninsula in Egypt supposedly aiming for Eilat in Israel and mistakenly hitting the Hotel InterContinental in Aqaba, killing one local taxi driver. On the morning of 4 August 2010 I packed a small bag and took a bus to Aqaba. I wanted to be there, in the middle of the hustle and bustle of the 'rocket affair'. I had that feeling that pushed me and I decided to take an eight-hour return bus trip. I did not acknowledge my feelings then; instead I invoked more academic motivations to travel to Aqaba, that is, to collect information and material for my research. In a way, I was like the tourists Arfan mentions next: 'really crazy'.

Detour to Iraq: fear in a hotspot: 'It makes you feel alive!'

Arfan: Yeah, oh yeah, oh yeah [I have met tourists coming here in this region because it is dangerous and because they want to see the conflict. For them it's just an adventure.] They told me, you know, even during the Iraqi war, when they started the Iraqi war in 2003 we still had tourists here and they said 'we are here, we want to see, we want to experience what people do, what people think'. You know, because for them it's just a new experience. I had tourists who came in 2003 when they started the war on Iraq and Iraq is on the border [with Jordan] and there were people here travelling and they said 'you know what it doesn't really scare us' . . . They always ask 'is it safe to leave the hotel?', 'is it safe to go and walk down in the market?'

Dorina: But if they came here because it was dangerous and because for them it was an adventure as you said, for them it shouldn't matter if is safe or not.

Arfan: No, no, no, they still, they still want to be here, it's like, you know what, they want to go back to their country and say 'do you know what I was in that region during the war', but there's still a little bit of fear. There's always fear.

           (Arfan, interview, 3 October 2010)

The conversation above is part of the interview I had with Arfan, a Jordanian tour guide in his early thirties. He acknowledged tourists' interests in places of (imagined) danger and fear. It seems that in his account, tourists' fear was more of an enticement factor than a deterrent, more a 'fun' emotion than a 'negative' one. The death drive may be traced in the fear that Arfan detected in those tourists, 'we are here, we want to see, we want to experience what people do, what people think . . . it [the neighbouring war] doesn't really scare us'. Arfan interpreted their wish to experience the war as a desire for fun and adventure, and to collect stories and dangerous places. In this quest to collect dangerous stories and places, tourists cross the fun/fear and life/death borders. The Jordanian tour guide continues:

Some people are really crazy, one guy said to me I wish I can be in Iraq now . . . Working with tourists you meet different people, different nationalities, different ways of thinking. There are people who want the adventure. There are people who are just too cheap to cancel their trip because they already paid for it and they will take the risk no matter what.

The death drive, which resists the life/death binary, seems to have penetrated Lacan's Symbolic and Imaginary orders as 'one guy' expressed in words 'I wish I can be in Iraq now.' Death drives seem to be important ingredients in danger-zone tourism at an embodied and emotional level of playing with fear and death. Danger-zone tourism draws on the productive and 'fun' aspect of danger and fear to disrupt and cross borders. Playing with fear (Saville, 2008), playing symbolically with death (Le Breton, 2000), the freedom to play with reality (Kane & Tucker, 2004) are expressions used to refer to fear as productive and possibly playful. In analyses of agoraphobia, fear of crime, fear of violence, geographers have positioned fear as an unwanted feeling, as a 'pejorative' emotion generated by 'physical vulnerability, powerlessness . . . isolation and loneliness' (Listerborn, 2002, p. 39). Listerborn mentions in passing that 'sometimes we experience fear intentionally (for example when we choose to see a "scary" movie)' (p. 35) alluding probably to those conscious desires to experience fear. My interest is in fear that does not repel, but perhaps even entices those who travel to danger-zones of political conflict and danger. Experiencing fear, whether intentionally and/or consciously (or not), in tourist places of ongoing troubles, disrupts the fun/fear and life/death oppositions.

Amru, a Jordanian tour guide, accompanied international journalists into Iraq on a couple of occasions including on 11 April 2003, the second day after Baghdad had fallen into the hands of the US-led 'Coalition of the Willing' (Newnham, 2008). Although he was paid to take journalists into Iraq, Amru had other, more personal motivations to travel to the war zone. He wanted to feel the fear that makes one feel alive:

> I am a fan of Paolo Coelho [a Brazilian lyricist and novelist]. 'Do you know this?' He writes about these things, the fear, it makes you alive sometimes. It is true, like you are in the middle of something or you need . . . I met this girl like from Turkey, she was a TV presenter . . . [She was] Turkish, [she] was 24 years [old,] stunningly beautiful and, and she's going there [Iraq] and I asked her 'what are you doing?' I said, I was joking with her like 'it's okay for me to die but you die no. It was, you know, teasing and she said 'I want to face my fear, fear of death', which is something that I put in mind. And you're always watching feeling this situation like how to control not control but, but feel the thing and, and just feel the fear, and deal with it, so I guess this is a personal thing.
>
> (Amru, interview, 2 October 2010)

Fear feels dangerous and danger feels like fear. Through fear, danger can be identified, and consequently dangerous things or situations that cause fear can be detected. Fear is embodied: muscles tighten; heart races, pulse quickens, breath shortens, eyes widen; so that 'these bodily changes seem to exhaust the feeling of fear' (Prinz, 2008, p. 150). The body can be felt through fear, which awakes senses, making Amru feel alive. Fear, however, manifests more than physiologically. Fear is not easily defined or measured; it is disorienting and pervasive, it can be both emotion and affect. Fear is the way through which the body is in contact with its vitality. There is affect that escapes the body; these escapes are perceived, sensed and captured. Continuous escapes of affect are 'nothing less than the *perception of one's own vitality*, one's sense of aliveness' (Massumi, 2002a, p. 37, emphasis in original). This sense of one's own aliveness is a steady self-perception at unconscious levels, therefore not easily amenable to analysis. Bringing it into consciousness, and into words, allows affect to be analysed – 'as long as a vocabulary can be found for that which is imperceptible but whose escape from perception cannot but be perceived, as long as one is alive' (p. 36).

The context and place in which a 'sense of aliveness' comes by, is crucial. Amru attested that when he travelled to Iraq he feared for his body being infected with 'chemicals maybe left from the war. I said we walk on the street and something you never know that there is something that influences your [body]' (Amru, interview, 2 October 2010). The context of the war in Iraq made Amru's fear of death manifest as fear for his body being infested with harmful chemical substances, which resonates with Lacan's argument that 'fear of death is psychologically subordinate to the narcissistic fear of damage to one's own body' (trans. 1977a, p. 28). For Amru, travelling to Iraq gave him a different understanding of life and death through his feelings of fear connected to a sense of aliveness and vitality.

The death drive works towards the unity of the ego, towards its vitality. Vitality, sense of aliveness, represents the overlapping aspect between death drives and affects. Both of them, to an extent, are autonomous. Affect holds the body's vitality, or the potential for emotional interactions. The death drive 'steers' towards a sense of aliveness through purging and purification of 'memories embedded in our flesh through family myths and archaic traumas' (Ragland-Sullivan, 1995, p. 94). Thus, for Amru, travelling to an area of ongoing conflict, such as Iraq in 2003, seems to have had the purificatory effects of a rite of passage in which, I argue, he (un/consciously) sought to negotiate and even purge his own embedded trauma of fear of death. Amru mentioned that he hid from his family his plans to travel to Iraq's capital in April 2003, 'I told mum and dad that I'm going to Syria not to Baghdad, and they were still afraid that I went to Syria too' (Amru, interview, 2 October 2010). Once the rite of passage was performed, he informed his parents that he had travelled to Iraq.

Assertions such as 'I want to face my fear of death', 'I want to control my fear of death', 'I want to feel fear of death', point to a death drive which penetrates the Symbolic and can be expressed in words, which impacts fantasies and images (the Imaginary). Thus, fear of death – understood through the psychoanalytic concept of the death drive – is an existential, *sense-of-aliveness fear*, a fear that shakes bodies, wakes up senses and makes tourists feel alive. It is a fear that removes us from 'the comfort of fixity, which Lacan called "death"' (Ragland-Sullivan, 1995, p. 167). Affects such as death drives are initially impersonal and virtual; they 'are "almost", they are potential, they are syn(es)thetic' (Thien, 2005, p. 452) and express the 'motion of emotion' (p. 451). When crossing into the Symbolic, affects become emotions, since 'an emotion or feeling is a recognized affect, an identified intensity' (Massumi, 2002, p. 61).

The drive is a constant force (Braunstein, 2003) which insists in the conscious, thus Amru decided to act on his drive to face his fear of death in spite of 'friends and people around me put[ting] me down sometimes. I mean, they would say "Are you crazy?" and stuff. But I had this feeling that pushes me and said, I wanted to go' (Amru, interview, 2 October 2010). Again, Amru seems to be motivated by the death drive and not by the pleasure principle.

Danger-zone tourists in Iraq in the media

Some tourism companies organise tours to conflict zones. Media accounts of such trips confirm the stories shared by participants in my project. Tourism to conflict areas is on the rise, due to 'the repetitive framing and circulation of war zone imagery within the news media' (Lisle, 2007, p. 334). People are becoming increasingly as familiar with images of Lebanon, Dubrovnik, Sarajevo, Palestine and Iraq, amongst others, as they are with images of sunny Caribbean beaches. Tours to hot spots of conflict and danger that had appeared on television were organised by Massimo Beyerle, an Italian travel agent who took tourists to

Lebanon and Dubrovnik in 1992 and 1993 (Dann, 1998; Fedarko et al., 1993; Lisle, 2007). The 'October War Zone tour', as it was called, came with a hefty price of US$25,000 for two weeks:

> Serious connoisseurs of violence, however, should call Massimo Beyerle in La Spezia, Italy, who is accepting bookings for his October War Zone tour of Lebanon. For $25,000, travelers can spend two weeks hunting for shrapnel in the Syrian-controlled Bekaa Valley, visiting the scene of the U.S. Marine barracks blown up in 1983 and dining in a Palestinian refugee camp.
>
> (Fedarko et al., para. 8, 1993)

In 1997, week-long tours to Sarajevo were organised by a tour operator based in Barcelona, Spain. During these trips, tourists would enjoy wartime meals of emergency rations in a dark cellar in the centre of the city (Newman, cited in Dann, 1998).

In September 2003, when the Iraqi war had officially ended, but violent clashes were still common, Hinterland Travel took tourists to Iraq, led by the company's managing director. Hinterland Travel is a tourism agency based in England, which caters for those who seek a change in their usual travel experiences by offering tours to areas of conflict. This tourism company's plans to take the first 'Western' tourists to Iraq in September 2003 shortly after the 'end' of the war were discussed in a magazine article, 'Why tourists are going back to Iraq'; the article opens with:

> A UK travel company is about to embark on the first post-war tour of Iraq. For these hardy travellers, the lure of visiting the cradle of civilisation overrides the very real dangers and difficulties to be faced in this scarred nation.
>
> (Lane, 2003, para. 1)

What type of cultural and historical sites and places can one visit in a country, which was invaded and bombed only a few months prior to the trip? Do such cultural and historical motivations allude to interests in, drives to (areas of) conflict and danger? Is this the death drive *calling*?

I wish to consider that for tourists travelling to Iraq less than six months after the March–April 2003 invasion 'the very real dangers and difficulties to be faced in this scarred nation' override more cultural and historical motivations of 'visiting the cradle of civilisation'. The death drive may be *calling* these tourists to engage with feelings in places that bear the marks of recent war. Witnessing the evidence of war, danger, death and feeling fear circulating around in the aftermath of war, are arguably important experiences while 'visiting the cradle of civilisation'.

Regarding the Iraq tour in September 2003, little is discussed about the tourists' feelings and emotions while travelling in a country which was at war only six months before. It can be challenging to see how conflict and danger are connected to tourism activities of foreign holidays (Lisle, 2000). This is, however, one of the three main aspects this book as a whole examines. To unpack connections between tourism, danger and conflict represents one of the three aims of this book, as discussed in the Introduction. This is done by analysing the ways in which the binaries fear/fun, safety/danger and also life/death are asserted and disrupted. I argue that there are some tourists who do not shy away from fears while travelling in areas of ongoing conflict. As morbid as some might consider them, there are those who indeed seek (consciously or not) fear in places of ongoing conflict. Their accounts are capitalised on by the media and become 'important' news. Seeking fear is encouraged by two interconnected mechanisms: media images of wars and conflicts, and opportunities to visit these places of dangers and fears (Lisle, 2004). Bombardments of media images of conflicts and wars seem to come from online media, print media and television.

The destinations promoted and sold by, for example, Hinterland Travel are usually countries that are on Western governments' travel warning lists. Armenia, Afghanistan, Kashmir, Pakistan, Iraq, Kurdistan, Iran are the countries where Hinterland Travel organises tours. Regarding trips to Afghanistan and Iraq, the website of Hinterland Travel notes:

> We are now regularly re-visiting Afghanistan after the years of International and Internal conflict in this starkly beautiful country. Some people will think that this is a little premature given that there is still internal dissension, and still only a tenuous groping toward Central Government control and that is certainly the British Govt Foreign Office advice [*sic*]. We prefer to state that Afghanistan is at the cutting edge of Adventure tourism, which in its self [*sic*] can offer benefits and progress. [Hinterland Travel, 2011, para. 1] . . . Tours to Iraq proper, or Mesopotamia as we like to call it, were on hold from 2004 until 2008, as we were unable to guarantee travel around Iraq and access to the sites despite our astonishing Post war tour in October 2003 [*sic*]. We began tours again in March 2009 when Geoff [the owner and managing director] had felt that the return was right. Since then we have operated throughout 2009 and 2010 with some very successful tours. The mood in Iraq is upbeat, vibrant with the security aspects improving all the time. For 2011 we have an improved and increased number of tours.
>
> (Hinterland Travel, 2011, para. 3)

Hinterland Travel capitalises on adventurous fears, with which danger-zone tourists engage affectively while travelling in areas of ongoing conflict. The company describes Afghanistan as the 'cutting edge of adventure tourism', defies travel advisories and openly markets such trips to areas of ongoing conflict. Most Hinterland trips are to areas of ongoing troubles and turmoil, which represent the pinnacle of adventure tourism for them. Intentionally seeking fear is not an aspect that can be acknowledged easily, either by tourism operators or tourists themselves. On their website, Hinterland Travel employs more 'socially accepted' motivations such as 'visiting a starkly beautiful country' or 'travel through historic Mesopotamia'.

Returning to the article about tourists in Iraq, the author mentions a suicide bomb that blew up in the United Nations headquarters in Baghdad just one month prior to the September 2003 tour. It is reported that the suicide bomber targeted civilians and killed twenty. News of a suicide bombing, which 'was the first of a string of attacks on civilian targets' (Lane, 2003, para. 5) did not prevent Hinterland Travel from organising the first post-war tour to Iraq. The phenomenon of suicide bombing is a bodily technological weapon meant to evoke fear and cause destruction (Curti, 2008, p. 114) especially towards those against whom it is perpetrated. These are often those belonging to and living 'the Western godless way of life based on modern science' (Žižek, 2008, p. 69). To travel to a country with a high risk of being blasted by possible bombs shows a defiance of life, probably even an 'enthusiasm for fear' or a 'joy in fear'.

In 2009, Hinterland Travel organised for a group of Western tourists to visit Iraq; this received another broad wave of media attention. From the BBC to the American broadcaster NBC, television channels, online newspapers and magazines covered the news of the Western tourists in Iraq: 'No frills tourism – in Iraq' (Sykes, 2009), 'First Western tourists visit Iraq' (Gennaro, 2009), 'Some Adventure tourists choose Iraq' (Hareyan, 2009) are but a few titles. In another:

> Five British tourists, two Americans and a Canadian spent two nights there [the Sheraton Hotel in Baghdad] at the end of a tour of Iraq which has included historic sites as well as cities where extreme violence is still a possibility.
>
> (Sykes, 2009, para. 2)

The possible extreme danger, fear of death, kidnapping, or bombing did not deter or scare them away; just the contrary, opined one of the tourists. She admitted she would have rather died in a car bomb than in a geriatric hospital (Sykes, 2009). Another woman of the group said 'My friends certainly think I'm a bit mad – but I tend to go on holiday to places like Afghanistan, so I think they're used to it!' (cited in para. 17). In an interview with National Public Radio (NPR) (2009) in Washington, DC, the same tourist explained: 'We haven't had any security guards with us — we just travelled on the minibus — the eight tourists along with a driver and a translator. We kept a very low profile and we haven't had any concerns about security' (tourist in Iraq interviewed, National Public Radio, 2009).

In the BBC or NPR interviews, there were very few questions as to tourists' motivations to visit a war-torn region, emphasis was laid on whether they felt safe and secure and whether they had opportunities to interact with the locals. 'There have been difficulties because of the problems here, but we have had the opportunity to meet local people – we've gone into the shops, we've gone into the teahouses, and people have been very gracious' said the tourist (National Public Radio, 2009).

In the interviews with the group of tourists to Iraq in 2009, there were no actual questions regarding emotions possibly generated while witnessing outcomes left behind by war. There was also no discussion of how (un)ethical such tours might be. To some, such interest of travelling to places of ongoing violence 'may be simply a reflection of people's inherent morbid or ghoulish interest in the suffering or death of others – in a sense, extreme examples of rubbernecking' (Sharpley,

2005, p. 216). To others, it can be a sort of educational and political escapism of witnessing the ways in which war impacts people and places. To some others, travelling to a danger-zone is a journey of confrontation of hidden fears, a search for danger so as to awaken the body since 'The body comes to life when coping with difficulty' (Sennett, 1994, p. 310). Rather than readily dismissing these seemingly 'deviant' interests and practices because they are not 'proper' and 'respectable' tourism endeavours, researchers should take a closer look at the relationship between danger, fear and tourism.

Note

1 The conversation is an excerpt from an interview between King Abdullah II of Jordan and Jon Stewart (2010), host of the *Daily Show*, a US television programme, which employs a 'reality'-based analysis of current events, politics, sports and entertainment.
2 To locate Madaba on the map please see Figures 5.2 and 5.3 in Chapter 5.

Part IV

Re-tour

9   Conclusions

Affect and emotion are what moves us into re/action and into *feeling*. Emotions matter because they affect the ways we travel, how we interact with others and with places. Affective tourism deals with circulations of emotions, affect and feelings between and among touring bodies, places and things. Emotions, feelings and affects have been at the periphery of tourism studies, in spite of some calls for closer engagement with emotional dimensions in tourism. The critical turn has become more visible, vocal and prominent in tourism studies. I have maintained that this book goes some way towards addressing affects, emotions, feelings, senses and death drives in tourism studies. I have offered just a sliver of the many affective and emotional engagements in tourism to places of ongoing sociopolitical turmoil. My intention was not to be exhaustive, but to offer examples from social and cultural geography, as well as from psychoanalysis, that provide insights into the rich world of affects and emotions.

In this book, I have examined affective tourism by engaging with these questions: how do tourists affectively and viscerally experience places? What emotions and senses circulate amongst and between tourists and local tourism industry representatives in such places? How do politics of affect and emotion shape tourism encounters in places of conflict? As I tackled these questions I had three aims.

First, I delved into affective and emotional geographies of that which circulates in tourist places. I employed social, cultural and spatial theories of affect and emotion to examine the data collected through ethnographic fieldwork using individual interviews, focus groups, written diaries and non-commercial photographs. This helped me explore what emotions do in a tourism context and track affective performances of tourists and local tourism industry representatives.

Second, I considered the ways in which binaries such as fun/fear, safety/danger, peace/war and life/death are asserted, disrupted and transgressed in tourism spaces by those who travel to/in places of ongoing conflict, such as Jordan and Palestine/Israel. Such places offer opportunities to reflect on, negotiate and sometimes purge embedded family and archaic traumas, a process explored using the psychoanalytic concept of the death drive. This helped me argue that danger-zone tourist subjectivities can be understood beyond the morbid and ghoulish labels attached to those travelling to areas of ongoing conflicts.

Third, I unravelled the *tourism–danger–conflict* nexus and examined the ways tourism has been constructed as opposite to conflict and danger. I turned to dark tourism literature to offer me a framework within which to expand research on danger-zone tourism. Danger-zone tourists are alluded to in literature on dark tourism as being those in the vanguard of dark tourism, that is, those who travel to the 'world's most dangerous places' (Lennon & Foley, 2000, p. 9). Danger-zone tourism exists and tourism researchers have failed to recognise its importance. The relationship between tourism, danger and ongoing socio-political conflict has been taken for granted, with tourism understood as being excluded from places of danger and ongoing conflicts.

In relation to the *first aim*, I analysed affective and emotional geographies in danger-zone tourist sites. I call for the affective and emotional turn in social and cultural geography, sociology and cultural studies to (*re-)route* towards tourism studies as well. Or better yet, for tourism studies to welcome the turn to affect and emotion. There is some engagement with emotions and feelings in tourism studies, but those approaches quantify and objectify emotions, use them as measuring factors for tourist loyalty and satisfaction. I draw on work that considers affect as intensities and resonances that shape encounters between bodies and places, circulate around and represent '*other than* conscious' ways of knowing the world (Seigworth & Gregg, 2010, p. 1, emphasis in the original). To be sure, inviting the affective to turn in tourism studies is not an epochal call, but a genuine encouragement to consider affects, emotions and drives in tourism theories and methodologies. Perhaps, this could find an adequate outlet within the critical turn in tourism studies.

Geographical theories on emotions, feelings and affects offered a great route to further the understanding of danger-zoners' performances in places (in the proximity) of ongoing conflict. In so doing, I levelled wider critique concerning the considerable degree of ignorance regarding emotions, feelings and affects in dark tourism in particular, and tourism studies in general. I maintained that the majority of studies on dark tourism have managerial and business approaches which focus on numerical aspects of supply and demand. While these studies provide valuable insights, they frame dark tourists to sites of conflict as entirely passive consumers (Lisle, 2007). I proposed that by considering affects and emotions encountered in areas of conflict, danger-zone tourists could be understood as emotional and sensuous subjectivities.

Bringing emotions into the debate on danger-zone tourism, I responded to Tucker's (2009) and Waitt and colleagues (2007) calls for closer engagements with emotional and bodily dimensions in tourism encounters. In this book, I concurred with Jamal and Hollinshead (2001), who observed that emotions have been noted and addressed by very few tourism scholars. This research project provided a different understanding of emotions in tourism studies, not as quantifiable variables of tourist satisfaction, but as gut-wrenchingly personal, fluid, pervasive and interconnected with feelings and affects.

Focusing on fear felt in places of conflict, and on the haptic sense of touch, I argued that fear makes one feel alive. Fear was considered to be both affect and emotion, sometimes sought (even if not always intentionally and consciously), always productive and not entirely 'negative'. The connotation 'negative' was not used lightly since I did not intend to dichotomise emotions or affects. I pointed out that feeling fear bespoke of a death drive engaged in a place of turmoil overlapping with affect as an *other than* conscious way of experiencing socio-political conflicts. In this respect, fear in the death drive is different from, for example, agoraphobia or fears of nature.

In Jordan, some tourists experience this layer of fear, especially at sites near the Jordanian–Palestinian/Israeli border, imbued with regional tensions representative of the Israeli–Palestinian conflict. Some tourist sites, such as Bethany Beyond the Jordan, are located along the border which is guarded by armed soldiers on each side; thus some tourists flirt with conflict and danger while taking pictures of soldiers, and fences or even looking for signs of landmines. The dynamics in these border places were analysed to challenge the image that local tourism industry representatives often present of Jordan – that of an 'oasis of peace and stability' or the 'Switzerland of the Middle East'. Jordan signed a peace treaty with Israel in 1994, so from this perspective the country is not directly involved in the ongoing Israeli–Palestinian conflict and can be considered 'peaceful'.

Historical entanglements between Jordan, Israel and Palestine tell a different story. With eastern parts of Jerusalem and the West Bank having been part of Jordan between 1950 and 1967 (West Bank, 2011), with the presence of numerous Jordanians of Palestinian descent and Palestinian refugees in Jordan, the implications of/for Jordan in this conflict could not be simply solved with the 1994 Peace Treaty. Moreover, the physical distance between Amman and Jerusalem is about 60 kilometres. I have, therefore, underlined in this book that Jordan is not merely an 'onlooker', a neutral party, but is directly concerned with and involved in the regional politics of the conflict. The image of Jordan as the Switzerland of the Middle East is troubled by the emotional politics of Jordanian tour guides working at tourist sites located near the Palestinian/Israeli border. The politics of tour guiding in Jordan challenge the sanitising apparatus which is intended to extricate Jordanian tourism from the conflict.

Emotions and politics interconnect in Palestinian tourism as well. Elements representative of the Israeli–Palestinian conflict – such as the separation wall, checkpoints and refugee camps – have become tourist attractions, which are incorporated by Palestinian tourism companies into tourist itineraries. At these sites, a mix of emotions and feelings are experienced by tourists and local tour guides. Tourists in Palestine walk along the wall, cross checkpoints and visit refugee camps, amongst other tourist activities. In this engagement with 'icons' of the conflict, some tourists feel these places through the haptic sense of touch. I contended that, by engaging emotionally and sensuously, tourists in Palestine in general, and danger-zoners in particular, disrupt binaries such as fun/fear, peace/war, safety/danger and even life/death. This represented the *second aim* of this book.

The psychoanalytic concept of the death drive was employed to understand how the binary oppositions mentioned above are asserted and resisted in Jordanian and Palestinian tourism spaces. I mainly focused on Freud's and Lacan's conceptualisations of the death drive and interpretations offered by Ragland-Sullivan (1992,

1995) and Boothby (1991). Geographers' works on emotions, affects and psycho-analysis were also used to introduce this potentially controversial concept in stud-ies of tourism (Anderson & Smith, 2001; Davidson et al., 2005; Dewsbury, 2009; Kingsbury, 2004, 2007, 2009a, 2009b; Smith et al., 2009). Focusing on the death drive to understand danger-zone tourists' affective and emotional experiences in an area of conflict, this book also contributed to the scarce and belated dialogue between critical tourism research and psychoanalysis (Kingsbury & Brunn, 2003).

I did not advocate for a clinical employment of the concept, but for an emo-tional and affective approach. Since affect is thought to reside in the unconscious and be ineffable, it overlaps with psychoanalytic drives, especially the death drive. As an invisible presence, 'infinitely connectable [and] impersonal' (Seigworth & Gregg, 2010, p. 4), affect connects with (death) drives. When affect escapes, it comes closer to emotions (Massumi, 1995). It is within this connection between emotions, affects and drives that crossing of boundaries can be understood. While dealing with affect and emotions circulating in danger-zones, in particular fear and the death drive were helpful in understanding how fun/fear, safety/danger, peace/war and life/death were asserted, disrupted and transgressed.

The death drive exists at the junction between life and death; when accessed in places of ongoing conflict, some danger-zone tourists cross this junction. Desire for *jouissance*, that is, satisfaction of drives, represents a component of the death drive. Enticement to travel to areas (in the proximity) of ongoing conflict, I pro-posed, can be understood through the seeking of *jouissance*, which is the ultimate satisfaction. Satisfaction of the death drive, Freud maintained, can be achieved through the repetition compulsion principle, the tendency of repeating repressed and therefore unpleasant memories. He argued that what caused displeasure to one system could give pleasure to another one. I employed this understanding of the death drive to examine affective and emotional tourist experiences in Jordan and Palestine, especially tourists originating from countries like South Korea, India, or Saudi Arabia, which are in the proximity of an ongoing conflict. Repeating repressed (traumatic) memories of conflict when travelling in a country in turmoil bespeaks of a repetition compulsion in the Freudian sense. It points to engage-ments with the death drive.

Lacan reconceptualised the death drive beyond the repetition compulsion, as the desire for new experiences through which one can achieve *jouissance*. Another of Lacan's innovations was that the death drive is not anchored in biol-ogy and does not refer to the death of the biological organism. He mentioned the existence of two deaths, one that is brought about by life and another one that brings life. Thus, Lacan argued that it was death that sustained existence. It is this fuzzy boundary between life and death that some danger-zone tourists cross while accessing the death drive in places of ongoing conflict.

In relation to the *third aim* of understanding the relationship between tour-ism, danger and conflict, I argued that there exist tourists who travel to places of ongoing socio-political conflict. The mainstream tourism discourse (Hall, 1994; Hall et al., 2003; Pizam & Mansfeld, 1996) contends that tourism and conflict are located at opposite ends of the continuum and are, therefore, mutually exclusive.

Considering Adams's (2001) research on danger-zone tourism, which challenges this mainstream discourse, I continued to maintain that some tourists travel to areas of political turmoil in spite of the danger, sometimes even enticed by it. The framework of dark tourism was useful as I could address 'desires and interests which are not supposed to have a legitimate existence within the secular, moral discourse of the 20th century' (Seaton, 1996, p. 224).

I located research on danger-zone tourism within the increased interest in dark tourism. The use of the term 'dark tourism' was preferred throughout the book. This was an informed decision as I sought to challenge constructions of dark tourism as an 'unhelpful term [with] negative connotations' whereby the word 'dark' refers to ghoulish and macabre interests (Sharpley & Stone, 2009b, p. 249). Some researchers prefer the use of the term 'thanatourism' to distance their research from the 'unhelpfulness' and 'negative' aspects of dark tourism (Dunkley et al., 2011). In an attempt to avoid construction of a binary between dark tourism – unhelpful and negative – and thanatourism – acceptable and academic – I employed the term 'dark tourism' to refer to the wider subfield of tourist interests in death, disaster and atrocity (Lennon & Foley, 2000).

Within the frame of dark tourism/thanatourism, I also discussed other terms such as conflict tourism, morbid tourism, war tourism and politically oriented tourism. I considered these forms of tourism in relation to danger-zone tourism and concluded that, for the most part, these studies had an inherent assumption that tourists would travel to sites of death, disaster and atrocity only after the turmoil has subsided. Danger-zone tourism represents active engagements in places of ongoing conflict.

My contribution to dark tourism is that I bring into discussion danger-zone tourism, a form of tourism that 'in most Western societies [is] morally proscribed' (Seaton, 1996, p. 220). As I examined this 'morally proscribed' form of tourism, I unpacked the interconnections between tourism, danger and conflict. I chose Jordan and Palestine as my case studies in order to understand the intimate links between tourism and conflict. I made use of qualitative methods such as individual in-depth interviews, small group interviews, non-commercial photographs, written diaries and participant observation. I employed these methods with international tourists, tourism industry representatives and governmental officials in Jordan and Palestine. Findings show that danger and the ongoing conflict in the region do not necessarily act as deterrents for all tourists in Jordan and Palestine/Israel, but sometimes act even as impetuses for some.

The Israeli–Palestinian conflict has been ongoing for well over six decades, yet numbers of tourists in the region are increasing (Scott & Jafari, 2010). According to mainstream tourism discourses, which claim that tourism can only thrive in peaceful and tranquil situations, tourists should be deterred from visiting an area (in the proximity) of ongoing conflict such as Jordan and Palestine. Notwithstanding the rich cultural, historical and religious sites that Jordan and Palestine have, I argued that danger-zone tourists also experienced the conflict, the danger and the fear that makes one feel alive. In doing so, it was not my intention to portray Jordan and Palestine as dangerous places, but to understand the relationship between tourism and conflict, and to question the readiness with which some local tourism industry representatives present the area, especially Jordan, as an 'oasis of peace'. This research understood tourist engagements in places of danger and conflict beyond their frequent presentation 'as heritage, education or history' (Seaton, 1996, p. 224). In examining such experiences, socio-spatial and cultural theories on emotions, feelings and affects were used together with psychoanalytic theories on the death drive.

The book has brought together and examined dark tourism, affective geographies and psychoanalytic death drives to offer understandings of danger-zone tourism. I therefore proposed new ways of theorising danger-zone tourism by drawing on knowledges from these three academic areas.

Much more detailed work remains to be done. There is much potential for future research on affect, emotions, psychoanalysis and tourism. As I have insisted, emotions, feelings, affects and death drives are so pervasive they can be examined in relation to many forms of tourism. My comments on various subdisciplinary areas of tourism, geography and psychoanalysis are less informed than I would like, since it is impossible to be fully accomplished in all aspects that this project brings together.

Other future routes

The debates on danger-zone tourism presented in this book are not exhaustive. There still remains huge potential to delve into this form of tourism. I want to point out that danger-zone tourism and adventure tourism capitalise on the thrill of danger, thus future research could examine this interconnection. Concepts of risk, danger and adrenaline lie at the core of adventure travel. While both forms of tourism draw on danger and risk, danger-zone tourism differs from adventure tourism in that the latter refers to a wider range of activities including physically challenging activities such as bungee jumping or white water rafting (Adams, 2006; Kane & Tucker, 2004). While characteristics of adventure at a conceptual level may be shared by danger-zone and adventure tourism, the latter occurs out of a fascination with nature and a desire to push one's boundaries by practising types of extreme sports. Adventure means different things to different people and, according to the degree of risk involved, there is a range of adventurous activities from 'soft' to 'hard', that is, the higher the risk the harder the adventure (Shephard & Evans, 2005). Tourists may move along this continuum of intensity from 'soft' towards 'hard', as their level of curiosity increases and the level of risk perception alters.

Another exciting possibility for future research can examine risk and adventure narratives as a way to construct and enhance one's identity. Identity is regarded as an active, continuous process, as opposed to a static state (Elsrud, 2001). Risk-taking separates adventurers from the 'ordinary', 'mass', or 'package' tourists; the adventurous ones seek to drift away from the 'horde' in the search for 'true' experiences and to add to their travel narratives thus constructing their life story and identity. Being an adventurer gives one the prospects of class distinction, of collecting and bringing back stories of danger. Forming and maintaining class differentiation is achieved by creating lifestyles through commodities that include both objects and experiences acquired through travels (Bourdieu, 1984). Drawing on Bourdieu's theory of habitus, it is maintained that cultural and symbolic capital, as ingredients for class distinction, are also 'accumulated through journeys to remote and hazardous regions' (Mowforth & Munt, 2009, p. 126). Tales, stories and histories legitimise the process of travelling to dangerous places by sensationalising it, making it appear dangerous and risky (Elsrud 2001; Mowforth & Munt, 2009).

As identities can be defined along several social categories such as age, gender, race, sex, sexuality and so on, future research on danger-zone tourism can delve into such aspects. Examining danger-zone tourists' gendered and sexualised identities can challenge heteronormativity in tourism studies, which 'often continues to presume heterosexuality, or alternatively to present an asexual terrain, a world seemingly devoid of lust, passion and sex (Waitt et al., p. 782).

Using Bourdieu's theory of class differentiation, future research could examine how cultural and symbolic capital is sought by travelling to dangerous places. Tour guides to the world's most dangerous places could be analysed through the lens of this theory. Such a guide is Pelton's book *The World's Most Dangerous Places* (2000, 2003). The first edition was printed in 1998 and, in the following five years, four more editions received interesting if not positive reviews from most of the Western media, such as comments on the fifth edition's cover: 'The book your travel agent does not want you to read. Lucid, albeit insane' (*Weekend Australian*); 'A rampage through war-torn, disease-ridden, desperate lands' (*USA Today*, both cited in Pelton 2003). The guide has a corresponding website *Come Back Alive* and a mascot as well in the form of a skull laughing defiantly, mouth wide open, face adorned with big black sunglasses and a green baseball cap embossed with the 'DP' (dangerous places) logo.

Throughout Pelton's book, the narratives depicting Middle Eastern countries such as Lebanon, Iraq, Iran, Israel, underline the danger generated by the ongoing conflict in the area, with descriptions of suicide bombings or attacks of different sorts between Muslims and Jews. Danger is scaled on a five-star rating, with one star indicating the least danger. A symbol depicting a hand showing the 'full stop' gesture is awarded for the most dangerous places. Tourists can acquire symbolic capital by travelling to as many places, with high risk, as possible.

Another guide to 'dangerous places' is *Adventure Travel in the Third World: Everything You Need to Know to Survive in Remote and Hostile Destinations* (Randall & Perrin, 2003). This guide caught my attention because of its bold use of the concept of 'the Third World'. The East is constructed by this travel and 'survival' guide as the Third World, a place brand where 'normal' tourists do not dare, a place full of dangerous, exotic and inconceivable surprises: 'no matter how benign and peaceful it may seem getting to your destination, when you travel in the Third World, nothing is predictable' (p. 71). Everything here is described as being of poor quality, from photo films with 'poor-quality developing fluids and cheap photo paper' to primitive airports with 'no security when it comes to baggage' (pp. 29–42). The label 'Third World' has become a projection of Western representations of poverty, starvation, famine, corruption, political instabilities, religious fundamentalism and wars, amongst other unpredictable, inconsistent and pejorative facts. Prospects of class distinction are alluded to by opportunities of 'bringing back the stories an average tourist will never be able to tell' (p. 131).

Tourism and conflict are linked throughout the guides' descriptions which conjure up images of dangers, and fears in the minds of some hard-core danger-zone tourists. An interesting avenue of research could also be the analysis of vocabulary and images used throughout these guides that potentially glorify the horrors of danger, conflict and wars. Danger-zone tourists walk the ethical fine line of glorifying danger, fear, conflicts and wars. Research on danger-zone tourism can be enriched by further investigations into such ethical considerations.

In regards to the dialogue between tourism and psychoanalysis, there also remain great resources to be tapped into. In this book, Freud and Lacan's theories on the death drive are employed. These are, however, critiqued by Irigaray (1985). She critically asserts that 'in psychoanalytic parlance, the death drive can be worked out only by man, never, under any circumstances by woman. She merely "services" the work of the death instincts. Of man' (Irigaray, 1985, p. 53). Irigaray further maintains that in Freudian and Lacanian psychoanalysis, woman must suppress her drives 'by pacifying them and making them passive . . . In her role as "wife" she will be assigned to maintain coital homeostasis, "constancy"'(p. 53). Man, on the contrary, has the power 'to trans-form his death drives . . . in order to use his life to ward off death for as long as it takes to choose a death, man will have to work on building up his ego' (p. 54). Such a critical reading of the death drive could inform further research into the interconnections between tourism and psychoanalysis. By focusing on the death drive as conceptualised by Freud and Lacan, and interpreted by Ragland-Sullivan (1995) and Boothby (1991), my goal was to offer tourism studies a starting point of engagements with the death drive.

Concepts like fantasy and voyeurism, for example, can be further teased out to examine emotions, affects, drives and motivations in danger-zone tourism. In psychoanalysis, fantasy is a complex concept. In tourism studies, 'fantasy' is a term that speaks about tourist imagination and invokes exotic images of holiday places and activities (Kingsbury & Brunn, 2004). Fantasy refers to conscious fantasies or daydreams that can be in contrast with reality. It is different to phantasy, which represents an unconscious psychological activity (Frosch, 2003). Frosch has argued that the distinction between reality and fantasy/phantasy is a problematic one and will always break down, the reason being the activity and dynamism of the unconscious, which Freud maintained, pervaded all of our thinking. For Freud, phantasies are responses to frustrations, substitutes for what cannot be achieved in reality (Frosch, 2003). For Lacan, phantasy is akin to a frozen scene from a jammed reel in a film projector before a traumatic event happens (Kingsbury & Brunn, 2004). An interesting aspect to examine could be the ways tourism taps into fantasies and phantasies, dreams, desires and fears to conjure up enticing images of desirable and dangerous activities and locations.

Voyeurism represents another psychoanalytic concept that can be employed to examine desires to visit places that embody the danger and violence of a conflict (Lisle, 2000, 2004, 2007). In psychoanalysis, voyeurism refers to any sexual satisfaction obtained from vision; it usually is associated with a keyhole aspect and a violation of space, such as Freud's example of the Peeping Tom looking through the shutters at Lady Godiva (Sarup, 1992). Considered broadly, psychoanalytic theories of voyeurism could be applied to the desire to gaze upon something that is (socially constructed) as forbidden. This could be a place that embodies the violence and danger of an ongoing conflict such as a border, a checkpoint, or even a town located at the heart of the conflict. The desire to look upon something that is forbidden is counteracted by a repulsion of the object of desire since 'Repulsion operates from the direction of the conscious upon what is to be repressed . . . attraction is exercised by what was primarily repressed upon everything with which it can establish a connection' (Freud, trans. 1984, p. 148). This almost simultaneous attraction to and repulsion of the object under scrutiny is manifested by some tourists' disconcerting feelings to see soldiers with machine guns at a tourist site, and then immediate desire to take a picture of the whole situation as a souvenir of the moment. What is repressed and is in relation with the repulsion–attraction mechanism is the pleasure that is derived from such tense situations in a site of conflict.

Affective geographies and psychoanalysis present many exciting possibilities to further research on danger-zone tourism in particular, and tourism studies in general. This book has offered a nexus of tourism, socio-cultural geography and psychoanalysis to critically examine the diverse ways danger-zone tourism exists. It focused on the ways in which tourism is affectively as well as emotionally felt and practised in Jordanian and Palestinian places of conflict. It has shown that tourism and conflict do not mutually exclude each other; rather, tourism can exist in spaces of ongoing socio-political conflict. Some tourists are actually not deterred by, and in fact at times are even enticed, by the danger of the conflict. I focused on danger-zone tourist subjectivities and local guides as experiencing and performing sites of danger and conflict in embodied, emotional and sensuous ways. This book contributes to current critical understandings in tourism studies of dark tourism, affects, emotions and psychoanalysis.

Bibliography

Abu Tarboush, Y. (2010). Jerusalem vists sparks debate. *The Star*. Retrieved from www. star.com.jo.

Adams, K. M. (2001). Danger-zone tourism: Prospects and problems for tourism in tumultuous times. In P. Teo, T. C. Chang & K. C. Ho (eds), *Interconnected worlds: Tourism in Southeast Asia* (pp. 265–281). Oxford: Pergamon.

Adams, K. M. (2003). Global cities, terror, and tourism: The ambivalent allure of the urban jungle. In R. Bishop, J. Phillips & W.-W. Yeo (eds), *Postcolonial urbanism: Southeast Asian cities and global processes* (pp. 37–59). New York: Routledge.

Adams, K. M. (2006). Terror and tourism: Charting the ambivalent allure of the urban jungle. In C. Minca & T. Oakes (eds), *Travels in paradox: Remapping tourism* (pp. 205–228). Lanham, MD: Rowman & Littlefield.

Adamski, M. (2007). *Star Bulletin – Boxed In*. Retrieved from http://archives.starbulletin. com/2007/11/10/features/adamski.html.

Ahmed, S. (1997). Intimate touches: Proximity and distance in international feminist dialogues. *Oxford Literary Review, 19*(1), 19–46. doi: 10.3366/olr.1997.002.

Ahmed, S. (2004a). Collective feelings or the impressions left by others. *Theory, Culture & Society, 21*(2), 25–42.

Ahmed, S. (2004b). *The cultural politics of emotion*. New York: Routledge.

Ahmed, S. (2010). Happy objects. In M. Gregg & S. J. Seigworth (eds), *The affect theory reader* (pp. 29–51). London, England: Duke University Press.

Aitchison, C. C. (2005). Feminist and gender perspectives in tourism studies. *Tourist Studies, 5*(3), 207–224. doi:10.1177/1468797605070330.

Aitchison, C. C. (2007). Marking difference or making a difference: Constructing places, policies and knowledge of inclusion, exclusion and social justice in leisure, sport and tourism. In I. Ateljevic, A. Pritchard & N. Morgan (eds), *The critical turn in tourism studies: Innovative research methodologies* (pp. 77–90). Amsterdam, Netherlands: Elsevier.

Al Jazeera. (2011, 28 January). Thousands protest in Jordan. *Al Jazeera*. Retrieved from http://www.aljazeera.com/news/middleeast/2011/01/2011128125157509196.html.

Al Mahadin, S. (2007). Tourism and power relations in Jordan: Contested discourses and semiotic shifts. In R. Daher (ed.), *Tourism in the Middle East: Continuity, change, and transformation* (pp. 308–325). Clevedon, OH: Channel View Publications.

Alaszewski, A. (2006). *Using diaries for social research*. London: Sage.

Alternative Business Solutions. (2011). *Visit Palestine: Your guide to Palestine*. Retrieved from http://visitpalestine.ps/.

Alternative Tourism Group. (2008). *Palestine & Palestinian: Guidebook.* Ramallah, Palestine: Alternative Tourism Group.

Altinay, L., & Bowen, D. (2006). Politics and tourism interface: The case of Cyprus. *Annals of Tourism Research, 33*(4), 939–956. doi:10.1016/j.annals.2006.03.020.

Altinay, L., & Paraskevas, A. (2008). *Planning research in hospitality and tourism.* Amsterdam, Netherlands: Elsevier: Butterworth-Heinemann.

Alvesson, M., & Sköldberg, K. (2000). *Reflexive methodology: New vistas for qualitative research.* London: Sage.

Anastas, C. (2011). *Palestinian gifts and accommodation in Bethlehem – Palestine.* Retrieved from http://www.anastas-bethlehem.com/.

Anderson, K., & Gale, F. (1999). *Cultural geographies* (2nd edn). Melbourne, Vic., Australia: Longman.

Anderson, K., & Smith, S. J. (2001). Editorial: Emotional geographies. *Transactions of the Institute of British Geographers, 26*(1), 7–10. doi:10.1111/1475-5661.00002.

Andrews, H. (2005). Feeling at home: Embodying Britishness in a Spanish charter tourist resort. *Tourist Studies, 5*(3), 247–266. doi:10.1177/1468797605070336.

Araña, J. E., & León, C. J. (2008). The impact of terrorism on tourism demand. *Annals of Tourism Research, 35*(2), 299–315. doi:10.1016/j.annals.2007.08.003.

Arendt, H. (1970). *On violence.* New York: Harcourt Brace & World.

Ashcroft, B. (2004). Representation and its discontents: Orientalism, Islam and the Palestinian crisis. *Religion, 34*(2), 113–121. doi:10.1016/j.religion.2003.12.003.

Ashworth, G. J. (2002). Holocaust tourism: The experience of Kraków-Kazimierz. *International Research in Geographical and Environmental Education, 11*(4), 363–367. doi:10.1080/10382040208667504.

Askjellerud, S. (2003). The tourist: A messenger of peace? *Annals of Tourism Research, 30*(3), 741–744. doi:10.1016/S0160-7383(03)00049-5.

Ateljevic, I., Pritchard, A., & Morgan, N. (eds) (2007). *The critical turn in tourism studies: Innovative research methodologies.* Amsterdam, Netherlands: Elsevier.

ATG Alternative Tourism Group. (2010). *Alternative Tourism Group Palestine webpage.* Retrieved from http://www.atg.ps/.

Ayikoru, M., & Tribe, H. (2007). Enhancing the interpretive and critical approaches to tourism education enquiry through a discursive analysis. In I. Ateljevic, A. Pritchard & N. Morgan (eds), *The critical turn in tourism studies: Innovative research methodologies* (pp. 279–292). Amsterdam, Netherlands: Elsevier.

Bampton, R., & Cowton, C. J. (2002). The e-interview. *Forum: Qualitative Social Research, 3*(2), Article 9. Retrieved from http://www.qualitative-research.net/index.php/fqs/article/view/848/1843.

Bankey, R. (2002). Embodying agoraphobia: Rethinking geographies of women's fear. In L. Bondi (ed.), *Subjectivities, knowledges, and feminist geographies: The subjects and ethics of social research* (pp. 44–56). Lanham, MD: Rowan & Littlefield.

Baptism Site Commission. (2010). Baptism site visitors comparative chart [Unpublished manuscript]. Baptism Site Commission. Baptismal Site, Jordan.

Bar, D., & Cohen-Hattab, K. (2003). A new kind of pilgrimage: The modern tourist pilgrim of nineteenth century and early twentieth century Palestine. *Middle Eastern Studies, 39*(2), 131–148. doi:10.1080/714004511.

Bar-On, R. R. (1996). Measuring the effects on tourism of violence and of promotion following violent acts. In A. Pizam & Y. Mansfeld (eds), *Tourism, crime, and international security issues* (pp. 159–174). Chichester, England: John Wiley.

Bauman, Z. (2006). *Liquid fear*. Cambridge, England: Polity Press.

BBC. (2011). Jordan protests: Thousands rally over economic policies. Retrieved from http://www.bbc.com/news/world-middle-east-12257894.

Bedford, T., & Burgess, J. (2001). The focus-group experience. In M. Limb & C. Dwyer (eds), *Qualitative methodologies for geographers: Issues and debates* (pp. 121–135). London: Arnold.

Begley, L. (2009). The other side of fieldwork: Experiences and challenges of conducting research in the border area of Rwanda/eastern Congo. *Anthropology Matters, 11*(2), 1–11.

Beirman, D. (2002). Marketing of tourism destinations during a prolonged crisis: Israel and the Middle East. *Journal of Vacation Marketing, 8*(2), 167–176. doi:10.1177/135676670200800206.

Bell, D. (2009). Cyberspace/cyberculture. In R. Kitchin & N. Thrift (eds), *International encyclopedia of human geography* (pp. 468–472). Oxford: Elsevier.

Bennett, K. (2004). Emotionally intelligent research. *Area, 36*(4), 414–422. doi:10.1111/j.0004-0894.2004.00241.x.

Bennett, K. (2009). Challenging emotions. *Area, 41*(3), 244–251. doi:10.1111/j.1745-4959.2008.00872.x.

Bhattarai, K., Conway, D., & Shrestha, N. (2005). Tourism, terrorism and turmoil in Nepal. *Annals of Tourism Research, 32*(3), 669–688. doi:10.1016/j.annals.2004.08.007.

Bianchi, R. V. (2009). The 'critical turn' in tourism studies: A radical critique. *Tourism Geographies: An International Journal of Tourism Space, Place and Environment, 11*(4), 484–504. doi:10.1080/14616680903262653.

Bigné, J. E., & Andreu, L. (2004). Emotions in segmentation: An empirical study. *Annals of Tourism Research, 31*(3), 682–696. doi:10.1016/j.annals.2003.12.018.

Biran, A., & Hyde, K. F. (2013). Guest editorial: New perspectives on dark tourism. *International Journal of Culture, Tourism and Hospitality Research, 7*(3), 191–198.

Bishop, R., Phillips, J., & Yeo, W.-W. (eds) (2003). *Postcolonial urbanism: Southeast Asian cities and global processes*. New York: Routledge.

Blanchard, L., & Higgins-Desbiolles, F. (eds) (2013). *Peace through tourism: Promoting human security through international citizenship*. Abingdon, England: Routledge.

Blom, T. (2000). Morbid tourism – A postmodern market niche with an example from Althorp. *Norsk Geografisk Tidsskrift – Norwegian Journal of Geography, 54*(1), 29–36. doi:10.1080/002919500423564.

Bock, P. K. (1970). *Culture shock: A reader in modern cultural anthropology*. New York: Knopf.

Bondi, L. (1999a). Small steps: A reply to commentaries on 'stages on journeys'. *The Professional Geographer, 51*(3), 465–468. doi:10.1111/0033-0124.00183.

Bondi, L. (1999b). Stages on journeys: Some remarks about human geography and psychotherapeutic practice. *The Professional Geographer, 51*(1), 11–24. doi:10.1111/0033-0124.00141.

Bondi, L. (ed.) (2002). *Subjectivities, knowledges, and feminist geographies: The subjects and ethics of social research*. Lanham, MD: Rowan & Littlefield.

Bondi, L. (2003). Empathy and identification: Conceptual resources for feminist fieldwork. *ACME: An International E-journal for Critical Geographies, 2*(1), 64–76.

Bondi, L. (2005). Making connections and thinking through emotions: Between geography and psychotherapy. *Transactions of the Institute of British Geographers, 30*(4), 433–448. doi:10.1111/j.1475-5661.2005.00183.x.

Bondi, L., Davidson, J., & Smith, M. (2005). Introduction: Geography's 'emotional turn'. In J. Davidson, L. Bondi & M. Smith (eds), *Emotional geographies* (pp. 1–16). Aldershot, England: Ashgate.

Boothby, R. (1991). *Death and desire: Psychoanalytic theory in Lacan's return to Freud.* New York: Routledge.

Bornstein, A. (2008). Dispossession and empowerment in the ethnography of Palestinians in the occupied territories. *Dialectical Anthropology, 32*(4), 341–351.

Bosco, F. J., & Hermann, T. (2010). Interviewing: Fear and liking in the field. In D. DeLyser (ed.), *The SAGE handbook of qualitative geography* (pp. 193–207). Los Angeles, CA: Sage.

Botterill, D. (2007). A realist critique on the situated voice in tourism studies. In I. Ateljevic, A. Pritchard & N. Morgan (eds), *The critical turn in tourism studies: Innovative research methodologies* (pp. 121–129). Amsterdam, Netherlands: Elsevier.

Bourdieu, P. (1984). *Distinction: A social critique of the judgement of taste.* London: Routledge & Kegan Paul.

Bowman, G. (1991). Christian ideology and the image of a holy land: The place of Jerusalem pilgrimage in the various Christianities. In J. Eade & M. J. Sallnow (eds), *Contesting the sacred: The anthropology of Christian pilgrimage* (pp. 98–121). London: Routledge.

Bowman, G. (1995). The politics of tour guiding: Israeli and Palestinian guides in Israel and the Occupied Territories. In D. Harrison (ed.), *Tourism and the less developed countries* (pp. 121–134). Chichester, England: Wiley.

Bowman, G. (1996). Passion, power and politics in a Palestinian tourist market. In T. Selwyn (ed.), *The tourist image: Myths and myth making in tourism* (pp. 83–103). Chichester, England: John Wiley.

Bowman, G. (2001). The two deaths of Basem Rishmawi: Identity constructions and reconstructions in a Muslim-Christian Palestinian community. *Identities: Global Studies in Culture and Power, 8*(1), 47–81.

Bowman, G. (2007a). Israel's wall and the logic of encystation. *Focaal, 50*, 127–136. doi:10.3167/foc.2007.500109.

Bowman, G. (2007b). Viewing the Holy City: An anthropological perspectivalism. *Jerusalem Quarterly,* (31), 27–39.

Boym, S. (2001). *The future of nostalgia.* New York: Basic Books.

Braunstein, N. (2003). Desire and jouissance in the teachings of Lacan. In J.-M. Rabate (ed.), *The Cambridge companion to Lacan* (pp. 102–115). Cambridge, England: Cambridge University Press.

Braverman, I. (2011). Civilized Borders: A study of Israel's new crossing administration. *Antipode, 43*(2), 264–295. doi:10.1111/j.1467-8330.2010.00773.x.

Brin, E. (2006). Politically-oriented tourism in Jerusalem. *Tourist Studies, 6*(3), 215–243. doi:10.1177/1468797607076672.

Brin, E., & Noy, C. (2010). The said and the unsaid: Performative guiding in a Jerusalem neighbourhood. *Tourist Studies, 10*(1), 19–33. doi:10.1177/1468797610390982.

Bronfen, E. (1992). Death drive (Freud). In E. Wright (ed.), *Feminism and psychoanalysis: A critical dictionary* (pp. 52–57). Oxford: Blackwell.

Brookfield, S. (1990). *The skillful teacher: On technique, trust, and responsiveness in the classroom.* San Francisco, CA: Jossey-Bass Publishers.

Brown, D. (2002). Going digital and staying qualitative: Some alternative strategies for digitizing the qualitative research process. *3*(2). Retrieved from http://www.qualitative-research.net/index.php/fqs/article/view/851/1849.

Bruce, D., & Creighton, O. (2006). Contested identities: The dissonant heritage of European town walls and walled towns. *International Journal of Heritage Studies, 12*(3), 234–254. doi:10.1080/13527250600604498.

Bryman, A. (2004). *Social research methods* (2nd edn). Oxford: Oxford University Press.

B'Tselem. (2011). *B'Tselem: The Israeli information center for human rights in the Occupied Territories.* Retrieved from http://www.btselem.org/English/index.asp.

Buda, D. M. (2015). The death drive in tourism studies. *Annals of Tourism Research, 50,* 39–51. doi:10.1016/j.annals.2014.10.008.

Buda, D. M. (forthcoming 2015). Tourism in conflict areas: Complex entanglements in Jordan. *Journal of Travel Research.*

Buda, D. M., & McIntosh, A. J. (2013). Dark tourism and voyeurism: Tourist arrested for 'spying' in Iran. *International Journal of Culture, Tourism and Hospitality Research, 7*(3), 214–226.

Buda, D. M., d'Hauteserre, A. M., & Johnston, L. (2014). Feeling and Tourism Studies. *Annals of Tourism Research, 46,* 102–114.

Buda, D. M., & Shim, D. (2014). Desiring the dark: 'A taste for the unusual' in North Korean tourism? *Current Issues in Tourism,* pp. 1–6.

Burgess, J. (1999). The genesis of in-depth discussion groups: A response to Liz Bondi. *The Professional Geographer, 51*(3), 458–460. doi:10.1111/0033-0124.00181.

Burns, P., & Novelli, M. (eds) (2007). *Tourism and politics: Global frameworks and local realities.* Amsterdam, Netherlands: Elsevier.

Buscher, M., & Urry, J. (2009). Mobile methods and the empirical. *European Journal of Social Theory, 12*(1), 99–116. doi:10.1177/1368431008099642.

Butler, J. (2003). No, it's not anti-semitic. *London Review of Books, 25*(16), 19–21. Retrieved from http://www.lrb.co.uk/v25/n16/judith-butler/no-its-not-anti-semitic.

Cahoone, L. E. (ed.) (2002). *From modernism to postmodernism: An anthology* (2nd edn, Vol. 2). Malden, MA: Blackwell.

Calinescu, M. (1987). *Five faces of modernity: Modernism, avant-garde, decadence, kitsch, postmodernism.* Durham, NC: Duke University Press.

Callard, F. (2003). The taming of psychoanalysis in geography. *Social & Cultural Geography, 4*(3), 295–312. doi:10.1080/14649360309071.

Catherwood, C. (2006). *A brief history of the Middle East.* New York: Carroll & Graf.

Chambers, D. (2007). Interrogating the 'critical' in critical approaches to tourism research. In I. Ateljevic, A. Pritchard & N. Morgan (eds), *The critical turn in tourism studies: Innovative research methodologies* (pp. 105–119). Amsterdam, Netherlands: Elsevier.

Chen, A. S.-Y., Lin, Y.-C., & Sawangpattanakul, A. (2011). The relationship between cultural intelligence and performance with the mediating effect of culture shock: A case from Philippine laborers in Taiwan. *International Journal of Intercultural Relations, 35*(2), 246–258. doi:10.1016/j.ijintrel.2010.09.005.

Christians, C. G., & Chen, S.-L. S. (2004). Introduction: Technological environments and the evolution of social research methods. In M. D. Johns, S.-L. Chen & G. J. Hall (eds), *Online social research: Methods, issues & ethics* (pp. 15–24). New York: Peter Lang.

Cisneros-Puebla, C. A., Faux, R., & Mey, G. (2004). Qualitative researchers – stories told, stories shared: The storied nature of qualitative research. An introduction to the special issue: *FQS* interviews. *Forum: Qualitative Social Research, 5*(3), Article 37. Retrieved from http://nbn-resolving.de/urn:nbn:de:0114-fqs0403370.

Clarke, R. (2000). Self-presentation in a contested city: Palestinian and Israeli political tourism in Hebron. *Anthropology Today, 16*(5), 12–18.

Clifford, N. J., French, S., & Valentine, G. (eds) (2010). *Key methods in geography* (2nd edn). London: Sage.

Cloke, P. J., & Johnston, R. (2005). Deconstructing human geography's binaries. In P. J. Cloke & R. Johnston (eds), *Spaces of geographical thought: Deconstructing human geography's binaries* (pp. 1–20). London: Sage.

Clough, P. T. (2003). Affect and control: Rethinking the body 'beyond sex and gender'. *Feminist Theory, 4*(3), 359–364.

Clough, P. T. (2007). Introduction. In P. T. Clough, & J. Halley (eds), *The affective turn: Theorizing the social* (pp. 1–33). London: Duke University Press.

Clough, P. T. (2010). The affective turn: Political economy, biomedia, and bodies. In M. Gregg & S. J. Seigworth (eds), *The Affect Theory Reader* (pp. 206–225). London: Duke University Press.

Clough, P. T. & Halley, J. (eds) (2007). *The affective turn: Theorizing the social*. London: Duke University Press.

Cohen-Hattab, K. (2004a). Historical research and tourism analysis: The case of the tourist-historic city of Jerusalem. *Tourism Geographies: An International Journal of Tourism Space, Place and Environment, 6*(3), 279–302. doi:10.1080/146166804200 0249629.

Cohen-Hattab, K. (2004b). Zionism, tourism and the battle for Palestine: Tourism as a political-propaganda tool. *Israel Studies, 9*(1), 61–85.

Cohen-Hattab, K., & Katz, Y. (2001). The attraction of Palestine: Tourism in the years 1850–1948. *Journal of Historical Geography, 27*(2), 166–177.

Cohen-Hattab, K., & Shoval, N. (2007). Tourism development and cultural conflict: The case of 'Nazareth 2000'. *Social & Cultural Geography, 8*(5), 701–717. doi:10.1080/14649360701633220.

Cole, S. (2004). Shared benefits: Longitudinal research in eastern Indonesia. In J. Phillimore & L. Goodson (eds), *Qualitative research in tourism: Ontologies, epistemologies and methodologies* (pp. 292–310). New York: Routledge.

Cole, S. (2005). Action ethnography: Using participant observation. In B. W. Ritchie, P. Burns & C. Palmer (eds), *Tourism research methods: Integrating theory with practice* (pp. 63–72). Wallingford, England: CABI.

Coles, T. E., & Timothy, D. J. (eds) (2004). *Tourism, diasporas, and space*. London: Routledge.

Collins-Kreiner, N., & Mansfeld, Y. (2005). Mapping of the Holy Land: Contemporary religious mapping. *Tijdschrift voor Economische en Sociale Geografie, 96*(1), 105–120. doi:10.1111/j.1467-9663.2005.00442.x.

Collins-Kreiner, N., Mansfeld, Y., & Kliot, N. (2006). The reflection of a political conflict in mapping: The case of Israel's borders and frontiers. *Middle Eastern Studies, 42*(3), 381–408. doi:10.1080/00263200500521230.

Cook, I. (2000). *Cultural turns/geographical turns: Perspectives on cultural geography*. Harlow, England: Prentice Hall.

Cook Jr., W. J. (1990). The effect of terrorism on executives' willingness to travel internationally (Unpublished doctoral dissertation). City University of New York, New York.

Cope, M. (2009a). Grounded theory. In R. Kitchin & N. Thrift (eds), *International encyclopedia of human geography* (pp. 647–650). Oxford: Elsevier.

Cope, M. (2009b). Transcripts (coding and analysis). In R. Kitchin & N. Thrift (eds), *International encyclopedia of human geography* (pp. 350–354). Oxford: Elsevier.

Cope, M. (2010). Coding transcripts and diaries. In N. J. Clifford, S. French & G. Valentine (eds), *Key methods in geography* (2nd edn, pp. 440–452). London: Sage.

Crang, M. (2001). Field work: Making sense of group interviews. In M. Limb & C. Dwyer (eds), *Qualitative methodologies for geographers: Issues and debates* (pp. 215–233). London: Arnold.

Crang, M. (2002). Qualitative methods: The new orthodoxy? *Progress in Human Geography, 26*(5), 647–655. doi:10.1191/0309132502ph392pr.

Crang, M. (2003). Qualitative methods: Touchy, feely, look-see? *Progress in Human Geography, 27*(4), 494–504. doi:10.1191/0309132503ph445pr.

Crang, M. (2005). Qualitative methods: There is nothing outside the text? *Progress in Human Geography, 29*(2), 225–233. doi:10.1191/0309132505ph541pr.

Crang, M. (2010).Visual methods and methodologies. In D. DeLyser (ed.), *The SAGE handbook of qualitative geography* (pp. 208–224). Los Angeles, CA: Sage.

Crouch, D., & Desforges, L. (2003). The sensuous in the tourist encounter. *Tourist Studies,* *3*(1), 5–22. doi:10.1177/1468797603040528.

Crouch, M. D. (2012). *Flirting with space: Journeys and creativity.* Aldershot, England: Ashgate.

Crystal, D. (2003). *English as a global language* (2nd edn). Cambridge, England: Cambridge University Press.

Curti, G. H. (2008). From a wall of bodies to a body of walls: Politics of affect: Politics of memory: Politics of war. *Emotion, Space and Society, 1*(2), 106–118. doi:10.1016/j. emospa.2009.02.002.

Daher, R. (2007). *Tourism in the Middle East: Continuity, change, and transformation* (Vol. 9). Clevedon, OH: Channel View Publications.

D'Amore, L. J. (1988). Tourism – A vital force for peace. *Annals of Tourism Research, 15*(2), 269–270. doi:10.1016/0160-7383(88)90087-4.

Damasio, A. R. (2003). *Looking for Spinoza: Joy, sorrow, and the feeling brain.* New York: A Harvest Book Harcourt, Inc.

Dann, G. M. S. (1998). *The dark side of tourism* (Vol. 14). Aix-en-Provence, France: International Center for Research and Studies in Tourism.

Dann, G. M. S., & Seaton, A. V. (2001). *Slavery, contested heritage, and thanatourism.* New York: Haworth Hospitality Press.

Davidson, J. (2002). All in the mind?: Women, agoraphobia, and the subject of self-help. In L. Bondi (ed.), *Subjectivities, knowledges, and feminist geographies: The subjects and ethics of social research* (pp. 15–33). Lanham, MD: Rowan & Littlefield.

Davidson, J., & Milligan, C. (2004). Embodying emotion sensing space: Introducing emotional geographies. *Social & Cultural Geography, 5*(4), 523–532. doi:10.1080/146493 6042000317677.

Davidson, J., & Smith, M. (2003). Bio-phobias/techno-philias: Virtual reality exposure as treatment for phobias of 'nature'. *Sociology of Health & Illness, 25*(6), 644–661. doi:10.1111/1467-9566.00363.

Davidson, J., & Smith, M. (2009). Emotional geographies. In R. Kitchin & N. Thrift (eds), *International encyclopedia of human geography* (pp. 440–445). Oxford: Elsevier.

Davidson, J., Bondi, L., & Smith, M. (eds) (2005). *Emotional geographies.* Aldershot, England: Ashgate.

Davidson, J., Smith, M., Bondi, L., & Probyn, E. (2008). Emotion, space and society: Editorial introduction. *Emotion, Space and Society, 1*(1), 1–3. doi:10.1016/j.emospa.2008.10.002.

De Socio, M. (2010). Geographers mobilize: A network-diffusion analysis of the campaign to free Ghazi-Walid Falah. *Antipode, 42*(2), 310–335. doi:10.1111/j.1467-8330.2009.00749.x.

Dean, T. (2003). Lacan and queer theory. In J.-M. Rabate (ed.), *The Cambridge companion to Lacan* (pp. 238–252). Cambridge, England: Cambridge University Press.

Dear, M. (2001). The postmodern turn. In C. Minca (ed.), *Postmodern geography: Theory and praxis* (pp. 1–34). Oxford: Blackwell.

DeLyser, D. (ed.) (2010). *The SAGE handbook of qualitative geography.* Los Angeles, CA: Sage.

Denzin, N. K. (1991). *Images of postmodern society: Social theory and contemporary cinema.* London: Sage.

Denzin, N. K. (2004). Prologue: Online environments and interpretive social research. In M. D. Johns, S.-L. Chen & G. J. Hall (eds), *Online social research: Methods, issues & ethics* (pp. 1–14). New York: Peter Lang.

Denzin, N. K., & Lincoln, Y. S. (2000). *Handbook of qualitative research* (2nd edn). Thousand Oaks, CA: Sage.

Denzin, N. K., & Lincoln, Y. S. (2003). *Strategies of qualitative inquiry* (2nd edn). Thousand Oaks, CA: Sage.

Denzin, N. K., & Lincoln, Y. S. (eds) (2005). *The SAGE handbook of qualitative research* (3rd edn). Thousand Oaks, CA: Sage.

Desai, V., & Potter, R. B. (eds) (2006). *Doing development research*. London: Sage.

Dewsbury, J. D. (2009). Affect. In R. Kitchin & N. Thrift (eds), *International encyclopedia of human geography* (pp. 20–24). Oxford: Elsevier.

d'Hauteserre, A.-M. (2004). Postcolonialism, colonialism and tourism. In A. A. Lew, C. M. Hall & A. M. Williams (eds), *A companion to tourism* (pp. 235–245). Malden, MA: Blackwell.

d'Hauteserre, A.-M. (2011). Politics of imaging New Caledonia. *Annals of Tourism Research, 38*(2), 380–402. doi: 10.1016/j.annals.2010.09.004.

Dholakia, N., & Zhang, D. (2004). Online qualitative research in the age of e-commerce: Data sources and approaches. *Forum: Qualitative Social Research, 5*(2). Retrieved from http://www.qualitative-research.net/index.php/fqs/article/view/594/1290.

Dixon, D., & Straughan, E. (2010). Geographies of touch/touched by geography. *Geography Compass 4*(5), 449–549.

Dixon, D., Hawkins, H., & Straughan, E. (2012). Of human birds and living rocks: remaking aesthetics for post-human worlds. *Dialogues in Human Geography, 2*(3), 249–270.

Donge, J. K. V. (2006). Ethnography and participant observation. In V. Desai & R. B. Potter (eds), *Doing development research* (pp. 180–188). London: Sage.

Dowler, L. (2001). Fieldwork in the trenches: Participant observation in a conflict area. In M. Limb & C. Dwyer (eds), *Qualitative methodologies for geographers: Issues and debates* (pp. 153–164). London: Arnold.

Downes, P. (2007). Trapped in Bethlehem. *Hawaii Catholic Herald,* 30 November.

Duncan, J. S., Johnson, N. C., & Schein, R. H. (eds) (2004). *A companion to cultural geography*. Malden, MA: Blackwell.

Dunkley, R. A. (2007). Re-peopling tourism: A 'hot approach' to studying thanatourism experiences. In I. Ateljevic, A. Pritchard & N. Morgan (eds), *The critical turn in tourism studies: Innovative research methodologies* (pp. 371–385). Amsterdam, Netherlands: Elsevier.

Dunkley, R. A., Morgan, N., & Westwood, S. (2011). Visiting the trenches: Exploring meanings and motivations in battlefield tourism. *Tourism Management, 32*(4), 860–868. doi:10.1016/j.tourman.2010.07.011.

Eagleton, T. (2003). *Sweet violence: The idea of the tragic*. Malden, MA: Blackwell.

Easthope, A. (2001). Postmodernism and critical and cultural theory. In S. Sim (ed.), *The Routledge companion to postmodernism* (pp. 15–27). London: Routledge.

Eco, U. (1987). *Travels in hyperreality: Essays*. London: Pan.

Eco, U. (2001). *Five moral pieces*. London: Secker & Warburg.

Edensor, T. (2000).Walking in the British countryside: Reflexivity, embodied practices and ways to escape. *Body & Society, 6*(3–4), 81–106. doi:10.1177/1357034x00006003005.

Edensor, T. (2001). Performing tourism, staging tourism. *Tourist Studies, 1*(1), 59–81. doi:10.1177/146879760100100104.

Edensor, T. (2007). Sensing the ruin. *The Senses and Society, 2*(2), 217(216).

Elliot, J. (1983). Politics, power, and tourism in Thailand. *Annals of Tourism Research, 10*(3), 377–393. doi:10.1016/0160-7383(83)90063-4.

Elliott, J. (1997). *Tourism: Politics and public sector management*. London: Routledge.

Elsrud, T. (2001). Risk creation in traveling: Backpacker adventure narration. *Annals of Tourism Research, 28*(3), 597–617. doi:10.1016/S0160-7383(00)00061-x.

Falah, G.-W. (2004a). Truth at war and naming the intolerable in Palestine. *Antipode, 36*(4), 596–600. doi:10.1111/j.1467-8330.2004.00437.x.

Falah, G.-W. (2004b). War, peace and land seizure in Palestine's border area. *Third World Quarterly, 25*(5), 955–975. doi:10.1080/0143659042000232054.

Falah, G.-W. (2005a). Speaking the truth to power: Jim Blaut, counter-memory and justice in Palestine. *Antipode, 37*(5), 1033–1037. doi:10.1111/j.0066-4812.2005.00552.x.

Falah, G.-W. (2005b). The geopolitics of 'enclavisation' and the demise of a two-state solution to the Israeli–Palestinian conflict. *Third World Quarterly, 26*(8), 1341–1372. doi:10.1080/01436590500255007.

Falah, G.-W. (2007). The politics of doing geography: 23 days in the hell of Israeli detention [Guest editorial]. *Environment and Planning D, 25*, 587–593. doi:10.1068/d2504ed.

Falah, G.-W. (2008). Geography in ominous intersection with interrogation and torture: Reflections on detention in Israel. *Third World Quarterly, 29*(4), 749–766. doi:10.1080/01436590802052706.

Falah, G.-W., Flint, C., & Mamadouh, V. (2006). Just war and extraterritoriality: The popular geopolitics of the United States' war on Iraq as reflected in newspapers of the Arab world. *Annals of the Association of American Geographers, 96*(1), 142–164. doi:10.1111/j.1467-8306.2006.00503.x.

Fallon, F. (2003). After the Lombok riots: Is sustainable tourism achievable? In C. M. Hall, D. J. Timothy & D. T. Duval (eds), *Safety and security in tourism: Relationships, management, and marketing* (pp. 139–158). Binghamton, NY: Haworth.

Farish, M. (2009). Maps and the State. In R. Kitchin & N. Thrift (eds), *International encyclopedia of human geography* (pp. 442–454). Oxford: Elsevier.

Farrell, S., & Kershner, I. (2010, August 2). Rocket hits resort on border of Jordan and Israel. *New York Times*. Retrieved from http://www.nytimes.com/2010/08/03/world/middleeast/03israel.html.

Faulkner, H. W., Fredline, L., Jago, L., & Cooper, C. P. (2003). *Progressing tourism research* (Vol. 9). Clevedon, OH: Channel View Publications.

Faullant, R., Matzler, K., & Mooradian, T. A. (2011). Personality, basic emotions, and satisfaction: Primary emotions in the mountaineering experience. *Tourism Management, 32*(6), 1423–1430. doi:10.1016/j.tourman.2011.01.004.

Fedarko, K., Beyer, L., Lea, E., & Hornik, R. (1993, August 23). Holidays in hell. *Time, 142*(8). Retrieved from http://content.time.com/time/magazine/article/0,9171,979078,00.html.

Feifer, M. (1986). *Tourism in history: From imperial Rome to the present*. New York: Stein and Day.

Feist, J. (director). (2001). *Jordan – The Royal Tour* [Television documentary]. Los Angeles, CA: The Travel Channel & Check Six Productions.

Feld, S. (2005). Places sensed, senses placed. In D. Howes (ed.), *Empire of the senses: The sensual culture reader* (pp. 171–191). Oxford: Berg.

Fielding, N., Lee, R. M., & Blank, G. (2008). *The SAGE handbook of online research methods*. Los Angeles, CA: Sage.

FightBack! News. (2009). *Minnesota activists jailed in Israel*. Retrieved from http://www.fightbacknews.org/2009/08/minnesota-activists-jailed-in-israel.htm.

Fink, B. (1995). The Lacanian subject: Between language and jouissance. Princeton, NJ: Princeton University Press.

Fisher, P. (2002). *The vehement passions*. Princeton, NJ: Princeton University Press.

Flint, C., & Falah, G.-W. (2004). How the United States justified its war on terrorism: Prime morality and the construction of a 'just war'. *Third World Quarterly, 25*(8), 1379–1399. doi:10.1080/0143659042000308429.

Foley, M., & Lennon, J. J. (1996). Editorial: Heart of darkness. *International Journal of Heritage Studies, 2*(4), 195–197. doi:10.1080/13527259608722174.

Foucault, M. (2002). *Archaeology of knowledge*. London: Routledge.

Francisco, R. A. (1983). The political impact of tourism dependence in Latin America. *Annals of Tourism Research, 10*(3), 363–376. doi:10.1016/0160-7383(83)90062-2.

Franklin, A. (2001). The tourist gaze and beyond. *Tourist Studies, 1*(2), 115–131. doi:10.1177/146879760100100201.

Franklin, A., & Crang, M. (2001). The trouble with tourism and travel theory? *Tourist Studies, 1*(1), 5–22. doi:10.1177/146879760100100101.

Freud, S. (1938). *The basic writings of Sigmund Freud* (A. A. Brill, Trans.). New York: The Modern Library.

Freud, S. (1984). *On metapsychology, the theory of psychoanalysis: Beyond the pleasure principle, the ego and the id, and other works* (J. Strachey, Trans., Vol. 2). Harmondsworth, England: Penguin Books.

Frohlick, S., & Johnston, L. (2011). Naturalizing bodies and places: Tourism media campaigns and heterosexualities in Costa Rica and New Zealand. *Annals of Tourism Research, 38*(3), 1090–1109. doi:10.1016/j.annals.2011.01.012.

Frohlick, S. (2013). *Sexuality, women and tourism: Cross-border desires through contemporary travel*. London: Routledge.

Frosch, S. (2003). *Key concepts in psychoanalysis*. New York: New York University Press.

Furnham, A. (1984). Tourism and culture shock. *Annals of Tourism Research, 11*(1), 41–57. doi:10.1016/0160-7383(84)90095-1.

Furnham, A., & Bochner, S. (1986). *Culture shock: Psychological reactions to unfamiliar environments*. London: Methuen.

Garcia, A. C., Standlee, A. I., Bechkoff, J., & Yan, C. (2009). Ethnographic approaches to the internet and computer-mediated communication. *Journal of Contemporary Ethnography, 38*(1), 52–84. doi:10.1177/0891241607310839.

Garrod, B. (2008). Exploring place perception a photo-based analysis. *Annals of Tourism Research, 35*(2), 381–401. doi:10.1016/j.annals.2007.09.004.

Gatrell, J. D., & LaFary, E. W. (2009). Space–time. In R. Kitchin & N. Thrift (eds), *International encyclopedia of human geography* (pp. 276–285). Oxford: Elsevier.

Gelbman, A. (2008). Border tourism in Israel: Conflict, peace, fear and hope. *Tourism Geographies: An International Journal of Tourism Space, Place and Environment, 10*(2), 193–213. doi:10.1080/14616680802000022.

Gelbman, A., & Timothy, D. J. (2010). From hostile boundaries to tourist attractions. *Current Issues in Tourism, 13*(3), 239–259. doi:10.1080/13683500903033278.

Gennaro. (2009). First Western tourists visit Iraq. Retrieved from http://www.enduring-wanderlust.com/first-tourists-visit-iraq/.

Gibson, C. (2010). Geographies of tourism: (Un)ethical encounters. *Progress in Human Geography, 34*(4), 521–527. doi:10.1177/0309132509348688.

Gilbert, M. R. (1994). The politics of location: Doing feminist research at 'home'. *The Professional Geographer, 46*(1), 90–96. doi:10.1111/j.0033-0124.1994.00090.x.

Goodson, L., & Phillimore, J. (2004). The inquiry paradigm in qualitative research. In J. Phillimore & L. Goodson (eds), *Qualitative research in tourism: Ontologies, epistemologies and methodologies* (pp. 30–45). New York: Routledge.

Gouk, P., & Hills, H. (2005). Towards histories of emotions. In P. Gouk & H. Hills *Representing emotions: New connections in the histories of art, music and medicine*. Surrey, England: Ashgate.

174   *Affective tourism*

Göymen, K. (2000). Tourism and governance in Turkey. *Annals of Tourism Research,* *27*(4), 1025–1048. doi:10.1016/S0160-7383(99)00127-9.

Graves-Brown, P. (2000). *Matter, materiality, and modern culture.* London: Routledge.

Gray, C. H. (1997). *Postmodern war: The new politics of conflict.* London: Routledge.

Gregg, M., & Seigworth, G. J. (eds) (2010). *The affect theory reader.* Durham, NC: Duke University Press.

Gregory, D. (2004a). *The colonial present: Afghanistan, Palestine, and Iraq.* Malden, MA: Blackwell.

Gregory, D. (2004b). Palestine under siege. *Antipode, 36*(4), 601–606. doi:10.1111/j.1467-8330.2004.00438.x.

Grosz, E. (1992). Voyeurism/exhibitionism/the gaze. In E. Wright (ed.), *Feminism and psychoanalysis: A critical dictionary* (pp. 447–450). Oxford: Blackwell.

Hack, S. (2007, January). A conversation with Jordan's King Abdullah II. *Conde Nast Traveler.* Retrieved from http://www.concierge.com/cntraveler/articles/10529?page Number=2.

Hall, C. M. (1994). *Tourism and politics: Policy, power, and place.* Chichester, England: Wiley.

Hall, C. M. (2004). Reflexivity and tourism research: Situating myself and/with others. In J. Phillimore & L. Goodson (eds), *Qualitative research in tourism: Ontologies, epistemologies and methodologies* (pp. 137–155). New York: Routledge.

Hall, C. M. (ed.) (2011). *Fieldwork in tourism: Methods, issues and reflections.* London: Routledge.

Hall, C. M., & O'Sullivan, V. (1996). Tourism, political stability and violence. In A. Pizam & Y. Mansfeld (eds), *Tourism, crime, and international security issues* (pp. 105–121). Chichester, England: Wiley.

Hall, C. M., Timothy, D. J., & Duval, D. T. (eds) (2003). *Safety and security in tourism: Relationships, management, and marketing.* Binghamton, NY: Haworth.

Hallward, M. C. (2009). Creative responses to separation: Israeli and Palestinian joint activism in Bil'in. *Journal of Peace Research, 46*(4), 541–558. doi:10.1177/0022343309334612.

Hardwick, S. W. (2009). Case study approach. In R. Kitchin & N. Thrift (eds), *International encyclopedia of human geography* (pp. 441–445). Oxford: Elsevier.

Hareyan, A. (2009). *Some adventure tourists choose Iraq.* Retrieved from http://www.huliq.com/1/78758/some-adventure-tourists-chose-iraq.

Harrison, D. (ed.) (1995). *Tourism and the less developed countries.* Chichester, England: Wiley.

Hartmann, R. (2009). Tourism to places with a difficult past: A discussion paper on recent research trends and concepts: Heritage tourism, dissonant heritage tourism, thanatourism, dark tourism, holocaust tourism [Unpublished manuscript]. University of Colorado, Department of Geography and Environmental Sciences. Denver, CO.

Hawkins, H., & Straughan, E. (2012). Nano-art, dynamic matter and the sight/sound of touch. *Geoforum 51,* 130–139.

Hazbun, W. (2008). *Beaches, ruins, resorts: The politics of tourism in the Arab world.* Minneapolis, MN: University of Minnesota Press.

Heller, A. (1999). *A theory of modernity.* Oxford: Blackwell.

Henderson, J. C. (2007). *Tourism crises: Causes, consequences and management.* Amsterdam, Netherlands: Butterworth-Heinemann.

Henderson, V. L. (2008). Is there hope for anger? The politics of spatializing and (re)producing an emotion. *Emotion, Space and Society, 1*(1), 28–37. doi:10.1016/j.emospa.2008.07.001.

Hesse-Biber, S. N., & Leavy, P. (2008). *Handbook of emergent methods*. New York: Guilford Press.

Hetherington, K. (2003). Spatial textures: Place, touch, and praesentia. *Environment and Planning A, 35*(11), 1933–1944. doi:10.1068/a3583.

Hill, B., Gibbons, D., Illum, S., & Var, T. (1995). International Institute for Peace Through Tourism. *Annals of Tourism Research, 22*(3), 709–709. doi:10.1016/0160-7383(94)00106-3.

Hine, C. (2005). *Virtual methods: Issues in social research on the Internet*. Oxford: Berg.

Hinterland Travel. (2011). *Hinterland Travel webpage*. Retrieved from http://www.hinterlandtravel.com/.

Holden, A. (2005). *Tourism studies and the social sciences*. Milton Park, England: Routledge.

Holy Land Trust. (2010). *Holy Land Trust*. Retrieved from http://www.holylandtrust.org/.

Hopkins, P. E. (2007). Thinking critically and creatively about focus groups. *Area, 39*(4), 528–535. doi:10.1111/j.1475-4762.2007.00766.x.

Hornby, A. S., Wehmeier, S., McIntosh, C., Turnbull, J., & Ashby, M. (eds) (2005). *Oxford advanced learner's dictionary of current English* (7th edn). Oxford: Oxford University Press.

Hottola, P. (2004). Culture confusion: Intercultural adaptation in Tourism. *Annals of Tourism Research, 31*(2), 447–466. doi:10.1016/j.annals.2004.01.003.

Hourani, A. (1991). *A history of the Arab peoples*. London: Faber.

House of Travel. (2011). *House of Travel website*. Retrieved from http://www.houseoftravel.co.nz.

Howes, D. (ed.) (2005). *Empire of the senses: The sensual culture reader*. Oxford: Berg.

Hoyt, R. G. (2000). Israel & Palestine. *Commonweal, 127*(1), 11.

International Court of Justice. (2004). *Legal consequences of the construction of a wall in the Occupied Palestinian Territory*. Retrieved from http://www.icj-cij.org/.

Ioannides, D., & Ioannides, M. C. (2004). Jewish past as a 'foreign country'. In T. E. Coles (ed.), *Tourism, diasporas, and space* (pp. 95–110). London: Routledge.

Irigaray, L. (1985). *Speculum of the other woman*. Ithaca, NY: Cornell University Press.

Isaac, R. K. (2010). Alternative tourism: New forms of tourism in Bethlehem for the Palestinian tourism industry. *Current Issues in Tourism, 13*(1), 21–36. doi:10.1080/13683500802495677.

Israel Guide: Hotels, Apartments, Car Rent, Touring. (2011). *One Day Tour to PETRA in Jordan*. Retrieved from http://www.israel-guide.com/touring/petra_tour.html.

Israeli Ministry of Defence. (2007). *Israel's security fence*. Retrieved from http://www.securityfence.mod.gov.il.

Jackson, P. (2001). Making sense of qualitative data. In M. Limb & C. Dwyer (eds), *Qualitative methodologies for geographers: Issues and debates* (pp. 199–214). London: Arnold.

Jacobs, J. (2010). Re-branding the Levant: Contested heritage and colonial modernities in Amman and Damascus. *Journal of Tourism and Cultural Change, 8*(4), 316–326.

Jafari, J. (1989). Tourism and peace. *Annals of Tourism Research, 16*(3), 439–443. doi:10.1016/0160-7383(89)90059-5.

Jamal, T., & Hollinshead, K. (2001). Tourism and the forbidden zone: The underserved power of qualitative inquiry. *Tourism Management, 22*(1), 63–82. doi:10.1016/S0261-5177(00)00020-0.

Jamal, T., & Robinson, M. (eds) (2009). *The SAGE handbook of tourism studies*. London: Sage.

James, W. (1884). What is an emotion? *Mind, 9*(34), 188–205.

Jameson, F. (2002). From 'The Cultural Logic of Late Capitalism' (L. E. Cahoone, Trans.). In L. E. Cahoone (ed.), *From modernism to postmodernism: An anthology* (2nd edn, Vol. 2). Malden, MA: Blackwell Publishers.

Jamieson, J. (2000). Negotiating danger in fieldwork on crime: A researcher's tale. In G. Lee-Treweek & S. Linkogle (eds), *Danger in the field: Risk and ethics in social research* (pp. 61–71). London: Routledge.

Jamoul, L. (2004). Palestine: In search of dignity. *Antipode, 36*(4), 581–595. doi:10.1111/j.1467-8330.2004.00436.x.

Jenkins, O. (2003). Photography and travel brochures: The circle of representation. *Tourism Geographies, 5*(3), 305–328. doi:10.1080/14616680309715.

Jerusalem (2011). *In Encyclopaedia Britannica.* Retrieved from http://www.britannica.com /EBchecked/topic/302812/Jerusalem.

Jerusalem (Reuters). (2011, May 16). Israel-Palestine: Violence erupts on three borders. *Huffington Post website.* Retrieved from http://www.huffingtonpost.com/2011/05/16/israel-palestine-violence_n_862450.html.

Johnston, L. (2001). (Other) bodies and tourism studies. *Annals of Tourism Research, 28*(1), 180–201. doi:10.1016/S0160-7383(00)00012-8.

Johnston, L. (2005a). Man/Woman. In P. J. Cloke & R. Johnston (eds), *Spaces of geographical thought: Deconstructing human geography's binaries* (pp. 119–141). London: Sage.

Johnston, L. (2005b). *Queering tourism: Paradoxical performances at gay pride parades.* London: Routledge.

Johnston, L. (2007). Mobilizing pride/shame: Lesbians, tourism and parades. *Social & Cultural Geography, 8*(1), 29–45. doi:10.1080/14649360701251528.

Johnston, L. (2012). Sites of excess: The spatial politics of touch for drag queens in Aotearoa New Zealand. *Emotion, Space and Society, 5*(1), 1–9. doi:10.1016/j.emospa.2010.02.003.

Jones, O. (2005). An ecology of emotion, memory, self and landscape. In J. Davidson, L. Bondi & M. Smith (eds), *Emotional geographies* (pp. 205–219). Aldershot, England: Ashgate.

Jordan. (2011). In *Encyclopaedia Britannica.* Retrieved from http://www.britannica.com. / EBchecked/topic/306128/Jordan.

Jordan Times (2011). UN supports Israeli claim on Lebanon clash. Retrieved from http://jordantimes.com/un-supports-israeli-claim-on-lebanon-clash.

Jordan Society of Tourism and Travel Agents. (2011). *Jordan Society of Tourism and Travel Agents webpage.* Retrieved from http://www.jsta.org.jo/english.htm.

Jordan Tourism Board. (2009). Travel and tourism Jordan. Executive summary: A committed government [Unpublished manuscript]. Jordan Tourism Board. Amman, Jordan.

Jordan Tourism Board. (2011). *Entry into Jordan – Visa requirements.* Retrieved from http://www.visitjordan.com/visitjordan_cms/GeneralInformation/EntryintoJordan/tabid/61/Default.aspx.

Kamberelis, G., & Dimitriadis, G. (2005). Focus groups: Strategic articulations of pedagogy, politics and enquiry. In N. K. Denzin & Y. S. Lincoln (eds), *The SAGE handbook of qualitative research* (3rd edn, pp. 887–907). Thousand Oaks, CA: Sage.

Kane, M. J., & Tucker, H. (2004). Adventure tourism: The freedom to play with reality. *Tourist Studies, 4*(3), 217–234. doi:10.1177/1468797604057323.

Karatnycky, A. (2005). *Freedom in the Middle East and North Africa: A freedom in the world special edition.* New York: Freedom House.

Kaur, R., & Hutnyk, J. (eds) (1999). *Travel worlds: Journeys in contemporary cultural politics.* London: Zed Books.

Kelly, M. (1998). Jordan's potential tourism development. *Annals of Tourism Research, 25*(4), 904–918. doi:10.1016/S0160-7383(98)00027-9.

Kim, S. S., Prideaux, B., & Prideaux, J. (2007). Using tourism to promote peace on the Korean Peninsula. *Annals of Tourism Research, 34*(2), 291–309. doi:10.1016/j. annals.2006.09.002.

Kingsbury, P. T. (2003). Psychoanalysis, a gay spatial science? *Social & Cultural Geography, 4*(3), 347–367. doi:10.1080/14649360309080.

Kingsbury, P. T. (2004). Psychoanalytic approaches. In J. S. Duncan, N. C. Johnson & R. H. Schein (eds), *A companion to cultural geography* (pp. 108–120). Malden, MA: Blackwell.

Kingsbury, P. T. (2005). Jamaican tourism and the politics of enjoyment. *Geoforum, 36*(1), 113–132. doi:10.1016/j.geoforum.2004.03.012.

Kingsbury, P. T. (2007). The extimacy of space. *Social & Cultural Geography, 8*(2), 235–258. doi:10.1080/14649360701360196.

Kingsbury, P. T. (2009a). Psychoanalysis. In R. Kitchin & N. Thrift (eds), *International encyclopedia of human geography* (pp. 480–486). Oxford: Elsevier.

Kingsbury, P. T. (2009b). Psychoanalytic theory/psychoanalytic geographies. In R. Kitchin & N. Thrift (eds), *International encyclopedia of human geography* (pp. 487–494). Oxford: Elsevier.

Kingsbury, P. (2010). Locating the Melody of the Drives. *The Professional Geographer, 62*(4), 519–533.

Kingsbury, P. (2014). Becoming literate in desire with Alan Partridge. *Cultural Geographies.* doi: 10.1177/1474474014536854.

Kingsbury, P. T., & Brunn, S. D. (2003). Traversing the fantasies of post-September 11 travel magazines. In C. M. Hall, D. J. Timothy & D. T. Duval (eds), *Safety and security in tourism: Relationships, management, and marketing* (pp. 39–61). Binghamton, NY: Haworth Press.

Kingsbury, P. T., & Brunn, S. D. (2004). Freud, tourism, and terror: Traversing the fantasies of post-September 11 travel magazines. *Journal of Travel & Tourism Marketing, 15*(2), 39–61. doi:10.1300/J073v15n02_03.

Kingsbury, P. T., & Pile, S. (eds) (2014). *Psychoanalytic geographies.* Farnham, England: Ashgate.

Kneale, J. (2001). Working with groups. In M. Limb & C. Dwyer (eds), *Qualitative methodologies for geographers: Issues and debates* (pp. 136–150). London: Arnold.

Knudsen, B. T. (2011). Thanatourism: Witnessing difficult pasts, *Tourist Studies 11*(1), 55–72.

Kreck, L. A. (1989). The semantics of the word 'peace'. *Annals of Tourism Research, 16*(3), 429–430. doi:10.1016/0160-7383(89)90054-6.

Lacan, J. (1977a). *Écrits: A selection* (A. Sheridan, Trans.). New York: Norton.

Lacan, J. (1977b). *The four fundamental concepts of psycho-analysis* (A. Sheridan, Trans.). London: Hogarth Press.

Lane, M. (2003). *Why tourists are going back to Iraq.* Retrieved from http://news.bbc. co.uk/2/hi/magazine/3076980.stm.

Latham, A. (2003). Research, performance, and doing human geography: Some reflections on the diary-photograph, diary-interview method. *Environment and Planning A, 35*(11), 1993–2017. doi:10.1068/a3587.

Le Breton, D. (2000). Playing symbolically with death in extreme sports. *Body & Society, 6*(1), 1–11. doi:10.1177/1357034x00006001001.

Lee, R. M. (1993). *Doing research on sensitive topics.* London: Sage.

Lee-Treweek, G., & Linkogle, S. (eds) (2000). *Danger in the field: Risk and ethics in social research.* London: Routledge.

Leiper, N. (2004). *Tourism management* (3rd edn). Sydney, NSW, Australia: Hospitality Press.

Lennon, J. J., & Foley, M. (2000). *Dark tourism*. London: Continuum.

Lew, A. A., Hall, C. M., & Williams, A. M. (eds) (2004). *A companion to tourism*. Malden, MA: Blackwell.

Lewis, B. (1995). *The Middle East: A brief history of the last 2,000 years*. New York: Scribner.

Lickorish, L. J., & Jenkins, C. L. (1997). *An introduction to tourism*. Oxford: Butterworth-Heinemann.

Limb, M., & Dwyer, C. (eds) (2001). *Qualitative methodologies for geographers: Issues and debates*. London: Arnold.

Linkogle, S. (2000). Realjo: Danger in the crowd. In G. Lee-Treweek & S. Linkogle (eds), *Danger in the field: Risk and ethics in social research* (pp. 132–146). London: Routledge.

Lisle, D. (2000). Consuming danger: Reimagining the war/tourism divide. *Alternatives: Global, Local, Political, 25*(1), 91–116.

Lisle, D. (2004). Gazing at Ground Zero: Tourism, voyeurism and spectacle. *Journal for Cultural Research, 8*(1), 3–21. doi:10.1080/1479758042000797015.

Lisle, D. (2007). Defending voyeurism: Dark tourism and the problem of global security. In P. Burns & M. Novelli (eds), *Tourism and politics: Global frameworks and local realities* (pp. 333–346). Amsterdam, Netherlands: Elsevier.

Listerborn, C. (2002). Understanding the geography of women's fear: Towards a reconceptualization of fear and space. In L. Bondi (ed.), *Subjectivities, knowledges, and feminist geographies: The subjects and ethics of social research* (pp. 34–43). Lanham, MD: Rowan & Littlefield.

Litvin, S. W., & Brewer, J. D. (2008). Charleston, South Carolina tourism and the presentation of urban slavery in an historic southern city. *International Journal of Hospitality & Tourism Administration, 9*(1), 71–84. doi:10.1080/15256480801910541.

Lloyd-Evans, S. (2006). Focus groups. In V. Desai & R. B. Potter (eds), *Doing development research* (pp. 153–162). London: Sage.

Lo, I. S., McKercher, B., Lo, A., Cheung, C., & Law, R. (2011). Tourism and online photography. *Tourism Management, 32*(4), 725–731. doi:10.1016/j.tourman.2010.06.001.

Lonely Planet. (2009). *Introducing Jordan*. Retrieved from http://www.lonelyplanet.com/jordan.

Longhurst, R. (1996). Refocusing groups: Pregnant women's geographical experiences of Hamilton, New Zealand/Aotearoa. *Area, 28*(2), 143–149.

Longhurst, R. (2003). Semi-structured interviews and focus groups. In N. J. Clifford & G. Valentine (eds), *Key methods in geography* (pp. 117–132). London: Sage.

Longhurst, R. (2009a). Embodied knowing. In R. Kitchin & N. Thrift (eds), *International encyclopedia of human geography* (pp. 429–433). Oxford: Elsevier.

Longhurst, R. (2009b). Interviews: In-depth, semi-structured. In R. Kitchin & N. Thrift (eds), *International encyclopedia of human geography* (pp. 580–584). Oxford: Elsevier.

Longhurst, R. (2010). Semi-structured interviews and focus groups. In N. J. Clifford, S. French & G. Valentine (eds), *Key methods in geography* (2nd edn, pp. 103–115). London: Sage.

Low, K. E. Y. (2005). Ruminations on smell as a sociocultural phenomenon. *Current Sociology, 53*(3), 397–417. doi: 10.1177/0011392105051333.

MacCannell, D. (1992). Jouissance. In E. Wright (ed.), *Feminism and psychoanalysis: A critical dictionary* (pp. 185–188). Oxford, England: Blackwell.

MacCannell, D. (1999). *The tourist: A new theory of the leisure class.* Berkeley, CA: University of California Press.

MacCannell, D. (2000). Postmodernism. In J. Jafari (ed.), *Encyclopedia of tourism* (pp. 457–458). London: Routledge.

MacCannell, D. (2001). Tourist agency. *Tourist Studies, 1*(1), 23–37. doi:10.1177/146879760100100102.

Macfie, A. L. (2000). Introduction. In A. L. Macfie (ed.), *Orientalism: A reader* (pp. 1–8). New York: New York University Press.

MacKay, K. J., & Couldwell, C. M. (2004). Using visitor-employed photography to investigate destination image. *Journal of Travel Research, 42*(4), 390–396. doi:10.1177/0047287504263035.

Macnaghten, P., & Urry, J. (2000). Bodies of nature: Introduction. *Body & Society, 6*(3–4), 1–11. doi:10.1177/1357034x00006003001.

Malkawi, K., & Qatamin, R. (2010, August 3). Rocket incident unlikely to affect Aqaba tourism. *Jordan Times.* Retrieved from http://www.jordantimes.com/index.php?news=28875.

Mann, C., & Stewart, F. (2000). *Internet communication and qualitative research: A handbook for researching online.* London: Sage.

Mansfeld, Y. (1994). The middle east conflict and tourism to Israel, 1967–90. *Middle Eastern Studies, 30*(3), 646–667. doi:10.1080/00263209408701016.

Mansfeld, Y. (1996). War, terrorism and the 'Middle East' factor. In A. Pizam & Y. Mansfeld (eds), *Tourism, crime, and international security issues* (pp. 265–278). Chichester, England: Wiley.

Maoz, D. (2006). The mutual gaze. *Annals of Tourism Research, 33*(1), 221–239. doi:10.1016/j.annals.2005.10.010.

Maoz, D. (2007). Backpackers' motivations: the role of culture and nationality. *Annals of Tourism Research, 34*(1), 122–140. doi:10.1016/j.annals.2006.07.008.

Maoz, D., & Bekerman, Z. (2010). Searching for Jewish answers in Indian resorts: The postmodern traveler. *Annals of Tourism Research, 37*(2), 423–439. doi:10.1016/j.annals.2009.10.015.

Markwell, K. W. (2000). Photo-documentation and analyses as research strategies in human geography. *Australian Geographical Studies, 38*(1), 91–98. doi:10.1111/1467-8470.00103.

Massumi, B. (ed.) (1993). *The politics of everyday fear.* Chicago, IL: University of Minnesota Press.

Massumi, B. (1995). The autonomy of affect. *Cultural Critique, 31*, The Politics of Systems and Environment, Part II (Autumn), 83–109.

Massumi, B. (1998). Requiem for our prospective dead (Toward a participatory critique of capitalist power). In E. Kaufman and K. J. Heller (eds), *Deleuze & Guattari: New mappings in politics, philosophy, and culture* (pp. 40–64). Minneapolis, MN: University of Minnesota Press.

Massumi, B. (2002a). *Parables for the virtual: Movement, affect, sensation.* Durham, NC: Duke University Press.

Massumi, B. (2002b). Introduction: Like a thought. In B. Massumi (ed.), *A shock to thought: Expression after Deleuze and Guattari* (pp. xiii–xxxix). London: Routledge.

Matthews, H. G. (1978). *International tourism: A political and social analysis.* Cambridge, MA: Schenkman.

Matthews, H. G., & Richter, L. K. (1991). Political science and tourism. *Annals of Tourism Research, 18*(1), 120–135. doi:10.1016/0160-7383(91)90043-B.

Maxwell, K. (2004). *Word of the week archive.* Retrieved from http://www.macmillandictionaries.com/wordoftheweek/archive/040821-grief-tourist.htm.

McDowell, L. (2010). Interviewing: Fear and liking in the field. In D. DeLyser (ed.), *The SAGE handbook of qualitative geography* (pp. 156–171). Los Angeles, CA: Sage.

McEwan, C. (2006). Using images, films and photography. In V. Desai & R. B. Potter (eds), *Doing development research* (pp. 231–240). London: Sage.

McGahey, S. (2006). Tourism development in Iraq: The need for support from international academia. *International Journal of Tourism Research, 8*(3), 235–239. doi:10.1002/jtr.571.

McGregor, J. (2006). Diaries and case studies. In V. Desai & R. B. Potter (eds), *Doing development research* (pp. 200–206). London: Sage.

McRae, L. (2003). Rethinking tourism. *Tourist Studies, 3*(3), 235–251. doi:10.1177/1468797603049658.

Mestrovic, S. G. (1991). *The coming fin de siecle: An application of Durkheim's sociology to modernity and postmodernism.* London: Routledge.

Meth, P. (2009). Diaries (Video, Audio or Written). In R. Kitchin & N. Thrift (eds), *International encyclopedia of human geography* (pp. 150–155). Oxford: Elsevier.

Mihalič, T. (1996).Tourism and warfare – the case of Slovenia. In A. Pizam & Y. Mansfeld (eds), *Tourism, crime, and international security issues* (pp. 231–246). Chichester, England: Wiley.

Mikula, G., Scherer, K. R., & Athenstaedt, U. (1998).The role of injustice in the elicitation of differential emotional reactions. *Personality & Social Psychology Bulletin, 24*(7), 769–783.

Miles, M. B., & Huberman, A. M. (1994).*Qualitative data analysis: An expanded sourcebook* (2nd edn). Thousand Oaks, CA: Sage Publications.

Miles, W. F. S. (2010). Dueling border tours: Jerusalem. *Annals of Tourism Research, 37*(2), 555–559. doi: 10.1016/j.annals.2009.11.003.

Milton-Edwards, B. (2007). *Contemporary politics in the Middle East* (2nd edn). Cambridge, England: Polity.

Mitas, O., Yarnal, C., & Chick, G. (2012). Jokes build community: Mature tourists' positive emotions. *Annals of Tourism Research, 39*(4), 1884–1905.

Morris, B. (2002). *The road to Jerusalem: Glubb Pasha, Palestine and the Jews.* London: I.B. Tauris.

Morris, I. L., Oppenheimer, J. A., & Sołtan, K. E. (eds) (2004). *Politics from anarchy to democracy: Rational choice in political science.* Stanford, CA: Stanford University Press.

Moser, S. (2008). Personality: A new positionality? *Area, 40*(3), 383–392. doi:10.1111/j.1475-4762.2008.00815.x.

Moufakkir, O., & Kelly, I. (eds) (2010). *Tourism, progress, and peace.* Wallingford, England: CAB International.

Mowforth, M., & Munt, I. (2009). *Tourism and sustainability: Development, globalisation and new tourism in the third world* (3rd edn). London: Routledge.

Mura, P. (2010). 'Scary . . . but I like it!' Young tourists' perceptions of fear on holiday. *Journal of Tourism and Cultural Change, 8*(1), 30–49. doi:10.1080/14766825.2010.482209.

Muzaini, H., Teo, P., & Yeoh, B. S. A. (2007). Intimations of postmodernity in dark tourism: The fate of history at Fort Siloso, Singapore. *Journal of Tourism and Cultural Change, 5*(1), 28–45. doi:10.2167/jtcc082.0.

Nast, H. J. (2000). Mapping the 'unconscious': Racism and the Oedipal Family. *Annals of the Association of American Geographers, 90*(2), 215–255. doi:10.1111/0004-5608.00194.

National Public Radio. (2009). Western tourist reflects on Iraq visit [Transcript of podcast]. Retrieved from http://www.npr.org/templates/story/story.php?storyId=102187982.

Neumayer, E. (2004). The impact of political violence on tourism: Dynamic cross-national estimation. *Journal of Conflict Resolution, 48*(2), 259–281. 10.1177/0022002703262358.

Neveu, N. (2010). Islamic tourism in Jordan: Sacred topography and state ambitions. In N. Scott & J. Jafari (eds), *Tourism in the Muslim world* (pp. 141–157). Bingley, England: Emerald.

New Open World Corporation. (2011). *Looking back looking foward.* Retrieved from http://www.new7wonders.com/archives/story/looking-back-looking-forward.

New Zealand Ministry of Foreign Affairs and Trade. (2011). *Jordan.* Retrieved from http://www.safetravel.govt.nz/jordan.

Newnham, R. (2008). 'Coalition of the bribed and bullied?' U.S. economic linkage and the Iraq war coalition. *International Studies Perspectives, 9*(2), 183–200. doi:10.1111/j.1528-3585.2008.00326.x.

Ngai, S. (2005). *Ugly feelings: Literature, affect, and ideology.* Cambridge, MA: Harvard University Press.

Nordstrom, C. (1995). War on the front lines. In C. Nordstrom & A. C. G. M. Robben (eds), *Fieldwork under fire: Contemporary studies of violence and survival* (pp. 129–153). Berkeley, CA: University of California Press.

Nordstrom, C., & Robben, A. C. G. M. (1995). *Fieldwork under fire: Contemporary studies of violence and survival.* Berkeley, CA: University of California Press.

Novelli, M. (ed.) (2005). *Niche tourism: Contemporary issues, trends and cases.* Oxford: Elsevier Butterworth-Heineman.

Noy, C. (2007). The language(s) of the tourist experience: An autoethnography of the poetic tourists. In I. Ateljevic, A. Pritchard & N. Morgan (eds), *The critical turn in tourism studies: Innovative research methodologies* (pp. 349–370). Amsterdam, Netherlands: Elsevier.

Noy, C. & Kohn, A. (2010). Mediating touristic dangerscapes: The semiotics of state travel warnings issued to Israeli tourists. *Journal of Tourism and Cultural Change, 8*(3), 206–222.

Oakes, T., & Minca, C. (2004). Tourism, modernity and postmodernity. In A. A. Lew, C. M. Hall & A. M. Williams (eds), *A companion to tourism* (pp. 280–290). Malden, MA: Blackwell.

Obrador-Pons, P. (2007). A haptic geography of the beach: Naked bodies, vision and touch. *Social & Cultural Geography, 8*(1), 123–141. doi:10.1080/14649360701251866.

O'Connor, H., Madge, C., Shaw, R., & Wellens, J. (2008). Internet-based interviewing. In N. Fielding, R. M. Lee & G. Blank (eds), *The SAGE handbook of online research methods* (pp. 271–289). Los Angeles, CA: SAGE.

Omari, R. (2010, September 16). No security threats detected within Kingdom. *Jordan Times.* Retrieved from http://www.jordantimes.com/no-security-threats-detected-within-kingdom.

Online Oxford Dictionaries. (2015). Dark tourism. Retrieved from http://www.oxforddictionaries.com/definition/english/dark-tourism?q=dark+tourism&searchDictCode=all.

Opdenakker, R. (2006). Advantages and disadvantages of four interview techniques in qualitative research. *Forum: Qualitative Social Research, 7*(4). Retrieved from http://www.qualitative-research.net/index.php/fqs/article/view/175/392.

Oxford English Dictionary. (2011). 'cyst, n'. Retrieved from http://www.oed.com/.

Oxford English Dictionary. (2011). 'haptic, adj. (and n.)'. Retrieved from http://www.oed.com/.

Pain, R. (2001). *Introducing social geographies*. London: Arnold.

Pain, R. (2010). The new geopolitics of fear. *Geography Compass, 4*(3), 226–240.

Pain, R. (2014). Everyday terrorism: Connecting domestic violence and global terrorism. *Progress in Human Geography, 38*(4), 531–550.

Paine, R. (1995). Behind the Hebron Massacre, 1994. *Anthropology Today, 11*(1), 8–15.

Palestine. (2011). In *Encyclopaedia Britannica*. Retrieved from http://www.britannica.com/EBchecked/topic/439645/Palestine.

Palestine Monitor. (2008). *The house with seven walls*. Retrieved from http://reliefweb.int/report/occupied-palestinian-territory/opt-house-seven-walls.

Pallister-Wilkins, P. (2011). The Separation Wall: A symbol of power and a site of resistance? *Antipode, 43*(5), 1851–1882. doi:10.1111/j.1467-8330.2010.00859.x.

Panksepp, J. (2007). Criteria for basic emotions: Is disgust a primary emotion? *Cognition & Emotion, 21*(8), 1819–1828. doi:10.1080/02699930701334302.

Pappe, I. (2004). *A history of modern Palestine: One land, two peoples*. New York: Cambridge University Press.

Paraskevas, A., & Arendell, B. (2007). A strategic framework for terrorism prevention and mitigation in tourism destinations. *Tourism Management, 28*(6), 1560–1573. doi:10.1016/j.tourman.2007.02.012.

Paterson, M. (2004). Caresses, excesses, intimacies and estrangements. *Angelaki, 9*(1), 165–177. doi:10.1080/0969725042000232478.

Paterson, M. (2005). The forgetting of touch. *Angelaki, 10*(3), 115–132. doi:10.1080/09697250500424387.

Paterson, M. (2006). Feel the presence: Technologies of touch and distance. *Environment and Planning D, 24*(5), 691–708. doi:10.1068/d394t.

Paterson, M. (2009a). Haptic geographies: Ethnography, haptic knowledges and sensuous dispositions. *Progress in Human Geography, 33*(6), 766–788. doi:10.1177/0309132509103155.

Paterson, M. (2009b). Introduction: Re-mediating touch. *The Senses and Society, 4*(2), 129–140.

Pearce, D. G., & Butler, R. (eds) (1999). *Contemporary issues in tourism development*. New York: Routledge.

Pedersen, P. (1995). *The five stages of culture shock: Critical incidents around the world*. Westport, CT: Greenwood Press.

Pelton, R. Y. (2000). *Robert Young Pelton's the world's most dangerous places* (4th edn). New York: Harper Resource.

Pelton, R. Y. (2003). *Robert Young Pelton's the world's most dangerous places* (5th edn). New York: Harper Resource.

Petra Israel. (2011). *One Day Tour of Petra from Israel*. Retrieved from http://www.petraisrael.com/index.php?option=com_content&view=article&id=106&Itemid=71.

Petra National Trust. (2011). *Entrance fees*. Retrieved from http://petranationaltrust.org/UI/ShowContent.aspx?ContentId=196.

Phillimore, J., & Goodson, L. (eds) (2004). *Qualitative research in tourism: Ontologies, epistemologies and methodologies*. New York: Routledge.

Philo, C. (2008). *Theory and methods: Critical essays in human geography*. Aldershot, England: Ashgate.

Phipps, P. (1999). Tourists, terrorists, death and value. In R. Kaur & J. Hutnyk (eds), *Travel worlds: Journeys in contemporary cultural politics* (pp. 74–93). London: Zed Books.

Picard, D. (2012). Tourism, awe and inner journeys. In D. Picard & M. Robinson (eds), *Emotion in motion: Tourism, affect and transformation*. Aldershot, England: Ashgate.

Picard, D., & Robinson, M. (eds) (2012). *Emotion in motion: Tourism, affect and transformation* (pp. 1–19). Aldershot, England: Ashgate.

Pieke, F. N. (1995). Witnessing the 1989 Chinese People's Movement. In C. Nordstrom & A. C. G. M. Robben (eds), *Fieldwork under fire: Contemporary studies of violence and survival* (pp. 62–79). Berkeley, CA: University of California Press.

Pile, S. (1991). Practising interpretative geography. *Transactions of the Institute of British Geographers, 16*(4), 458–469.

Pile, S. (1996). *The body and the city: Psychoanalysis, space, and subjectivity*. London: Routledge.

Pile, S. (2005). *Real cities: Modernity, space and the phantasmagorias of city life*. London: Sage.

Pile, S. (2010). Emotions and affect in recent human geography. *Transactions of the Institute of British Geographers, 35*(1), 5–20. doi:10.1111/j.1475-5661.2009.00368.x.

Pitts, W. J. (1996). Uprising in Chiapas, Mexico: Zapata lives – tourism falters. In A. Pizam & Y. Mansfeld (eds), *Tourism, crime, and international security issues* (pp. 215–227). Chichester, England: Wiley.

Pizam, A. (1996). Does tourism promote peace and understanding between unfriendly nations? In A. Pizam & Y. Mansfeld (eds), *Tourism, crime, and international security issues* (pp. 203–213). Chichester, England: Wiley.

Pizam, A., & Mansfeld, Y. (eds) (1996). *Tourism, crime, and international security issues*. Chichester, England: Wiley.

Pizam, A., Fleischer, A., & Mansfeld, Y. (2002). Tourism and social change: The case of Israeli ecotourists visiting Jordan. *Journal of Travel Research, 41*(2), 177–184. doi:10.1177/004728702237423.

Poirier, R. A. (1997). Political risk analysis and tourism. *Annals of Tourism Research, 24*(3), 675–686. doi:10.1016/S0160-7383(97)00019-4.

Pollock, G. (2003). Holocaust tourism: Being there, looking back and the ethics of spatial memory. In N. Lübbren & D. Crouch (eds), Visual culture and tourism (pp. 175–189). New York: Berg.

Preece, T., & Price, G. (2005). Motivations of participants in dark tourism: A case study Port Arthur, Tasmania, Australia. In C. Ryan, S. Page & M. Aicken (eds), *Taking tourism to the limits: Issues, concepts and managerial perspectives* (pp. 191–198). Oxford: Elsevier.

Preston, V. (2009). Questionnaire survey. In R. Kitchin & N. Thrift (eds), *International encyclopedia of human geography* (pp. 46–52). Oxford: Elsevier.

Prinz, J. J. (2008). Is emotion a form of perception? In L. Faucher & C. Tappolet (eds), *The modularity of emotions* (Vol. 32, pp. 137–160). Calgary, Canada: University of Calgary Press.

Pritchard, A., & Morgan, N. (2003). Mythic geographies of representation and identity: Contemporary postcards of Wales. *Journal of Tourism and Cultural Change, 1*(2), 111–130. doi:10.1080/14766820308668163.

Pritchard, A., & Morgan, N. (2005). 'On location'. *Tourist Studies, 5*(3), 283–302. doi:10.1177/1468797605070338.

Pritchard, A., & Morgan, N. (2007). De-centring tourism's intellectual universe, or traversing the dialogue between change and tradition. In I. Ateljevic, A. Pritchard & N. Morgan (eds), *The critical turn in tourism studies: Innovative research methodologies* (pp. 11–28). Amsterdam, The Netherlands: Elsevier.

Pritchard, A., Morgan, N., & Ateljevic, I. (2011). Hopeful tourism: A new transformative perspective. *Annals of Tourism Research, 38*(3), 941–963. doi:10.1016/j.annals.2011.01.004.

Pritchard, A., Morgan, N., Ateljevic, I., & Harris, C. (2007). *Tourism and gender: Embodiment, sensuality, and experience*. Wallingford, England: CAB International.

Probyn, E. (2003). The spatial imperative of subjectivity. In K. Anderson, M. Damosh, S. Pile & N. Thrift (eds), *Handbook of cultural geography* (pp. 290–299). London: Sage.

Probyn, E. (2004a). Everyday shame. *Cultural Studies, 18*(2–3), 328–349. doi:10.1080/09 50238042000201545.

Probyn, E. (2004b). Shame in the habitus. *The Sociological Review, 52,* 224–248. doi:10.1111/j.1467-954X.2005.00533.x.

Punch, S. (2012). Hidden struggles of fieldwork: Exploring the role and use of field diaries. *Emotion, Space and Society, 5*(2), 86–93. doi:10.1016/j.emospa.2010.09.005.

Rabate, J.-M. (2003). *The Cambridge companion to Lacan.* Cambridge, England: Cambridge University Press.

Raccah, P.-Y. (1995). Argumentation and natural language: Presentation and dis- cussion of four foundational hypotheses. *Journal of Pragmatics, 24*(1–2), 1–15. doi:10.1016/0378-2166(95)00029-R.

Ragland-Sullivan, E. (1987). *Jacques Lacan and the philosophy of psychoanalysis.* Urbana, IL: University of Illinois Press.

Ragland-Sullivan, E. (1992). Death drive (Lacan). In E. Wright (ed.), *Feminism and psy- choanalysis: A critical dictionary* (pp. 57–59). Oxford: Blackwell.

Ragland-Sullivan, E. (1995). *Essays on the pleasures of death: From Freud to Lacan.* New York: Routledge.

Raju, S. (2009). Polyvocality. In R. Kitchin & N. Thrift (eds), *International encyclopedia of human geography* (pp. 265–268). Oxford: Elsevier.

Randall, J., & Perrin, M. (2003). *Adventure in the third world: Everything you need to know to survive in remote and hostile destinations.* Boulder, CO: Paladin Press.

Reisinger, Y., & Turner, L. W. (2003). *Cross-cultural behaviour in tourism: Concepts and analysis.* Oxford: Butterworth-Heinemann.

Richards, G. (2005). Emotions into words – or words into emotions? In P. Gouk & H. Hills (eds), *Representing Emotions: New Connections in the Histories of Art, Music and Medicine* (pp. 49–65). Surrey, England: Ashgate.

Richter, L. K. (1983). Tourism politics and political science: A case of not so benign neglect. *Annals of Tourism Research, 10*(3), 313–335. doi:10.1016/0160-7383(83)90060-9.

Richter, L. K., & Richter, W. L. (1985). Policy choices in South Asian tourism development. *Annals of Tourism Research, 12*(2), 201–217. doi:10.1016/0160-7383(85)90057-X.

Ritchie, B. W., Burns, P., & Palmer, C. (eds) (2005). *Tourism research methods: Integrating theory with practice.* Wallingford, England: CAB International.

Rittichainuwat, N. (2008). Responding to disaster: Thai and Scandinavian tourists' motiva- tion to visit Phuket, Thailand. *Journal of Travel Research, 46*(4), 422–432.

Robin, C. (2004). *Fear: The history of a political idea.* Oxford: Oxford University Press.

Robins, P. (2004). *A history of Jordan.* New York: Cambridge University Press.

Robinson, M., & Novelli, M. (2005). Introduction. In M. Robinson & M. Novelli (eds), *Niche tourism: Contemporary issues, trends and cases.* Oxford: Elsevier Butterworth-Heinemann.

Rodaway, P. (1994). *Sensuous geographies: Body, sense, and place.* London: Routledge.

Rojek, C. (1993). *Ways of escape: Modern transformations in leisure and travel.* Basingstoke, England: Macmillan.

Ryan, C. (2005). Dark tourism: An introduction. In C. Ryan, S. Page & M. Aiken (eds), *Taking tourism to the limits: Issues, concepts and managerial perspectives* (pp. 187– 190). Oxford: Elsevier.

Ryan, C. (ed.) (2007a). *Battlefield tourism: History, place and interpretation.* Amsterdam, Netherlands: Elsevier.

Ryan, C. (2007b). Introduction. In C. Ryan (ed.), *Battlefield tourism: History, place and interpretation* (pp. 1–15). Amsterdam, Netherlands: Elsevier.

Ryan, C., & Cave, J. (2005). Structuring destination image: A qualitative approach. *Journal of Travel Research, 44*(2), 143–150. doi:10.1177/0047287505278991.

Ryan, C., & Kohli, R. (2006). The Buried Village, New Zealand: An example of dark tourism? *Asia Pacific Journal of Tourism Research, 11*(3), 211–226. doi:10.1080/10941660600753240.

Ryan, C., Page, S., & Aicken, M. (eds) (2005). *Taking tourism to the limits: Issues, concepts and managerial perspectives*. Oxford: Elsevier.

Said, E. W. (1993). *Culture and imperialism*. New York: Vintage Books.

Said, E. W. (1997). *Covering Islam: How the media and the experts determine how we see the rest of the world*. New York: Vintage Books.

Said, E. W. (2003). *Orientalism*. London: Penguin Books.

Said, E. W. (2004). *From Oslo to Iraq and the road map*. New York: Pantheon Books.

Salamone, G. (2009, March 29). First western tourists visit Iraq. *Enduring Wanderlust*. Retrieved from http://www.enduringwanderlust.com/first-tourists-visit-iraq/.

Salazar, N. B. (2006). Building a 'culture of peace' through tourism: Reflexive and analytical notes and queries. *Universitas Humanística, 62*(2), 319–333.

Salibi, K. S. (1993). *The modern history of Jordan*. London: I.B. Tauris.

Sanders, R. (2009). Photographs. In R. Kitchin & N. Thrift (eds), *International encyclopedia of human geography* (pp. 157–162). Oxford: Elsevier.

Sarup, M. (1992). *Jacques Lacan*. New York: Harvester Wheatsheaf.

Saville, S. J. (2008). Playing with fear: Parkour and the mobility of emotion. *Social & Cultural Geography, 9*(8), 891–914. doi:10.1080/14649360802441440.

Schlomka, F. (2011). *Green Olive Tours*. Retrieved from http://www.toursinenglish.com/.

Schwanen, T. (2009). Time–space diaries. In R. Kitchin & N. Thrift (eds), *International encyclopedia of human geography* (pp. 294–300). Oxford: Elsevier.

Scott, N., & Jafari, J. (2010). Introduction: Islam and tourism. In N. Scott & J. Jafari (eds), *Tourism in the Muslim world* (pp. 1–13). Bingley, England: Emerald.

Seaton, A. V. (1996). Guided by the dark: From thanatopsis to thanatourism. *International Journal of Heritage Studies, 2*(4), 234–244. doi:10.1080/13527259608722178.

Seaton, A. V. (1999). War and thanatourism: Waterloo 1815–1914. *Annals of Tourism Research, 26*(1), 130–158. doi:10.1016/S0160-7383(98)00057-7.

Seaton, T. (2009). Thanatourism and its discontents: An appraisal of a decade's work with some future issues and directions. In T. Jamal & R. Mike (eds), *The Sage handbook of tourism studies* (pp. 521–542). London: Sage.

Secor, A. J. (2009). Focus groups. In R. Kitchin & N. Thrift (eds), *International encyclopedia of human geography* (pp. 200–201). Oxford: Elsevier.

Seddighi, H., Lawler, K. A., & Katos, A. V. (2000). *Econometrics: A practical approach*. London: Routledge.

Segal, R., & Weizman, E. (2003). Occupation in space and time. *Index on Censorship, 32*(3), 186–193. doi:10.1080/03064220308537271.

Seigworth, G. J., & Gregg, M. (2010). An inventory of shimmers. In M. Gregg & S. J. Seigworth (eds), *The Affect Theory Reader* (pp. 1–25). London: Duke University Press.

Selwyn, T. (ed.) (1996). *The tourist image: Myths and myth making in tourism*. Chichester, England: John Wiley.

Sennett, R. (1994). *Flesh and stone: The body and the city in Western civilization*. New York: Norton.

Shakeela, A., & Weaver, D. (2012). Resident reactions to a tourism incident: Mapping a Maldivian Emoscape. *Annals of Tourism Research, 39*(3), 1337–1358.

Sharpley, R. (2005). Travels to the edge of darkness: Towards a typology of 'dark tourism'. In C. Ryan, S. Page & M. Aicken (eds), *Taking tourism to the limits: Issues, concepts and managerial perspectives* (pp. 215–226). Oxford: Elsevier.

Sharpley, R. (2009). Shedding light on dark tourism: An introduction. In R. Sharpley & P. Stone (eds), *The darker side of travel: The theory and practice of dark tourism* (pp. 3–22). Bristol, England: Channel View Publications.

Sharpley, R., & Stone, P. (eds) (2009a). *The darker side of travel: The theory and practice of dark tourism*. Bristol, England: Channel View Publications.

Sharpley, R., & Stone, P. (2009b). Life, death and dark tourism: Future research directions and concluding remarks. In R. Sharpley & P. Stone (eds), *The darker side of travel: The theory and practice of dark tourism* (pp. 247–251). Bristol, England: Channel View Publications.

Sharpley, R., & Sundaram, P. (2005). Tourism: A sacred journey? The case of Ashram tourism, India. *International Journal of Tourism Research, 7*, 161–171.

Shaw, W. S. (2011). Researcher journeying and the adventure/danger impulse. *Area*, advance online. doi:10.1111/j.1475-4762.2011.01032.x.

Sheller, M., & Urry, J. (2004). *Tourism mobilities: Places to play, places in play*. London: Routledge.

Shephard, G., & Evans, S. (2005). Adventure tourism: Hard decisions, soft options and home for tea: Adventure on the hoof. In M. Novelli (ed.), *Niche tourism: Contemporary issues, trends and cases* (pp. 201–209). Oxford: Elsevier Butterworth-Heinemann.

Sheridan, A. (1977). Translator's note (A. Sheridan, Trans.). In J. Lacan (ed.), *Écrits: A selection* (pp. vii–xii). New York: Norton.

Sianne, N. (2009). *Ugly feelings*. Cambridge, MA: Harvard University Press.

Sibley, D. (1999). Comments on 'stages on journeys' by Liz Bondi. *The Professional Geographer, 51*(3), 451–452. doi:10.1111/0033-0124.00179.

Sibley, D. (2003). Geography and psychoanalysis: Tensions and possibilities. *Social & Cultural Geography, 4*(3), 391–399. doi:10.1080/14649360309070.

Silver, I. (1993). Marketing authenticity in third world countries. *Annals of Tourism Research, 20*(2), 302–318. doi:10.1016/0160-7383(93)90057-A.

Sim, S. (ed.) (2001). *The Routledge companion to postmodernism*. London: Routledge.

Siraj Center. (2011). *Siraj Center for Holy Land Studies*. Retrieved from http://www.siraj-center.org.

Skelton, T. (2001). Cross-cultural research: Issues of power, positionality and 'race'. In M. Limb & C. Dwyer (eds), *Qualitative methodologies for geographers: Issues and debates* (pp. 87–100). London: Arnold.

Skelton, T. (2009). Cross-cultural research. In R. Kitchin & N. Thrift (eds), *International encyclopedia of human geography* (pp. 398–403). Oxford: Elsevier.

Smith, M., Davidson, J., Cameron, L., & Bondi, L. (eds) (2009). *Emotion, place, and culture*. Aldershot, England: Ashgate.

Smith, M., & Duffy, R. (2003). *The ethics of tourism development*. London: Routledge.

Smith, N., & Croy, W. G. (2005). Presentation of dark tourism: To Wairoa, the buried village. In C. Ryan, S. Page & M. Aicken (eds), *Taking tourism to the limits: Issues, concepts and managerial perspectives* (pp. 199–214). Oxford: Elsevier.

Smith, V. L. (1996). War and its tourist attractions. In A. Pizam & Y. Mansfeld (eds), *Tourism, crime, and international security issues* (pp. 247–264). Chichester, England: Wiley.

Smith, V. L. (1998). War and tourism: An American ethnography. *Annals of Tourism Research, 25*(1), 202–227. doi:10.1016/S0160-7383(97)00086-8.

Smyth, R., Nielsen, I., & Mishra, V. (2009). 'I've been to Bali too' (and I will be going back): Are terrorist shocks to Bali's tourist arrivals permanent or transitory? *Applied Economics, 41*(11), 1376–1378.

Sneddon, A. (2008). Two views of emotional perception. In L. Faucher & C. Tappolet (eds), *The modularity of emotions* (pp. xxxi, 288). Calgary: University of Calgary Press.

Solomon, R. C. (2003). *What is an emotion? Classic and contemporary readings.* Oxford: Oxford University Press.

Solomon, R. C., & Stone, L. D. (2002). On 'positive' and 'negative' emotions. *Journal for the Theory of Social Behaviour, 32*(4), 417–435. doi:10.1111/1468-5914.00196.

Sönmez, S. F. (1998). Tourism, terrorism, and political instability. *Annals of Tourism Research, 25*(2), 416–456. doi:10.1016/S0160-7383(97)00093-5.

Sönmez, S. F., & Graefe, A. R. (1998). Influence of terrorism risk on foreign tourism decisions. *Annals of Tourism Research, 25*(1), 112–144. doi:10.1016/S0160-7383(97)00072-8.

Steiner, C. (2010). Impacts of September 11: A two-sided neighbourhood effect. In N. Scott & J. Jafari (eds), *Tourism in the Muslim world* (pp. 181–204). Bingley, England: Emerald.

Stewart, J. (Anchorman). (2010). Exclusive – King Abdullah II of Jordan extended interview [Transcript of podcast]. Retrieved from http://thedailyshow.cc.com/videos/04hplh/exclusive-king-abdullah-ii-of-jordan-extended-interview.

Stone, P. (2006). A dark tourism spectrum: Towards a typology of death and macabre related tourist sites, attractions and exhibitions. *TOURISM: An Interdisciplinary International Journal, 54*(2), 145–160.

Stone, P. (2009). Making absent death present: Consuming dark tourism in contemporary society. In R. Sharpley & P. Stone (eds), *The darker side of travel: The theory and practice of dark tourism* (pp. 23–38). Bristol, England: Channel View Publications.

Stone, P., & Sharpley, R. (2008). Consuming dark tourism: A thanatological perspective. *Annals of Tourism Research, 35*(2), 574–595. doi:10.1016/j.annals.2008.02.003.

Strange, C., & Kempa, M. (2003). Shades of dark tourism: Alcatraz and Robben Island. *Annals of Tourism Research, 30*(2), 386–405. doi:10.1016/S0160-7383(02)00102-0.

Straughan, E. R. (2012). Touched by water: The body in scuba diving. *Emotion, Space and Society, 5*(1), 19–26. doi:10.1016/j.emospa.2010.10.003.

Sudilovsky, J. (2011, May 19). Israel removes land mines from site of Jesus' baptism. *Huffington Post.* Retrieved from http://www.huffingtonpost.com/2011/05/19/israel-removes-land-mines_n_863811.html.

Swain, M. B. (2004). (Dis)embodied experience and power dynamics in tourism research. In J. Phillimore & L. Goodson (eds), *Qualitative research in tourism: Ontologies, epistemologies and methodologies* (pp. 102–118). New York: Routledge.

Swedenburg, T. (1995). With Genet in the Palestinian Field. In C. Nordstrom & A. C. G. M. Robben (eds), *Fieldwork under fire: Contemporary studies of violence and survival* (pp. 25–40). Berkeley, CA: University of California Press.

Sykes, H. (2009). *No frills tourism – in Iraq.* Retrieved from http://news.bbc.co.uk/2/hi/middle_east/7957974.stm.

Tansey, S. D., & Jackson, N. A. (2008). *Politics: The basics.* London: Routledge.

Tarlow, P. (2005). Dark tourism – the appealing 'dark' side of tourism and more. In M. Novelli (ed.), *Niche tourism: Contemporary issues, trends and cases* (pp. 47–57). Oxford: Elsevier Butterworth-Heinemann.

Tawil-Souri, H. (2011). Qalandia checkpoint as space and nonplace. *Space and Culture, 14*(1), 4–26. doi:10.1177/1206331210389260.

Teo, P., Chang, T. C., & Ho, K. C. (eds) (2001). *Interconnected worlds: Tourism in Southeast Asia*. Oxford: Pergamon.

Terada, R. (2001). *Feeling in theory: Emotion and the 'Death of the Subject'*. Cambridge, MA: Harvard University Press.

Teye, V. B. (1986). Liberation wars and tourism development in Africa: The case of Zambia. *Annals of Tourism Research, 13*(4), 589–608. doi:10.1016/0160-7383(86)90004-6.

Teye, V. B. (1988). Coups d'etat and African tourism: A study of Ghana. *Annals of Tourism Research, 15*(3), 329–356. doi:10.1016/0160-7383(88)90026-6.

Thapa, B. (2003). Tourism in Nepal: Shangri-La's troubled times. In C. M. Hall, D. J. Timothy & D. T. Duval (eds), *Safety and security in tourism: Relationships, management, and marketing* (pp. 117–138). Binghamton, NY: Haworth.

Thien, D. (2005). After or beyond feeling? A consideration of affect and emotion in geography. *Area, 37*(4), 450–454. doi:10.1111/j.1475-4762.2005.00643a.x.

Thien, D. (2009). Feminist methodologies. In R. Kitchin & N. Thrift (eds), *International encyclopedia of human geography* (pp. 71–78). Oxford: Elsevier.

Thomas, M. E. (2009). Auto-photography. In R. Kitchin & N. Thrift (eds), *International encyclopedia of human geography* (pp. 244–251). Oxford: Elsevier.

Thompson, E. (2000). *Colonial citizens: Republican rights, paternal privilege, and gender in French Syria and Lebanon*. New York: Columbia University Press.

Thrift, N. (2004). Intensities of feeling: Towards a spatial politics of affect. *Geografiska Annaler: Series B, Human Geography, 86*(1), 57–78. doi: 10.1111/j.0435-3684.2004.00154.x.

Thrift, N. (2008). *Non-representational theory: Space, politics, affect*. London: Routledge.

Till, K. E. (2009). Ethnography. In R. Kitchin & N. Thrift (eds), *International encyclopedia of human geography* (pp. 626–631). Oxford: Elsevier.

Timothy, D. J. (2001). *Tourism and political boundaries*. London: Routledge.

Travel Link The True Israel Specialists. (2015). *Petra Day Tour*. Retrieved from http://www.travelinkuk.com/internal_group_tours_main.php/275/Petra_(1_day)_from_Eilat.

Tribe, J. (2007). Critical tourism: Rules and resistance. In I. Ateljevic, A. Pritchard & N. Morgan (eds), *The critical turn in tourism studies: Innovative research methodologies* (pp. 29–39). Amsterdam, Netherlands: Elsevier.

Trotta, J. (2006). *Grief tourism definition*. Retrieved from http://www.grief-tourism.com/grief-tourism-definition/.

Tuan, Y. F. (1979). *Landscapes of fear*. Oxford: Basil Blackwell Publisher.

Tucker, H. (2003). *Living with tourism: Negotiating identities in a Turkish village*. London: Routledge.

Tucker, H. (2005). Narratives of place and self. *Tourist Studies, 5*(3), 267–282. doi:10.1177/1468797605070337.

Tucker, H. (2007a). Performing a young people's package tour of New Zealand: Negotiating appropriate performances of place. *Tourism Geographies: An International Journal of Tourism Space, Place and Environment, 9*(2), 139–159. doi:10.1080/14616680701278497.

Tucker, H. (2007b). Undoing shame: Tourism and women's work in Turkey. *Journal of Tourism and Cultural Change, 5*(2), 87–105. doi:10.2167/jtcc089.0.

Tucker, H. (2009). Recognizing emotion and its postcolonial potentialities: Discomfort and shame in a tourism encounter in Turkey. *Tourism Geographies: An International Journal of Tourism Space, Place and Environment, 11*(4), 444–461. doi:10.1080/14616680903262612.

Turnbull, C. M. (1986). Sex and gender: The role of subjectivity in field research. In T. L. Whitehead & M. E. Conaway (eds), *Self, sex, and gender in cross-cultural fieldwork* (pp. 17–27). Urbana, Il: University of Illinois Press.

Turner, B. (2004). Edward W. Said: Overcoming Orientalism. *Theory, Culture & Society, 21*(1), 173–177. doi:10.1177/0263276404041958.

UNOCHA (UN Office for Coordination of Humanitarian Affairs) occupied Palestinian territory (UN OCHA oPT). (2010). West Bank movement and access. (Special Focus, June 2010). Retrieved from http://www.ochaopt.org/results.aspx?id= 4770047.

United Nations Security Council. (1980). *Resolutions 465, 468, 476, 478, 480, 484.* Retrieved from http://www.un.org/documents/sc/res/1980/scres80.htm.

UNWTO (United Nations World Tourism Organisation). (2006). *Tourism highlights: 2006 edition.* Retrieved from http://www.unwto.org/factsandfigures.

UNWTO (United Nations World Tourism Organisation). (2008). *Tourism highlights: 2008 edition.* Retrieved from http://www.unwto.org/factsandfigures.

UNWTO (United Nations World Tourism Organisation). (2013). *Tourism highlights: 2013 edition.* Retrieved from http://www.unwto.org/factsandfigures

Uriely, N. (1997). Theories of modern and postmodern tourism. *Annals of Tourism Research, 24*(4), 982–985. doi:10.1016/S0160-7383(97)00029-7.

Uriely, N., Maoz, D., & Reichel, A. (2007). Rationalising terror-related risks: The case of Israeli tourists in Sinai. *International Journal of Tourism Research, 9*(1), 1–8. doi:10.1002/jtr.587.

Uriely, N., Ram, Y., & Malach-Pines, A. (2011). Psychoanalytic sociology of deviant tourist behavior. *Annals of Tourism Research, 38*(3), 1051–1069. doi:10.1016/j. annals.2011.01.014.

Urry, J. (1990). *The tourist gaze: Leisure and travel in contemporary societies.* London: Sage.

Urry, J. (2005). The place of emotions within place. In J. Davidson, L. Bondi & M. Smith (eds), *Emotional geographies* (pp. 77–86). Aldershot, England: Ashgate.

van Hoven, B. (2011). Multi-sensory tourism in the Great Bear Rainforest. *Landabréfið 25,* 31–49.

Var, T., Brayley, R., & Korsay, M. (1989). Tourism and world peace: Case of Turkey. *Annals of Tourism Research, 16*(2), 282–286. doi:10.1016/0160-7383(89)90078-9.

Var, T., Schlüter, R., Ankomah, P., & Lee, T.-H. (1989). Tourism and world peace: The case of Argentina. *Annals of Tourism Research, 16*(3), 431–434. doi:10.1016/0160-7383(89)90055-8.

Veijola, S., & Jokinen, E. (1994). The body in tourism. *Theory Culture & Society, 11*(3), 125–151.

Visit Palestine. (2011). *General information: Getting there.* Retrieved from http://www. visitpalestine.ps/index.php?lang=en&page=122709564391.

Wahab, S. (1996). Tourism and terrorism: Synthesis of the problem with emphasis on Egypt. In A. Pizam & Y. Mansfeld (eds), *Tourism, crime, and international security issues* (pp. 175–186). Chichester, England: Wiley.

Waikato Times (2010, August 5). Rockets raining on resorts.

Waitt, G., Figueroa, R., & McGee, L. (2007). Fissures in the rock: Rethinking pride and shame in the moral terrains of Uluru. *Transactions of the Institute of British Geographers, 32*(2), 248–263. doi:10.1111/j.1475-5661.2007.00240.x.

Waitt, G., Markwell, K., & Gorman-Murray, A. (2008). Challenging heteronormativity in tourism studies: Locating progress. *Progress in Human Geography, 32*(6), 781–800. doi:10.1177/0309132508089827.

Wall, G. (1996). Terrorism and tourism: An overview and an Irish example. In A. Pizam & Y. Mansfeld (eds), *Tourism, crime, and international security issues* (pp. 143–158). Chichester, England: Wiley.

Walsh, K. (2009). Participant observation. In R. Kitchin & N. Thrift (eds), *International encyclopedia of human geography* (pp. 77–81). Oxford: Elsevier.

Wang, N. (2000). *Tourism and modernity: A sociological analysis.* Amsterdam, Netherlands: Pergamon.

Ward, C. A., Bochner, S., & Furnham, A. (2001). *The psychology of culture shock* (2nd edn). Hove, England: Routledge.

Warner, J. (1999). North Cyprus: Tourism and the challenge of non-recognition. *Journal of Sustainable Tourism, 7*(2), 128–145. doi:10.1080/09669589908667331.

Wearing, S., & McDonald, M. (2003). Interconnected worlds: Tourism in Southeast Asia [Book Review]. *Annals of Tourism Research, 30*(3), 752–753. doi:10.1016/S0160-7383(03)00053-7.

Wearing, S., & Wearing, B. (2001). Conceptualizing the selves of tourism. *Leisure Studies, 20*(2), 143–159. doi:10.1080/02614360110051631.

Weizman, E. (2006). Seeing through walls: The split sovereign and the one-way mirror. *Grey Room, 24,* 88–99.

Weizman, E. (2012). *Hollow land: Israel's architecture of occupation.* London: Verso Books.

Werman, M. (2009). *Interview with Robert Reid* (podcast). Retrieved from Public Radio International: The World. http://www.pri.org/stories/2009-11-09/danger-tourism.

West Bank. (2011). *In Encyclopaedia Britannica.* Retrieved from http://www.britannica.com/EBchecked/topic/640076/West-Bank.

White, L., & Frew, E. (eds) (2013). *Dark tourism and place identity: Managing and interpreting dark places.* London: Routledge.

Whitehead, T. L., & Conaway, M. E. (eds) (1986). *Self, sex, and gender in cross-cultural fieldwork.* Urbana, IL: University of Illinois Press.

Widdowfield, R. (2000). The place of emotions in academic research. *Area, 32*(2), 199–208. doi:10.1111/j.1475-4762.2000.tb00130.x.

Wilks, J. (2006). Preface. In J. Wilks, D. Pendergast & P. A. Leggat (eds), *Tourism in turbulent times: Towards safe experiences for visitors* (pp. xxiii–xxiv). Amsterdam, Netherlands: Elsevier.

Wilks, J., Pendergast, D., & Leggat, P. A. (eds) (2006). *Tourism in turbulent times: Towards safe experiences for visitors.* Amsterdam; Netherlands: Elsevier.

Williams, S. (ed.) (2004). *Tourism* (Vol. 1). London: Routledge.

Willis, K. (2006). Interviewing. In V. Desai & R. B. Potter (eds), *Doing development research* (pp. 144–152). London: Sage.

Wilson, F. L. (2002). *Concepts and issues in comparative politics: An introduction to comparative analysis* (2nd edn). Upper Saddle River, NJ: Prentice Hall.

Wilson, M. C. (1987). *King Abdullah, Britain, and the making of Jordan.* Cambridge, England: Cambridge University Press.

Wiseman, G. (2005). Pax Americana: Bumping into diplomatic culture. *International Studies Perspectives, 6*(4), 409–430. doi:10.1111/j.1528-3577.2005.00218.x.

Wittel, A. (2000). Ethnography on the move: From field to net to Internet. *Qualitative Research Net, 1*(1). Retrieved from http://www.qualitative-research.net/index.php/fqs/article/view/1131/2518.

Wolff, K., & Larsen, S. (2014). Can terrorism make us feel safer? Risk perceptions and worries before and after the July 22nd attacks. *Annals of Tourism Research, 40,* 200–209.

Woodward, K., Dixon, D. P., & Jones III, J. P. (2009). Poststructuralism/Poststructuralist Geographies. In R. Kitchin & N. Thrift (eds), *International Encyclopedia of Human Geography* (pp. 396–407). Oxford: Elsevier.

Wright, E. (ed.) (1992). *Feminism and psychoanalysis: A critical dictionary.* Oxford: Blackwell.

Yang, R. (2001). An obstacle or a useful tool? The role of the English language in internationalizing Chinese universities. *Journal of Studies in International Education, 5*(4), 341–358. doi:10.1177/102831530154005.

Yiftachel, O. (2004). Contradictions and dialectics: Reshaping political space in Israel/Palestine. An indirect response to Lina Jamoul. *Antipode, 36*(4), 607–613. doi:10.1111/j.1467-8330.2004.00439.x.

Yüksel, A., & Yüksel, F. (2007). Shopping risk perceptions: Effects on tourists' emotions, satisfaction and expressed loyalty intentions. *Tourism Management, 28*(3), 703–713. doi:10.1016/j.tourman.2006.04.025.

Žižek, S. (2008). *Violence: Six sideways reflections*. London: Profile.

Index

fantasy 162
fascination 116–31
Fatah 64, 65
fatality, fields of 42
Fatimid dynasty 66
fear 13, 18, 30–1, 133–52, 156–7; between affect and emotion 26–8; fun/fear binary 68, 133–43; in a hotspot 145–52; sense of 143–5; separation wall and checkpoints 116, 117, 126, 129–30
'fearful' dangers 27
feelings 23, 155, 156; ugly 27; *see also* affect, emotion
fields of fatality 42
fieldwork 'in conflict' 7–11
Finland–USSR frontier 97
First World War 60; battlefield tours 25–6
flags 95, 97, 98
Foley, M. 15, 43
For Ever Love and Peace Shop, Madaba 82
France 60–1
Freud, S. 4, 132, 143, 162–3; death drive 34–6, 158
Frosch, S. 162
frustration 116–31
fun/fear binary 68, 133–43

gambler's fallacy 75–6
Gaza Strip 61, 63
gender politics of research 21–2
Germany 142–3
glorification, vocabulary of 162
Goldstein, B. 112
Göreme, Turkey 25
graffiti 118, 119, 123
Green Line 107, 131
Green Olive Tours 107–8, 109
Gregory, D. 117
grief tourism 45, 50–1

habitus 161
Hamas 65
haptic geographies 13, 28–31; separation wall and checkpoints 116, 120, 121–4, 127
haptic shock 30, 128
haptic system 28–9
Hashemite family 58–60, 63
hate 87–8, 103

Hazbun, W. 63
Hebron/Al Khalil 112–15
Hine, C. 10
Hinterland Travel 149, 150–1
Hollinshead, K. 25, 156
holocaust tourism 16
Holy Land Trust (HLT) 106, 109
horror 50–1, houses of 42
humiliation 126
Hussein, King 60, 61

Ibrahimi Mosque 112, 113, 115
identity 160–1
Imaginary, the 39, 72
India 135
inside-out model of fear 27
Institute for Dark Tourism Research 15
intensity of affect 109–10
International Journal of Heritage Studies 15, 16
International Solidarity Movement 111–12
interviews 8
intifadas 64, 65, 66, 87
intrigued tourists 53
inward-oriented rationalisations 75
Iraq 58, 59, 145–52; danger-zone tourists in the media 148–52
Irigaray, L. 162
Islamic tourism 57
Islamophobia 88, 100
Israel 3, 4, 13, 30, 59, 157; Arava/Aqaba border 85–91, 94; Baptismal Site 7, 91–9, 138–42, 144–5; connections between Jordan, Palestine and 61–5; establishment of the state 106; fieldwork 8–11; peace treaty with Egypt 64; peace treaty with Jordan (1994) 4, 58, 60, 77, 78, 157; recognition of the state of 103; tourism between Jordan and 100–3
Israeli flags 95, 97
Israeli–Palestinian conflict 4, 13, 18, 49–50, 58, 78–9, 157, 159

Jamal, T. 25, 156
Jerusalem/Al Quds 45, 49–50, 63; East Jerusalem 61, 63; Muslim Quarter 110–11
Jewish 'Disneyland' tours 108
John Paul II, Pope 139